TENOR GUITAR METHOD in GDAE TUNING

by
Todd Montgomery M.A.

Online Audio

To access the online audio, scan the QR code above or go to:
www.melbay.com/31166MEB

Tenor guitar photos

Cover: Ulrich tenor guitar by Craven tenor guitars.

Back Cover: Session King by Nigel Forster

Photos courtesy of:

Craven Tenor Guitars @ craventenorguitars.com

Nigel Forster @ nkforsterguitars.com

Eastwood Guitars @ eastwoodguitars.com.

I0808768

WWW.MELBAY.COM

Online Audio Contents

Preface

This method offers an alternative to learning music through practicing scales. Instead, we'll focus on learning 5 inversions of each major, minor, and dominant seventh chord, and ingrain into muscle memory the important triad notes within each chord shape, and with practice begin to create melodies from those arpeggio notes. Learn to get to the melodic point faster and with more harmonic confidence using the entire fretboard of the tenor guitar for your music.

Table of Contents

Who is this book for?

Here are the players I had in mind when making this book: 1.) relative beginners who have learned a few first position chords and simple songs who would like to learn new chords and begin playing up the neck and adding melodies, riffs, and improvisations to their playing; 2.) the high school violin player and/or Irish dance tune player who has experience with GDAE tuning but would like to branch out into new styles of music afforded by the extended range of the acoustic or electric tenor guitar; 3.) intermediate players seeking key notes to seemlessly connect the scales they already know and; 4.) the regular guitar player who is ready to explore a different musical voice. For musicians at any level, this book is a handy reference for major, minor, and dominant 7th triads/arpeggios within each chord inversion.

Introduction

Welcome to your GDAE tenor guitar method. In this book you will find exercises that will help you to memorize and access the harmonic skeleton of major, minor, and dominant 7th chords and their related arpeggios anywhere on the fretboard! (These musical terms will become clear as progress through the book.)

This book is not a "song book". In the simplest terms possible, this collection of exercises and tips for the GDAE tenor guitar provides a quicker, and more useful, way to see and use the entire fretboard of the tenor guitar for musical creations. This collection of exercises and tips for the GDAE tenor is information put in the simplest terms possible, that I wish that I had known decades ago when I first started learning how to play the mandolin, which is also tuned GDAE. I initially found my way around the fretboard mostly by learning songs and memorizing scales. This tenor guitar method is designed to present a "skeleton key" that will allow for a quicker understanding of how to use the entire fretboard. This chord/arpeggio based method clarifies and illuminates how the tenor fretboard can be looked as organized with interlocking chord shapes (inversions) and arpeggios, and how that understanding will help you know where you are (musically) and where you want to go. Once ingrained in your muscle memory, these important arpeggio notes can then be embellished with whatever scales you like to use and can benefit a musician learning any style of music.

Why play the tenor guitar in the first place? Why not just play a regular guitar, and why is GDAE a good tuning to use?

The tenor guitar is a relatively easy to learn instrument due to its symmetrical tuning in fifths. All four strings are tuned at equal intervals from one another, unlike the guitar which switches its interval at the b-string. This makes the tenor less complicated than a typical 6-string guitar. This is why I think the tenor guitar is a good "first" instrument to learn. Also, for people that have played violin in the high school orchestra, or learned fiddle tunes, but want to branch out into other types of music, the GDAE tuning is the same. If this is you, then you already have a huge head start to begin making music on a tenor guitar! It's a unique and fresh voice to bring into your music.

Let's spend some time unlocking the fretboard as we improve our dexterity with practice so we can enjoy making music on the entire fretboard faster and more confidently than by other methods. I came to see this method's effectiveness after nearly four decades of exploring the GDAE fretboard.

I learned mostly in an oral tradition from friends and a few great teachers and books along the way. Sometimes, players use a song approach, learning a few chords in the first position. Others see the neck from a perspective of major, minor, or blues scales. While other musicians focus on fiddle tunes. I have tried all of these methods, but I believe that this chord shape/arpeggio method can be incorporated into the other methods and will help you learn the tenor guitar fretboard faster.

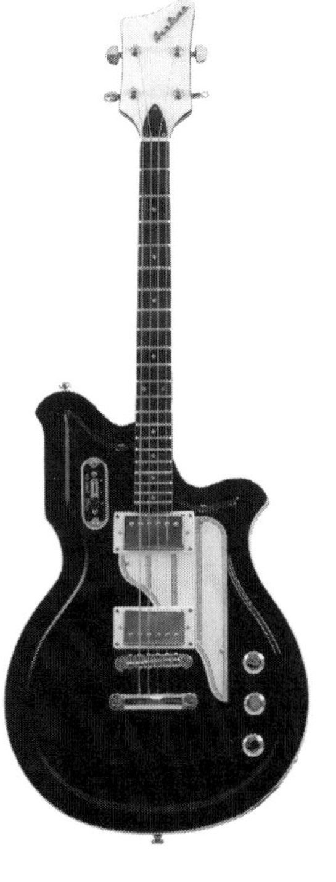

Map tenor guitar by Eastwood

The tuning of the tenor guitar in GDAE is one octave below a mandolin or violin. When comparing the notes of the tenor guitar to a regular guitar, the low G-string on the tenor is equal to fretting the 3rd fret on the low-E string, the tenor D note is equal to the open D note on the guitar, the A note is equal to fretting the guitar's G-string at the 2nd fret, and the open high E strings are the same on both instruments.

GDAE Tenor guitar compared to the piano: G=G2, D=D3, A=A3, E=E5.

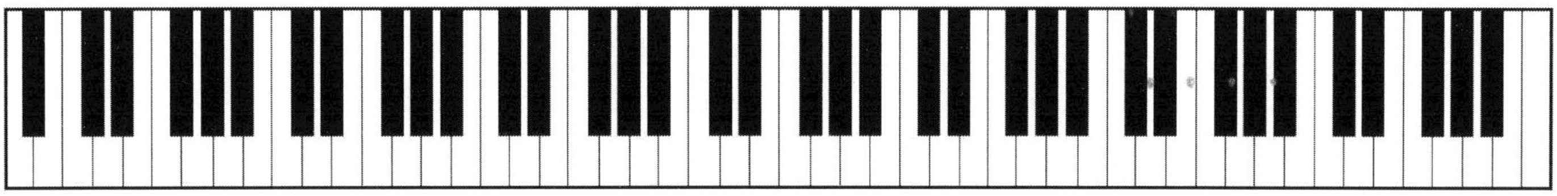

G2 D3 A4 E5

On the sheet music you will notice a small 8 symbol below the treble clef. The 8 means that the music we play on our tenor guitars will sound one octave lower than it is written on the staff. This is common for guitar sheet music. We will finger our notes by reading the music exactly as you have done if you have played the mandolin or fiddle. Tablature is included for each exercise in case you haven't yet learned to read sheet music.

The lessons in this book are designed as my sitar teacher might have done if he was teaching a CAGED system for GDAE tenor guitar. This book is presents a series of progressive exercises with the hope of increasing your knowledge and facility with the tenor guitar so that you can apply these skills and use them as a framework for your own music. We are aiming for understanding how chords and important scale tones fit together, the underlying structure that is useful to know for any style of music. Meanwhile, we get to experience the simple joy of practicing our fingering to play each sequence of notes as musically as possible.

I had the great fortune to study classical sitar with Harihar Rao, who was Ravi Shankar's oldest student and collaborator. He taught me sections of one raga for nearly two years! Each week, he would model a new melodic or rhythmic phrase that I was to master by the next lesson. And little by little, the phrases would grow in length and complexity. Finally, he told me, "Now you can play that Raga." All that time, I was studying the "heart" or "skeleton" of the raga, but I wasn't memorizing parts of a piece. I was being given the tools of how the raga fit together with the understanding that the musician brings its "framework" to life. That is my goal with this book; to pass on tools from this CAGED system as a framework for GDAE tenor guitar that you can apply to whatever music you like.

What is the CAGED system?

This book is my version of a CAGED system for the tenor guitar. C, A, G, E, and D are chord shapes that occur in this order up the fretboard to produce the same chord at different locations. Any regular chord has different inversions consisting of the member notes in different arrangements, not always with the root note on the lowest note of the chord. I have named each shape after the way I would play it in the first position down on the 1st or 2nd fret.

When a musician understands the CAGED system, they can play, for example, a C Major chord at the 2nd, 5th, 7th, 10th, 12th, 14th, and 17th frets! This system teaches the student to be able to access the key notes of the chord triad/arpeggios at each position! You will learn important notes and arpeggios as they relate to particular chord shapes. Learning these chord inversions enables a student to have quicker access to understanding how they all connect and how to better play up and down the neck as well as the hidden secrets within the 5 chord shapes. We will use these chords as the "trigger point" for our muscle memory, kind of like physical mnemonic devices for the arpeggios and scales that lie with the chords

The CAGED system makes it easier to learn the defining notes of each particular chord shape, and simplifies understanding of how they connect to each other as you move up the fretboard. If you learn where the important notes are in the context of a chord shape you can more confidently and directly focus your melodies and solos to be more harmonically related to the chord structure of the piece of music. In other words, instead of noodling in the G major scale over a song in the key of G, we can knowingly, and easily choose the arpeggio notes of any chord of the song to emphasize the chord changes as we create melodies.

The following exercises reveal the arpeggio notes of C, A, G, E, and D-shaped chords in major, minor and dominant seventh variations. Of course, you will usually want to add related scale notes other than just playing arpeggio notes when making music, but by using this method, you can choose your notes more confidently, thereby increasing your knowledge and intuition of finding them in any style of music or scale.

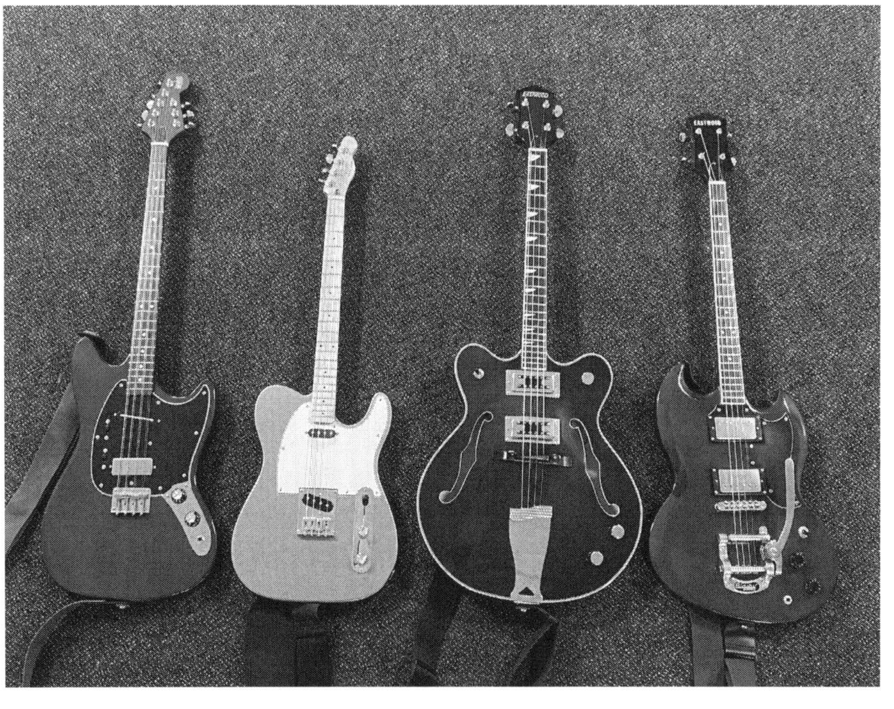

Eastwood Mandocello, Fender Tenor, Tele, Eastwood Classic and Astrojet

Objectives of this Tenor Guitar Method:

1. Memorize 15 chord shapes (5 shapes for each C-A-G-E-D, major, minor and 7th chord) and be able to immediately find the root note in each shape, which is the 1-note.
2. Memorize the arpeggio notes for each of the 15 chord shapes.
3. Play the arpeggios with the notes ringing out clearly and sustaining until you pluck the next note.
4. Play arpeggio notes through various chord changes.
5. Develop a strong and limber pinky for those long stretches.
6. Add notes of a particular scale to your arpeggio notes when creating melodies.
7. Become aware of the parallel structure of the rhythm in melodic phrasing from bar to bar.
8. Become aware of chord shape options when arranging chord progressions.
9. Learn to create melodies that respect the underlying chord structure of a progression.
10. Have fun practicing for its own sake!

Holding the Pick: The plane of the first finger nail is parallel to the side of the thumb. The pick is at near ninety degrees to that plane. Use a down/up alternating pick motion in most cases. For jigs, it is common to use a down-up-down, down-up-down triplet pattern to emphasize the first and fourth notes. Keep the wrist loose.

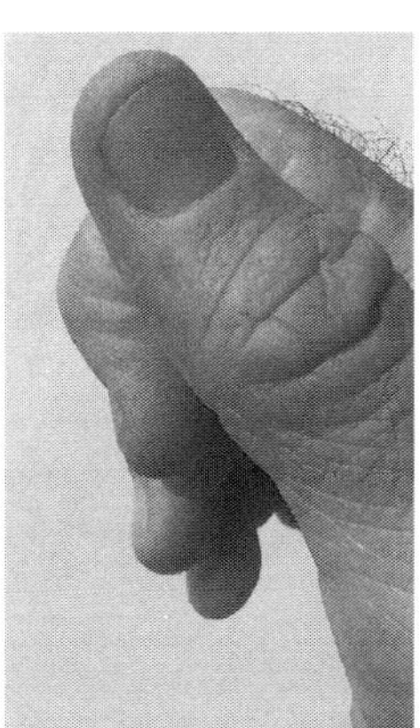
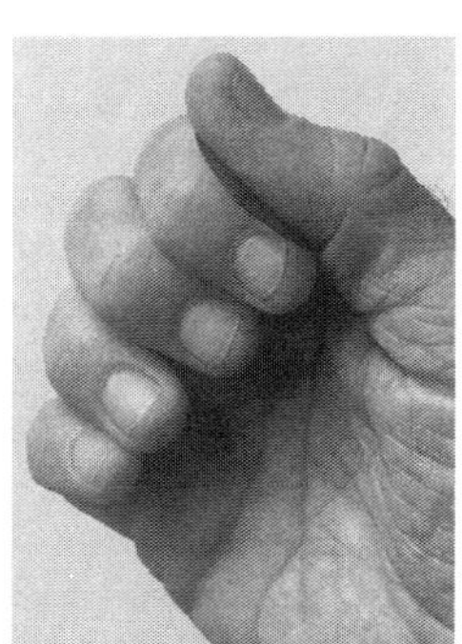
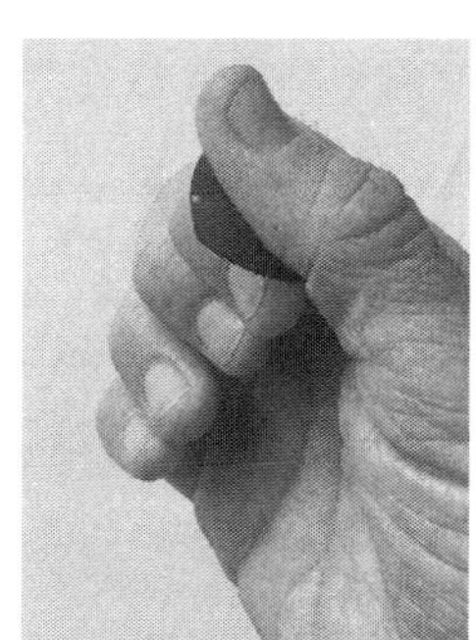
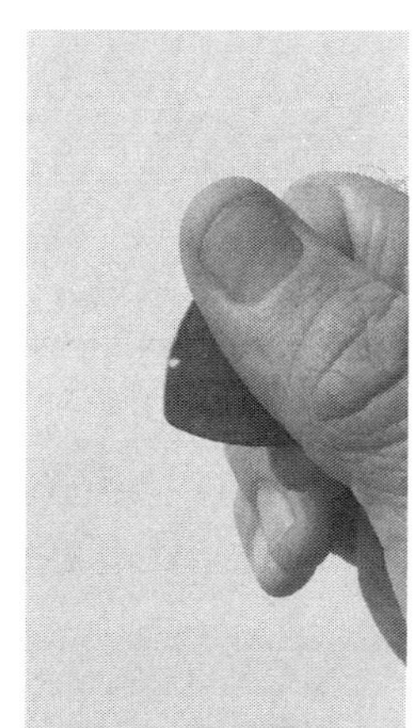

5 Major Chord Shapes

Here are each of the major chord shapes: C, A, G, E, and D. At the fret positions indicated, each of these is a C major chord. Try fingering each chord noticing where the shapes overlap. The fret numbers are on the left side of each chart. X marks the string you don't play; a square indicates the root, tonic, or "1" notes; and the numbers under the chord grid are fingering suggestions. I recommend using the pinky (4) often, but sometimes you may prefer to use your 3rd finger (3) where appropriate for you. As you can see, if you learn how these shapes connect, you will have much greater access to playing chord inversions up and down the entire tenor guitar fretboard. Learn the connecting or common tones between each chord shape.

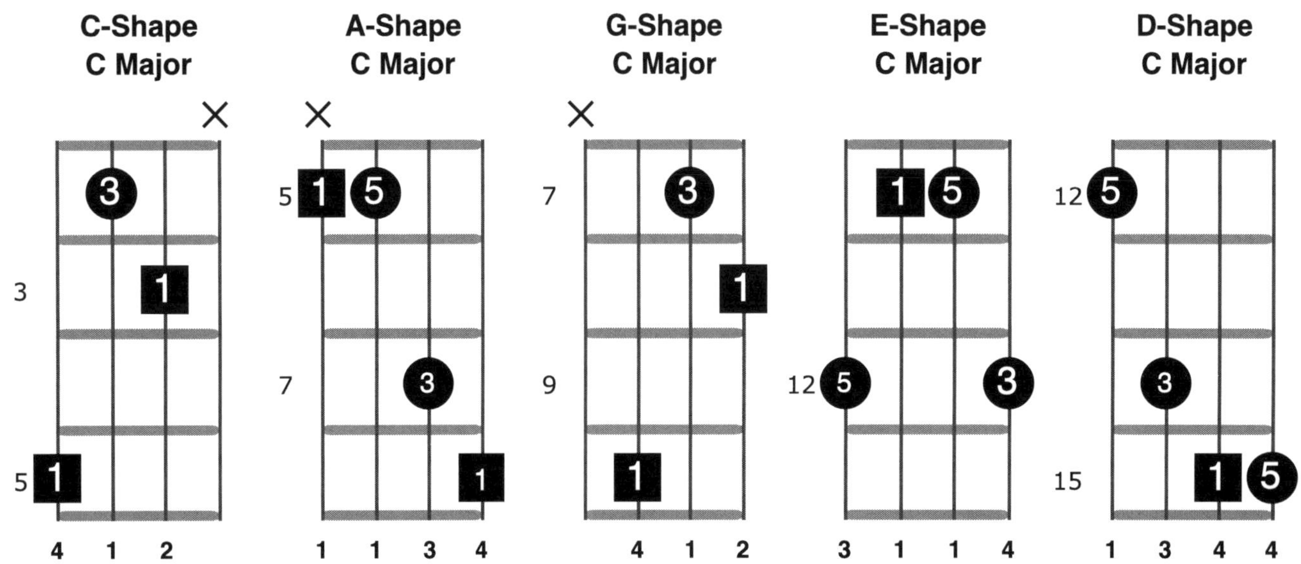

Note that chord shapes are all movable. Use the root notes to find the chords you want. For example: Within the A-shaped C major chord above, you can see the root or tonic note C at the 5th fret on the G-string. If you wanted to play an A-shaped D major chord you would find the D root or 1 note at the 7th fret on the low string and make the A-shaped major chord form there. Always be aware of where the root notes are in each chord shape. As you get better at this, it will be faster and easier to find the chords you want anywhere.

GDAE Tenor Guitar Fretboard

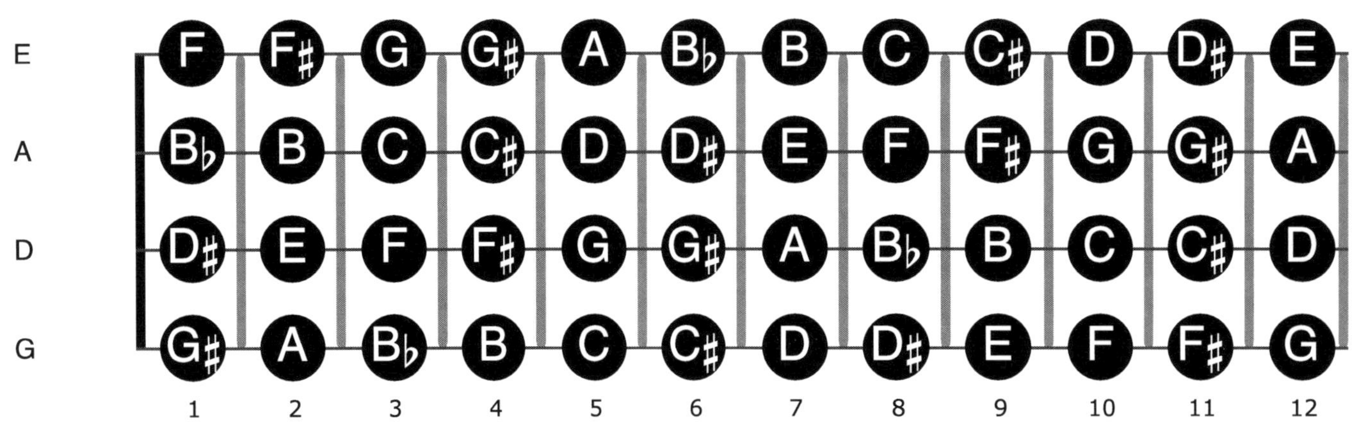

Notes on the GDAE tenor guitar fretboard (Open strings GDAE, bottom to top)

5 Minor Chord Shapes

Here are each of the minor chord shapes showing Em up the neck. Notice the E root notes (square).

E-Shape
E Minor

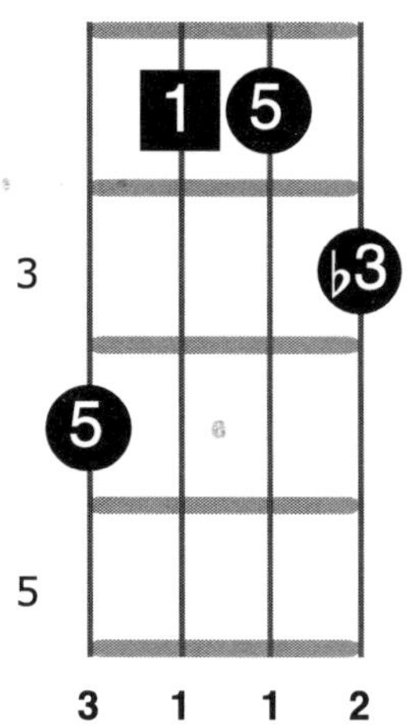

D-Shape
E Minor

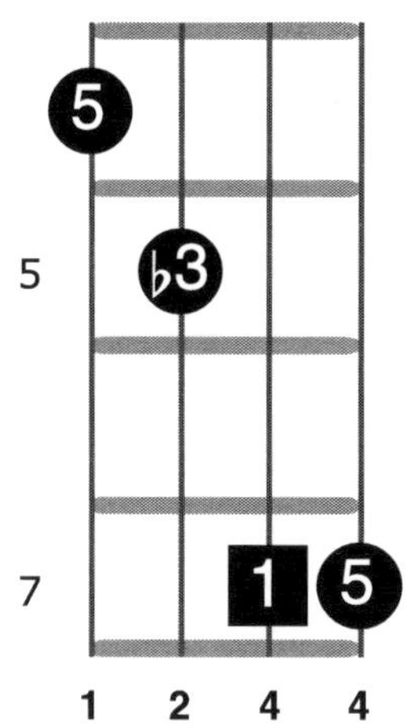

C-Shape
E Minor

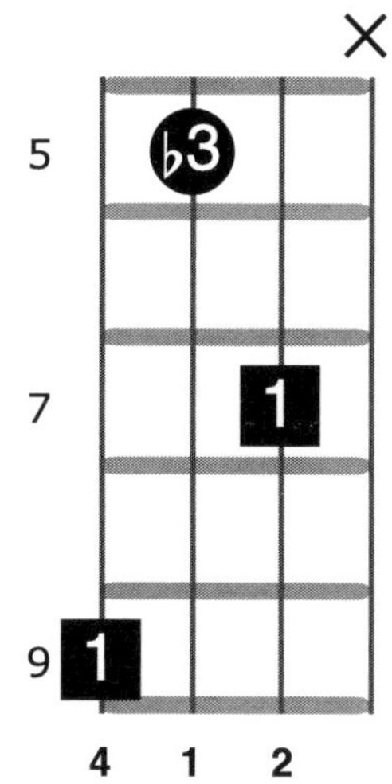

A-Shape
E Minor

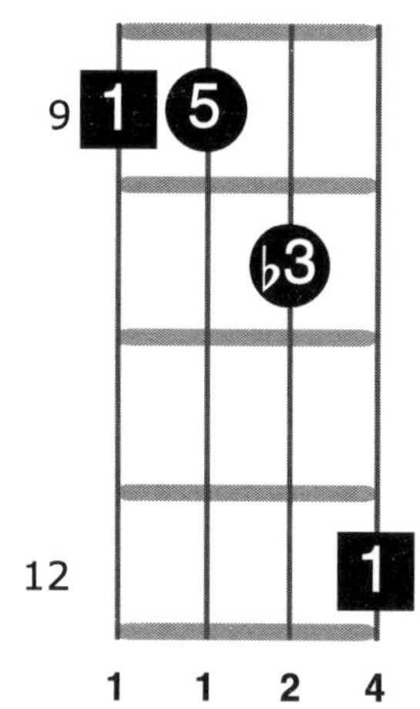

G-Shape
E Minor

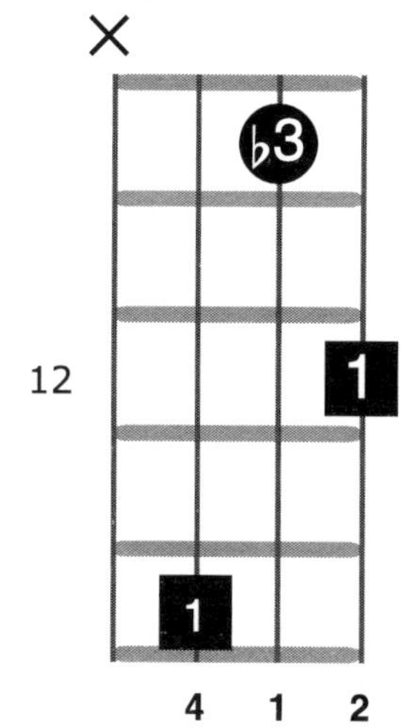

Five Dominant 7th Chord Shapes

Here are each of the 7th chord shapes showing A7 up the neck starting with the A-shape A7 chord. Notice the D-shape A7 chord has no A root note in the chord!

A-Shape
A7

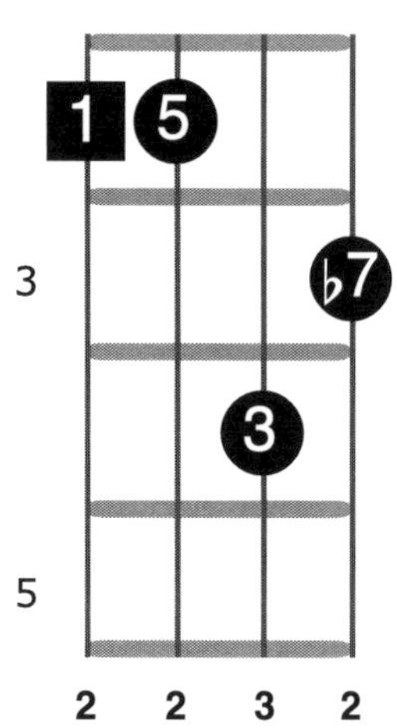

G-Shape
A7

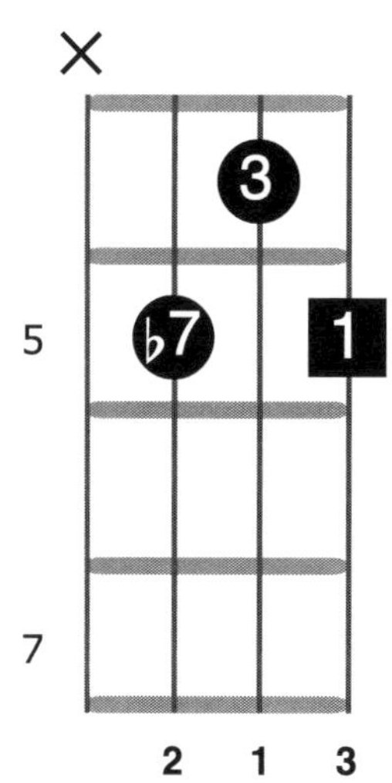

E-Shape
A7

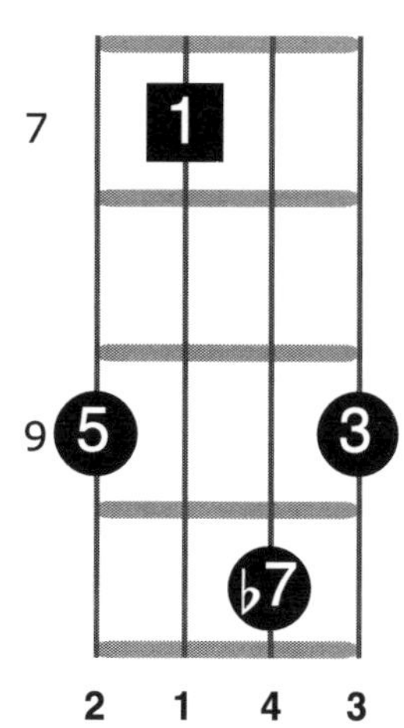

D-Shape
A7

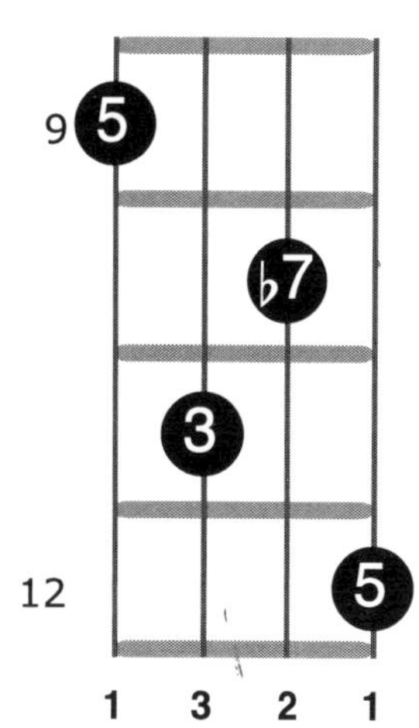

C-Shape
A7

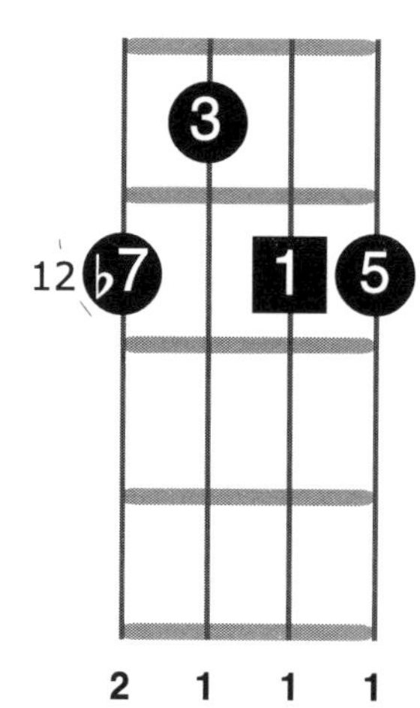

Book Organization

This book is organized in 7 chapters; Chapters 1-5 focus on each chord shape: C, A, G, E and D. Within each of these chord shape chapters are four sections featuring the chord shape, arpeggio, chord variations and finger dexterity exercises for: 1.) major chord, 2.) minor chord, 3.) 7th chord, and 4.) the last section of each chapter suggests melody ideas with examples of how to apply these particular chord shape arpeggios in a more musical context. Chapter 6 shows how to find major scale notes related to each chord shape, and Chapter 7 has exercises on how to create a melody while keeping the chord structure clear on a more complex song, "Waiting for Penny".

Here are the major chord forms that are the basis of this tenor guitar method. These shapes are all movable. The "1" is always the root note of the chord. For example, in the C-shape major chord,

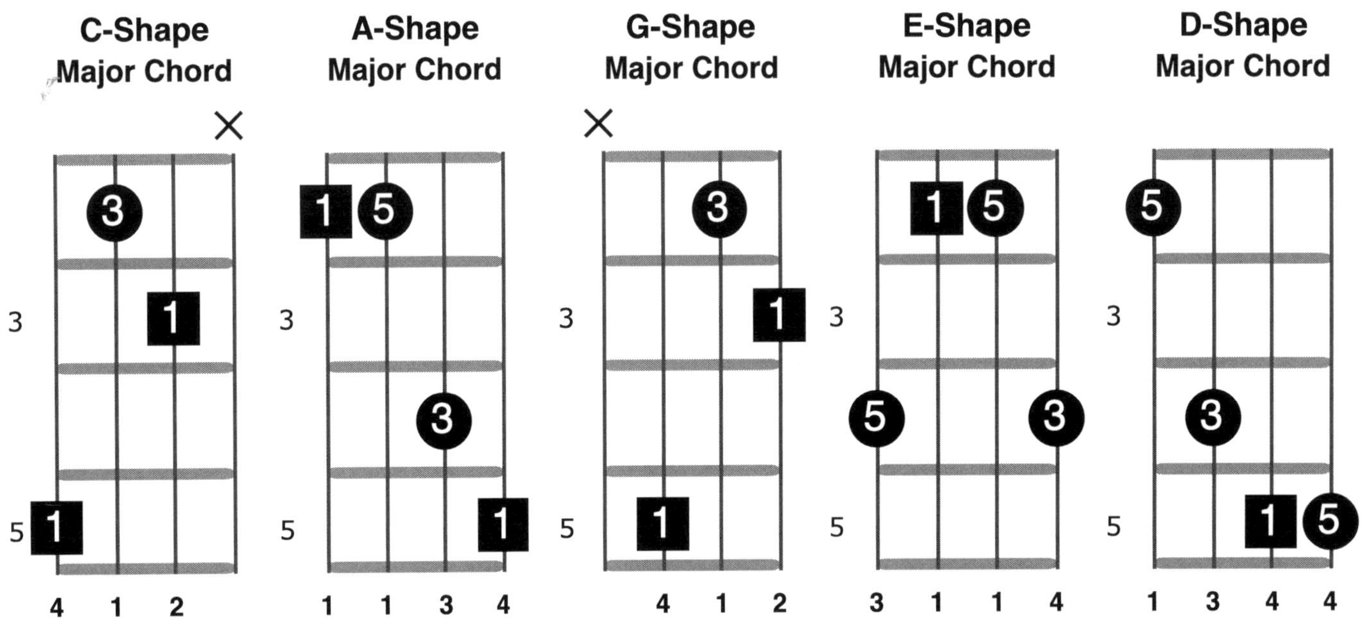

the two notes marked "1" are both root notes. The first and most important strategy is to learn and memorize where the "1" notes are in each chord shape; then, you will be able to quickly make the chords you want anywhere on the fingerboard. The numbers on the chord charts refer to the scale degree, which is also very valuable information.

What are arpeggios and what is this 1, 3, 5 stuff?

The term, scale degree simply refers to the numbered note of a diatonic scale used to indicate a chord. The major scale has 8 notes. In C Major, the notes are C, D, E, F, G, A, B, C. Major chords are made up of the first, third, and fifth notes of the major scale: C, E, and G in this case. Arpeggios consits of playing these notes of the chord in a broken or consectutive pattern rather than by strumming. If you want to play a melodic phrase over a major chord and you emphasize the arpeggio notes (1, 3, 5), your melody will sound like it belongs there because it will be harmonically in sync with the chord that is playing behind it. This method allows a good melody player to suggest underlying chord changes while playing a melody, riff, or solo. If this sounds like a good idea to you, let's get started! The word triad refers to a 3-note chord, usually the 1, 3, and 5 notes in a scale.

Chapter 1-1: C-Shape Major Chords and Arpeggio Exercises

C-Shape Major Chord

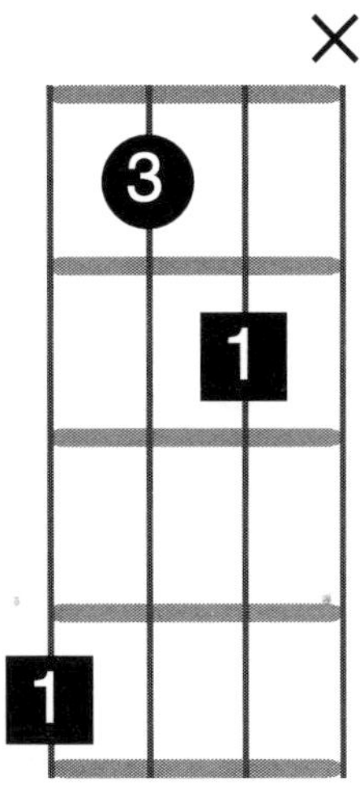

4 1 2

To move this chord anywhere on the neck, just locate the note you want on the low G string, make this shape and you have the major chord in the C-shape of the particular chord you want.

Here is the C-shape major chord. This shape has two root notes, with one of them falling on the lowest string. This gives the chord a strong fundamental root note that is clearly defined. This chord shape is made up of just the 1 note and the major third note.

The x means that the string is muted. When played with the low note at the fifth fret, the C-shape major chord is an actual C major chord, so you can let that high E string ring because it is another one of the arpeggio notes in the C major chord. But, when played elsewhere on the fretboard, most often you would want to mute the high string, which can be done by rotating your hand slightly so that the lower part of your first finger slightly touches the string.

At right, you'll see the notes of the C-shape major arpeggio with suggested fingering below the grid. Remember this shape can be moved anywhere on the fretboard. Whatever note is at the "1" position is the **root note** of the arpeggio.

C-Shape Major Arpeggio

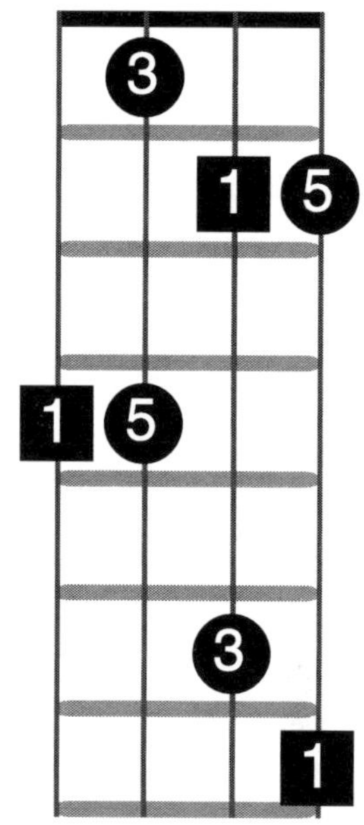

3 1 1 1
3 4 4

Alternative Chord Shapes

Oftentimes on the GDAE tenor guitar, we play chords that don't always have the 1, 3, and 5 notes in them, like our first C-shape major chord above. In these cases, you can substitute alternative major chords shapes, and use different combinations of the arpeggio notes.

C-Shape Major Chord Variation 1

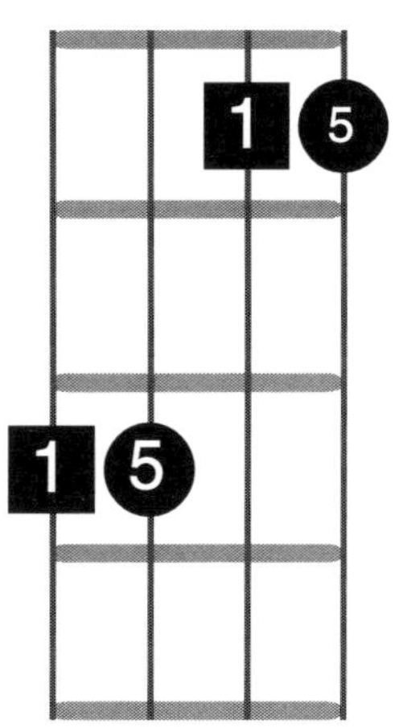

3 4 1 1

C-Shape Major Chord Variation 2

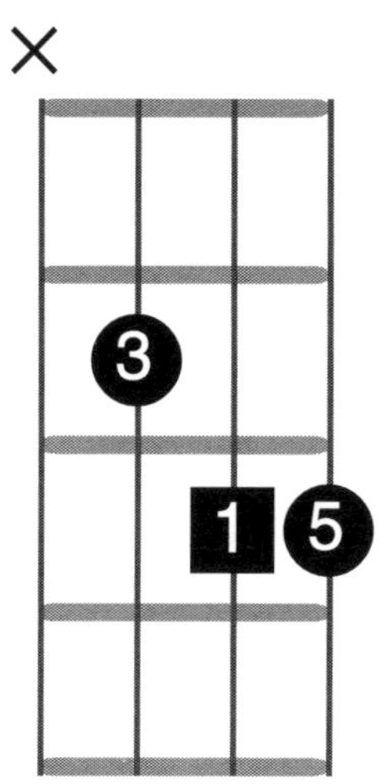

1 2 2

C-Shape Major Chord Variation 3

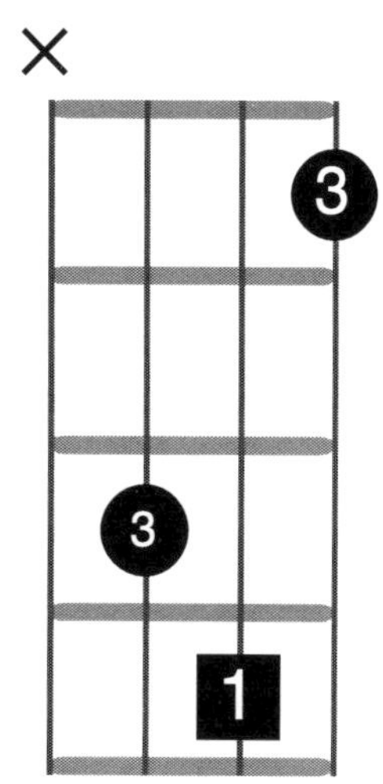

3 4 1

C-Shape Major Chord Variation 4

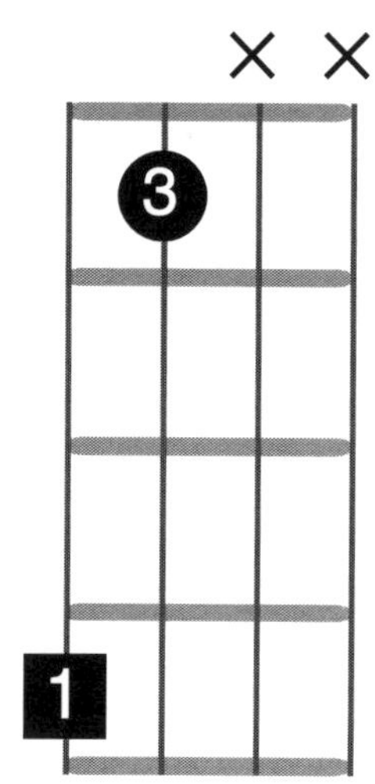

4 1

Set a metronome at a tempo that allows you to be able to play each note cleanly so that it rings out. Locate a C-shaped D major chord with the root note at 7th fret on the G-string - and run through this arpeggio up and down, over and over until it's automatic. Strum the D-major chord in between each pass to memorize the pattern as attached to the chord.

It's best to start out slowly. The goal is to play each note so that it rings out and sustains until we pluck the next one. Use a metronome to gaurantee you are playing at an even tempo. There are many free metronome apps and websites that have very flexible settings. At first, set the metronome at a slow tempo and play one note per beat. Notice that this arpeggio has a 6 fret spread. Let's start our practice with the D major chord in the C-shape.

C-Shape Major Exercise 1: Repeat this over and over until you can play it smoothly with each note ringing until the next note is plucked, and then gradually increase your speed. Also, try practicing the pattern at different locations up and down the neck. To repeat, it's important to strum the chord at the end, so that you are memorizing key arpeggio notes by muscle memory as connected to that chord shape.

C-Shape Major Exercise 1

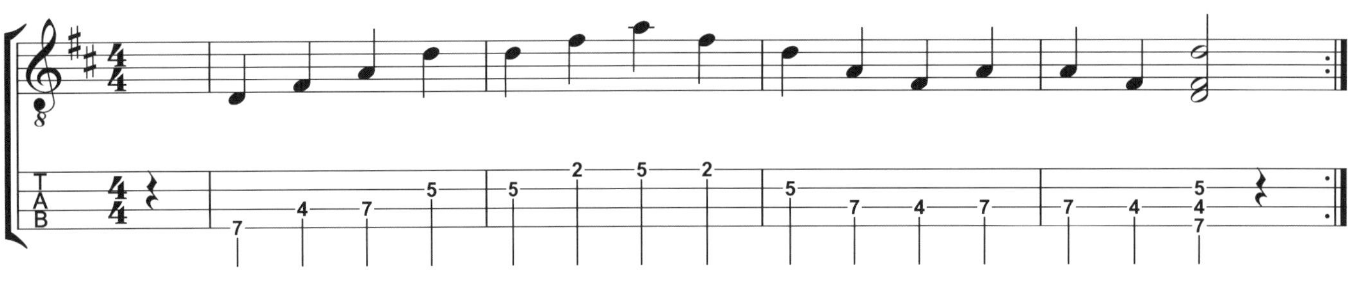

C-Shape Major Exercise 2: Now try the same arpeggio pattern double time. Play two notes per metronome beat at the same setting. Don't speed up until you can play it cleanly. Try to stay on your fingertips. After you have the pattern memorized and can play it without looking, try moving it to other C-shape major chords.

C-Shape Major Exercise 2

D Major

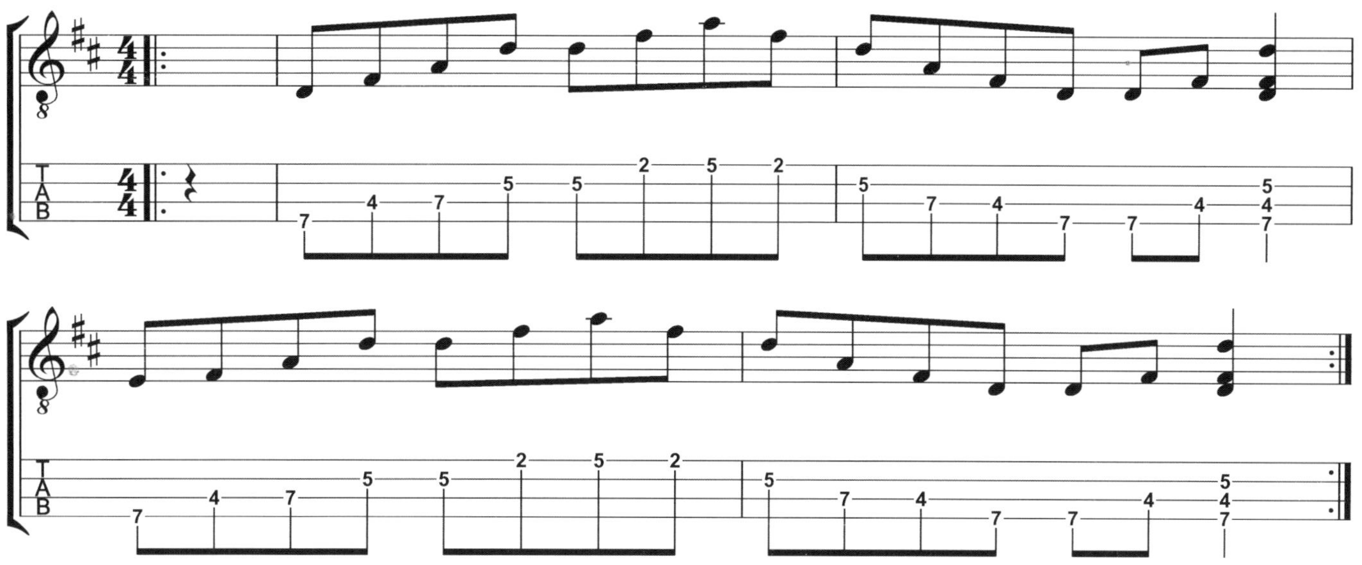

C-Shape Major Exercise 3: Move the major arpeggio between two chords, D major to E major, one step apart. One step equals two frets. The D major arpeggio can be found on the low string at the seventh fret, and the E moves up to the ninth fret. As you get better at moving the arpeggio around, practice moving between 3 chords, then 4. And when it gets really easy, experiment by altering the last 2-3 notes of each bar.

C-Shape Major Exercise 3

Moving from D Major to E Major

D Major

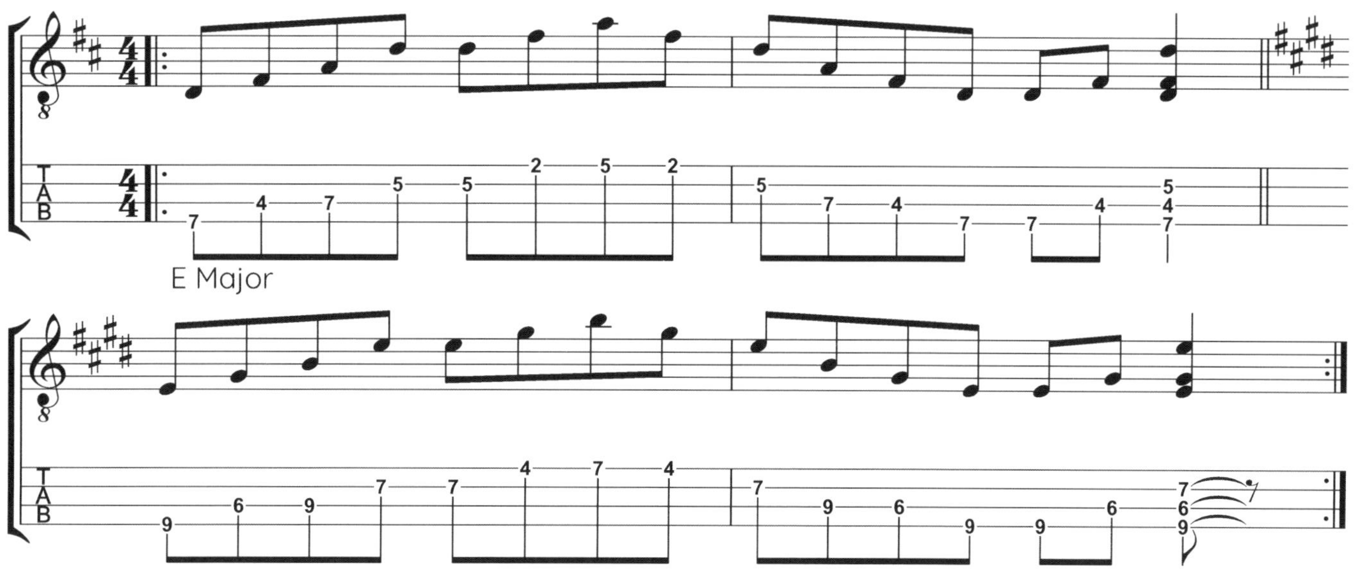

The Pinky and the Tenor Guitar

One of the challenges of playing an instrument with a long scale that is tuned in fifths is that the finger stretches can be quite long. It's important to develop strength and flexibility with the pinky. This next exercise will do that. Shorter scale instruments will be easier to play. The most common scale is 23". My tenors are this length. Often, I wish they were 20 or 21 inches. Another idea is to use a capo to play higher up the neck and shortened fret distances - until you get used to the stretch.

C-Shape Major Exercise 4: This exercise requires some finger stretching. In the second bar, try fretting the B note (9th fret D-string) with the pinky, the E (7th fret A-string) with the second or third finger, and the G♯ on the high string with the first finger. Try to leave your pinky in place (or nearly in place) so that it's already there when you pluck the E note again at the seventh fret on the A-string. In bar 3, you will need to shift your hand. Try fretting the G♯ on the high string with the first finger, and then move that first finger up to the B before stretching your pinky up to the 12th fret. Play the G♯ at the eleventh fret on the A-string with your third finger. Again, leave your third finger and pinky in place to start the next phrase at the second half of bar 3. This exercise is more difficult due to the position shifting and long stretches. Give it a try, nice and slow at first. Sometimes it's helpful to practice without the metronome until you have your finger positions sorted out in a way that works for you. Practice short sections until it's smooth.

4

C-Shape Major Exercise 4

E Major

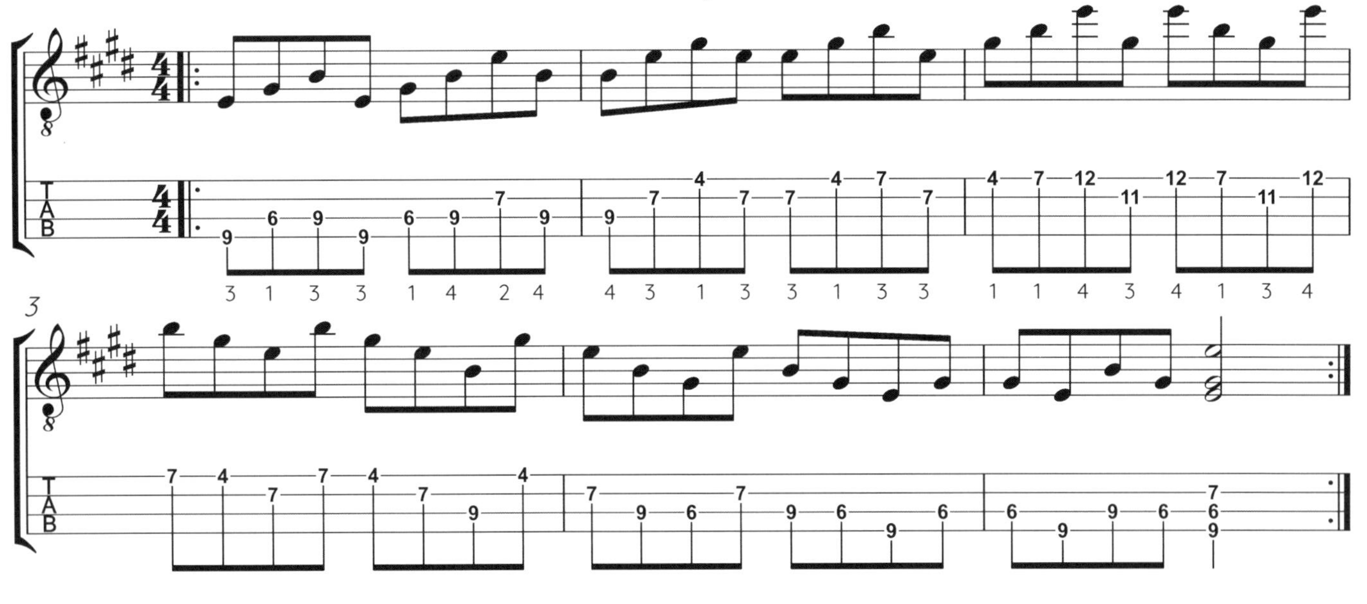

Practice Tip: Memorize Small Sections

Practice Tip: It's perfectly alright and you are encouraged to shorten practice phrases down to a few notes and play them over and over until you can play them smoothly and then add more notes. I like to learn 4 notes until I can play them without thinking, then add four more until those are down, then go back to the start and try to memorize 3 sections of four notes as so on until the whole exercise is memorized.

If you run into phrases that are difficult, don't rush through those and convince yourself you have them down, when you really don't. If you hear your pick clicking loudly instead of a clear ringing note, then you know it's time to keep practicing. The best players stop when they get to difficult sections, and focus on those until they are mastered. Then they go back and try to play them within the whole piece.

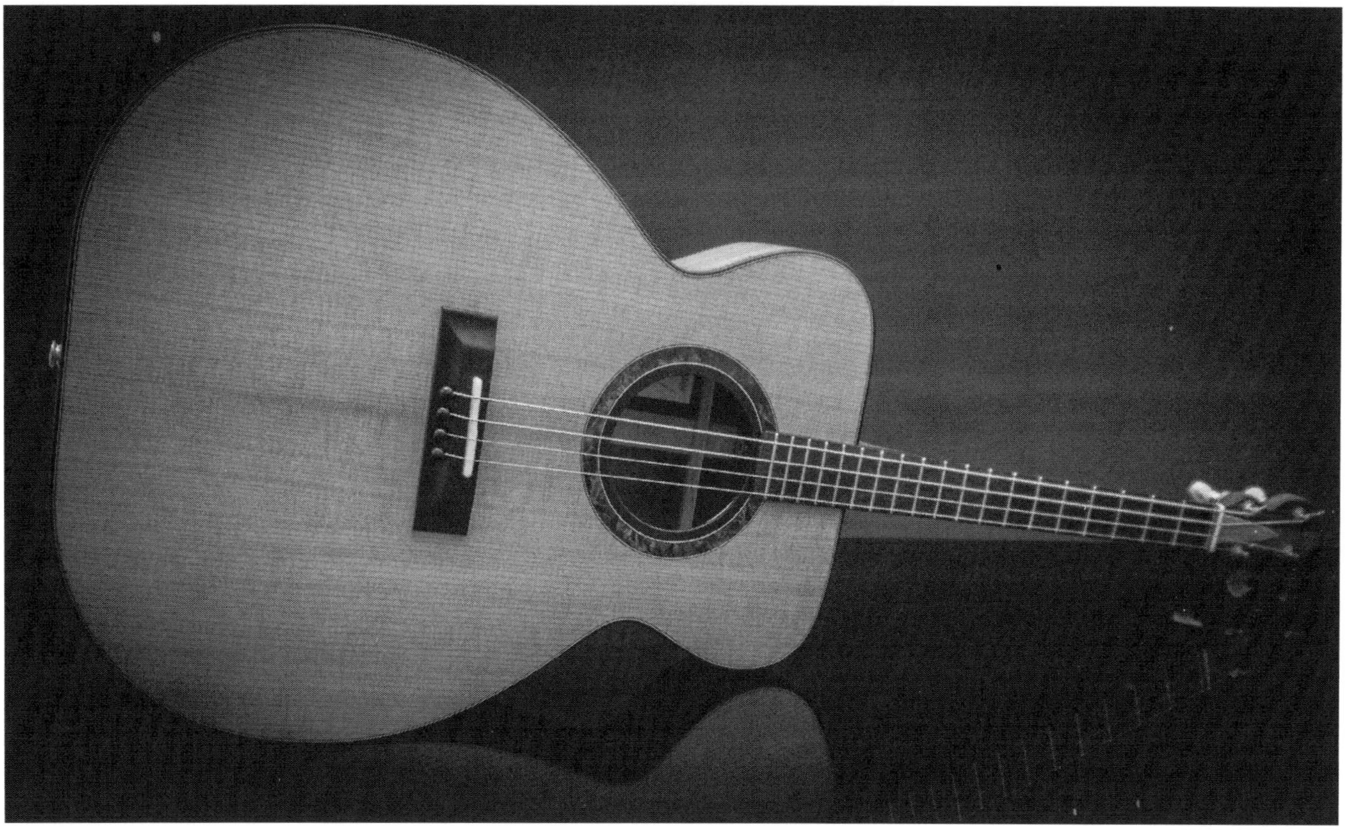

Session King by Nigel Forster

In general, it's most effective to alternate up and down pick strokes, especially for tunes in 4/4 time. In 6/8, it's good to emphasize the 1 and 4 notes, with a down-up-down, down-up-down triplet pattern. It's good to try to play the exercises with consistently plucked notes that ring with nearly similar volume and duration. Once you can do that, have fun making the exercises more musical with varying dynamics, and tempos, etc. Remember these exercises are a framework to build on, not an end in themselves.

Chapter 1-2: C-Shape Minor Chords and Arpeggio Exercises

C-Shape
Minor Chord

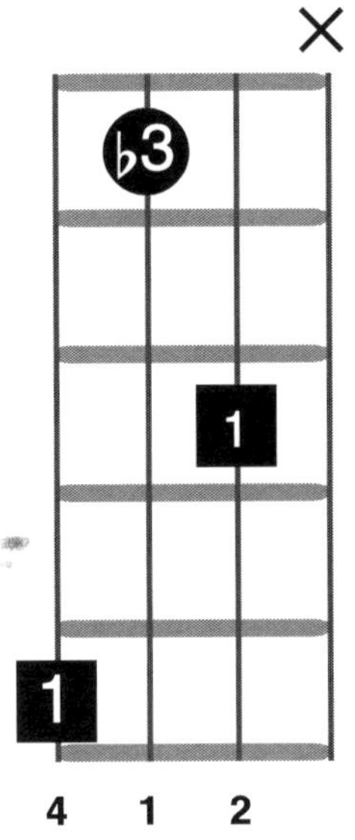

Here is the C-shape minor chord. Like the major chord, this shape has two root notes, with one of them falling on the lowest string. Also, like the C-shape major, this gives the chord a strong fundamental root note that is clearly defined. This chord shape is made up of just the 1 note and the minor third note. The only difference between the minor and major chords is that the third note moves down one half-step (one fret) from the major third to the flat third.

Before you try the finger exercises below, practice this arpeggio up and back, many times, while looking at the chart to aid visual memory, and until you can play it without thinking too much or looking at your fingers.

C-Shape
Minor Arpeggio

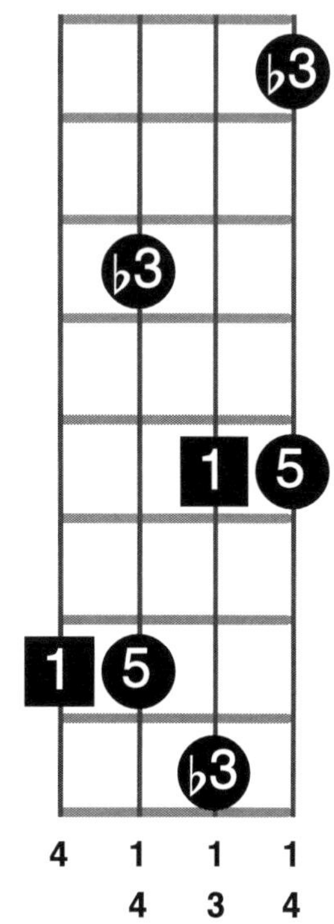

C-Shape Minor Chord Variations: Variation 1 uses the 1 and 5 notes, and can be used as a minor or major chord, since it has no major or minor third interval. Variation 2 only uses the lower two notes of the chord. Usually, you will want to mute the high strings with the side of your first finger. Variation 3 doesn't have the root note on the lowest string. Try muting the low string with your thumb around the back of the neck. And variation 4 is a long stretch. Try making your own variations!

C-Shape
Minor Chord
Variation 1

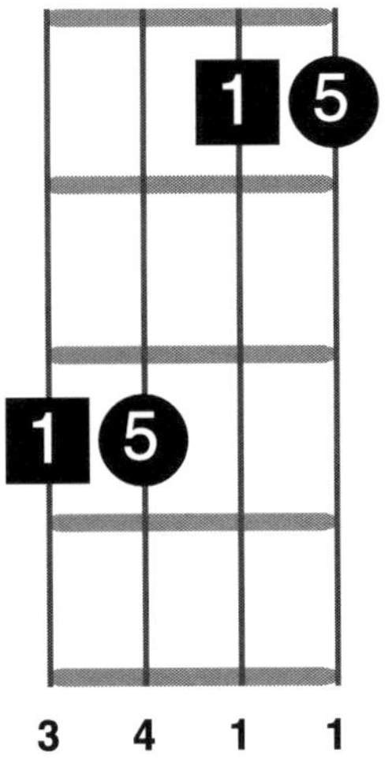

C-Shape
Minor Chord
Variation 2

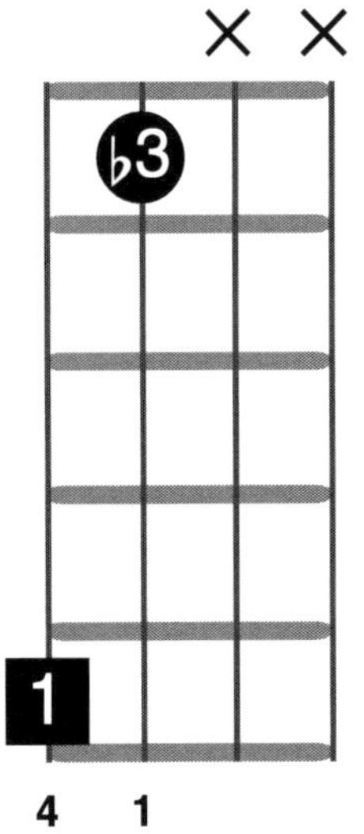

C-Shape
Minor Chord
Variation 3

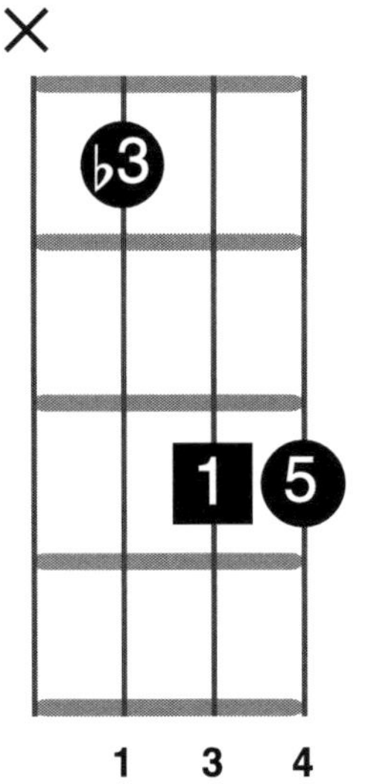

C-Shape
Minor Chord
Variation 4

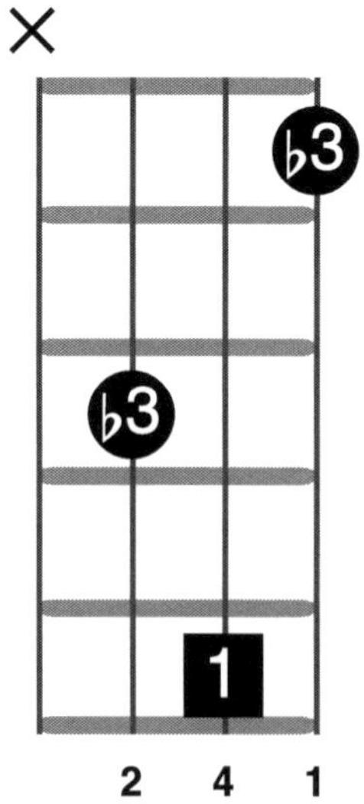

C-Shape Minor Exercise 1: Practice this C-shape minor arpeggio in E minor. This is a good arpeggio to get to know better, since Em is the relative minor of G major, which is commonly used for tenor guitar tuned GDAE. If we number our fretting fingers; 1, 2, 3, with 4 for the pinky, try this fingering in the first bar (4, 1, 4, 2, 4, 1, 4, 1). This will require a quick shift between the two E-notes from 2nd to 4th finger, between the 4th and 5th notes in bar 1. You might try this fingering (4, 1, 4, 4, 4, 1, 4, 1) which brings the pinky from the 9th to 7th fret between the 3rd and 4th note in bar 1. See which one works better for you. Remember, start slowly!

5

C-Shape Minor Exercise 1

E Minor

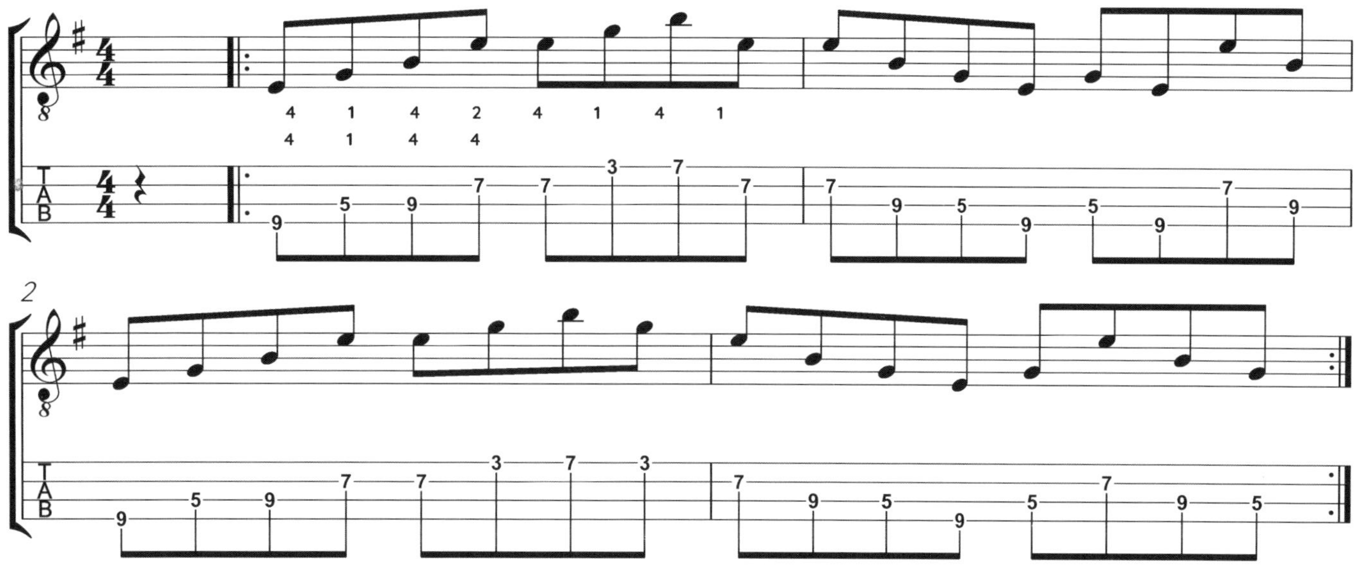

C-Shape Minor Exercise 2: Try a different pattern that changes direction and extends up to a higher note in the arpeggio. Let's keep practicing in E minor, but remember that once the fingering pattern is internalized in your muscle memory, you can move it anywhere on the neck for very useful notes within a minor chord arpeggio. The next exercise is a jig in 6/8.

6

C-Shape Minor Exercise 2

E Minor

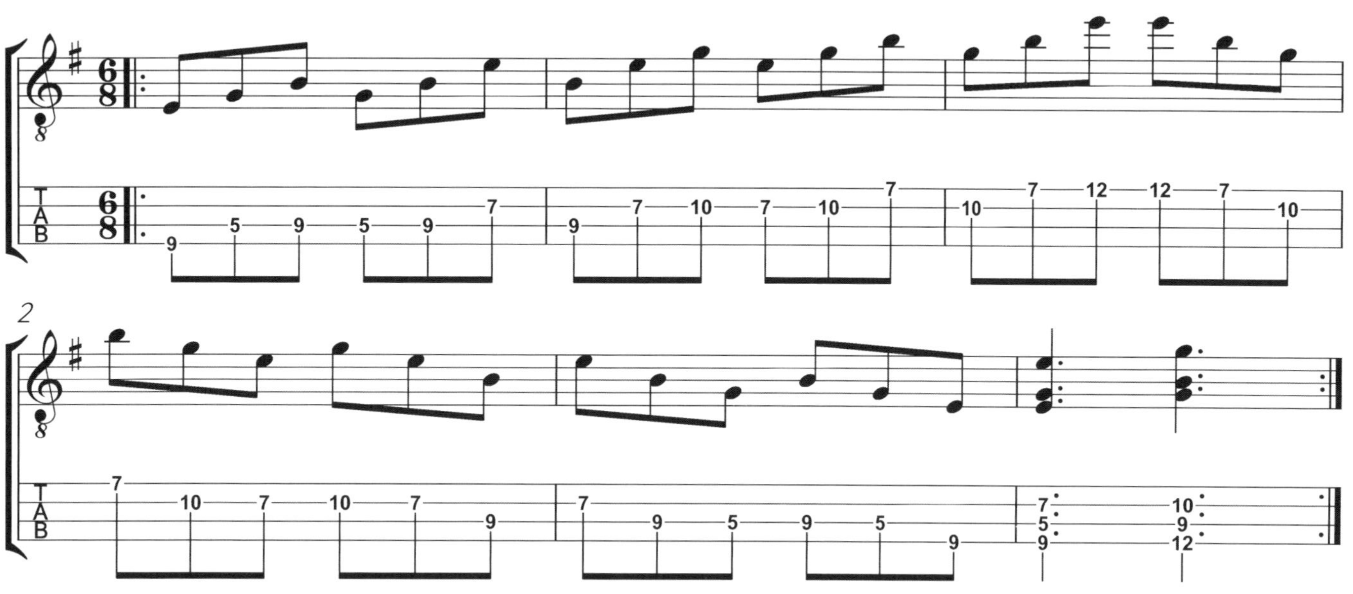

C-Shape Minor Exercise 3: Next, let's practice moving between C-shape minor and major arpeggios. E minor is the relative minor of G major. It's easy to find your relative minors for any major key. From your major root note, say G (12 fret on the low string), count down a step and a half (3 frets) to the E (9th fret, low string), and there's the relative minor. These chord intervals are heard in thousands of songs, so it's good for you to know them too!

7

C-Shape Minor Exercise 3

E Minor to G Major

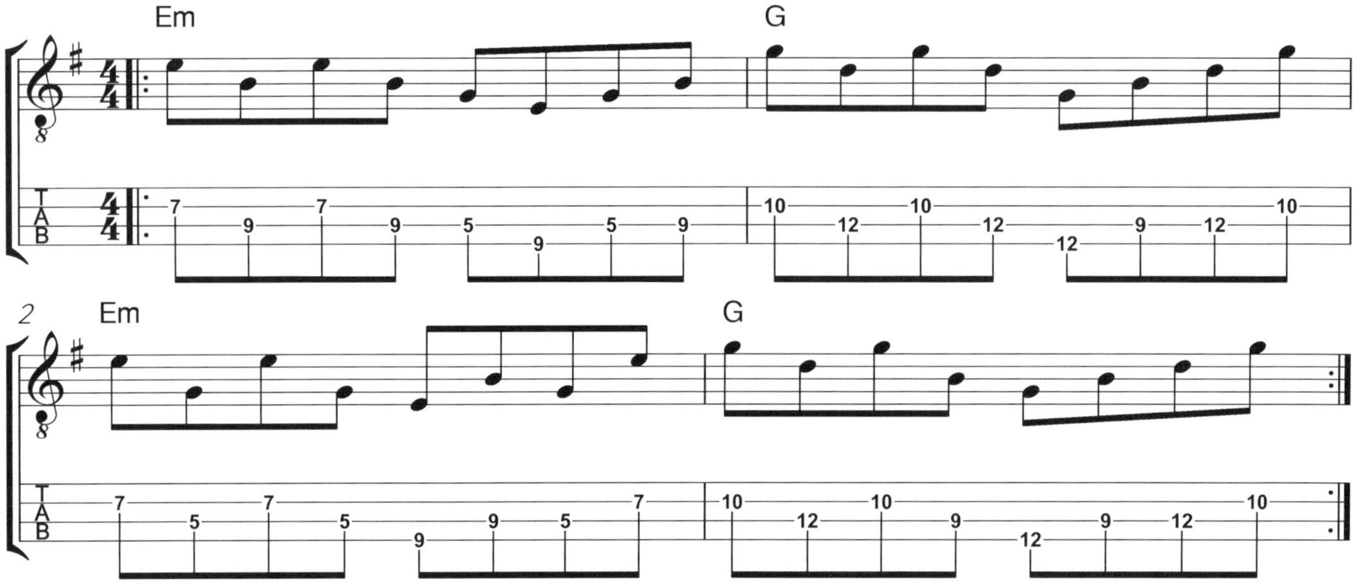

C-Shape Minor Exercise 4: Let's further cement the E minor to G major arpeggios connection with this rhythm exercise. Watch the time signature changes. Practice this over and over until you can smoothly sound each note and move between arpeggios without sliding your notes unintentionally. Move this around the neck to memorize your relative minor to major chord arpeggios. For practice variation, use this rhythm with different note patterns anywhere on the neck, with any scale or pattern you know. Use a metronome!

8

C-Shape Minor Exercise 4

Rhythm Practice

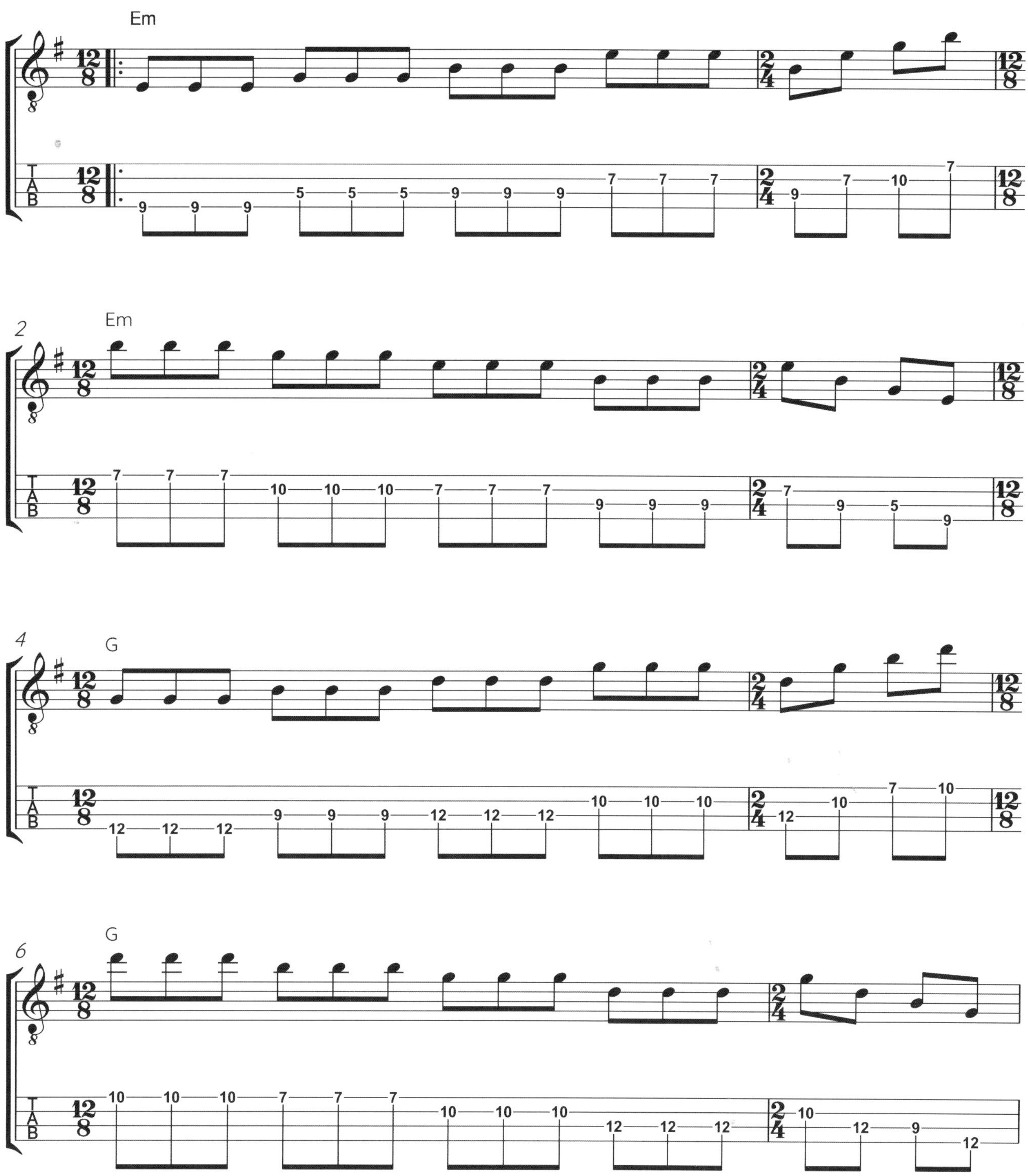

Practice Tip:

These practice patterns are just that, patterns. It's up to you to make them musical and fun for yourself. Try adding some of these new ideas to the songs you already know. There's a lot to learn and practice just within one bar; change the tempo, riff on two notes back-and-both, emphasize some notes while barely sounding others, strum a chord at intervals, play each note as a triplet, reverse directions, break the patterns apart, make little sing-songs phrases, change keys, etc. Then use them in your songs.

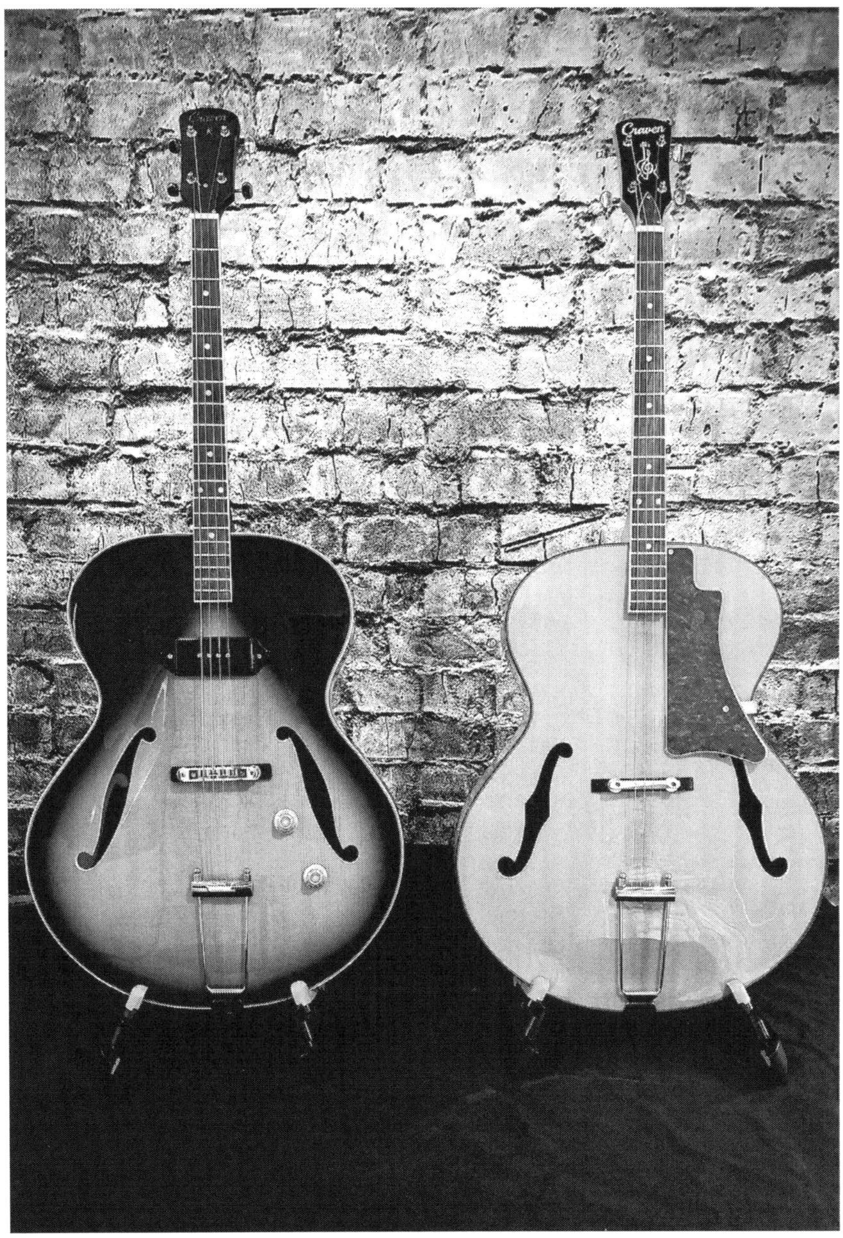

Arch top tenor guitars by Craven

Chapter 1-3: C-Shape Seventh Chords and Arpeggio Exercises

C-Shape
7th Chord

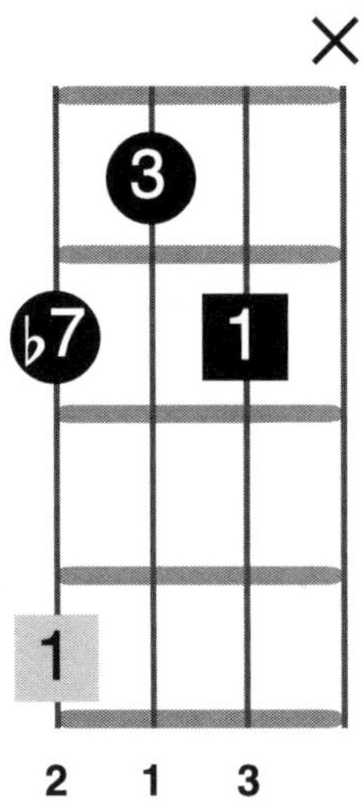

This shape emphasizes the note one step down from the root note, the flatted 7th note. The seventh chord in the C-shape doesn't have a strong low root note that is clearly defined. The C7 chord wants to resolve to another chord - F major. Sometimes it's helpful to reach up with the pinky and play the root note, or have someone else in the band emphasize the root note. This chord shape is made up of the ♭7, the major 3rd, and the highest note - the root note. To discover where to play this chord, just find the root note on the low string, and then move down 2 frets.

The C7 arpeggio is nearly the same as the major arpeggio, but adds one note, the flat 7- B♭. Also, notice the repeating "stair-step" pattern, where the pattern on the low two strings is repeated on the high two strings, shifted down toward the nut, 1 step. When practicing the arpeggios, remember to strum the chord that goes with it to lock into memory the arpeggio notes.

C-Shape
7th Arpeggio

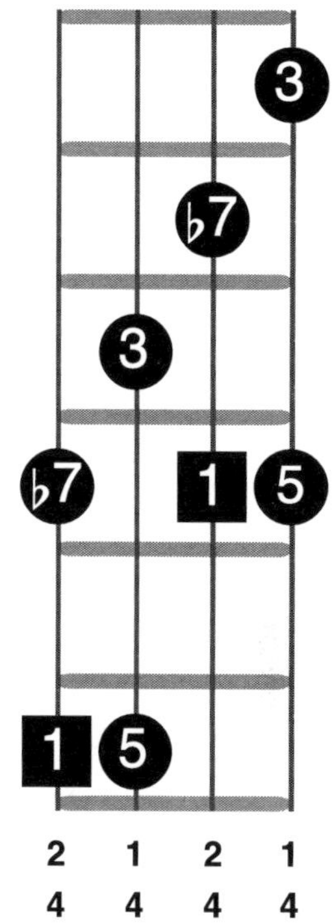

C-Shape 7th Chord Variations

Three of these C-shape 7th variations adds a fourth note which lets you strum all 4 strings. Variations 2 and 3 do not have the 1-note, and will sound less defined than other variations. Variation 4 has the root note back on the low string, but does require a finger stretch, and may be easier to finger higher up the neck.

C-Shape
7th Chord
Variation 1

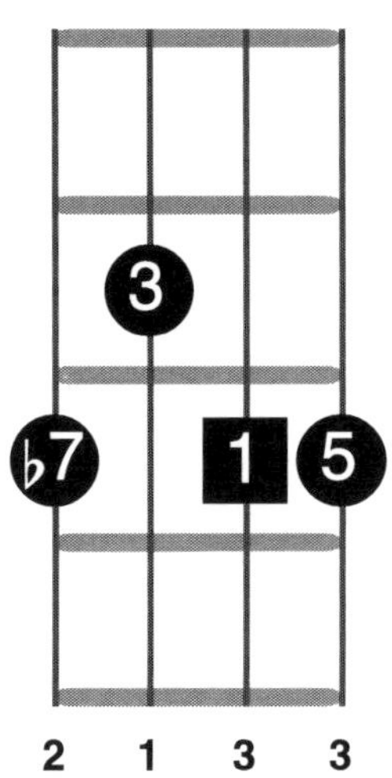

C-Shape
7th Chord
Variation 2

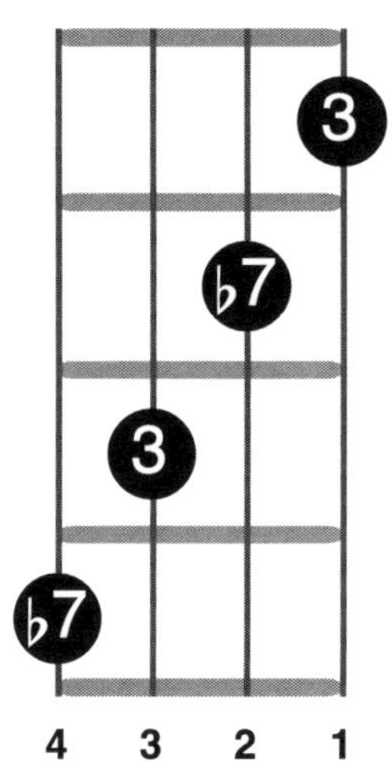

C-Shape
7th Chord
Variation 3

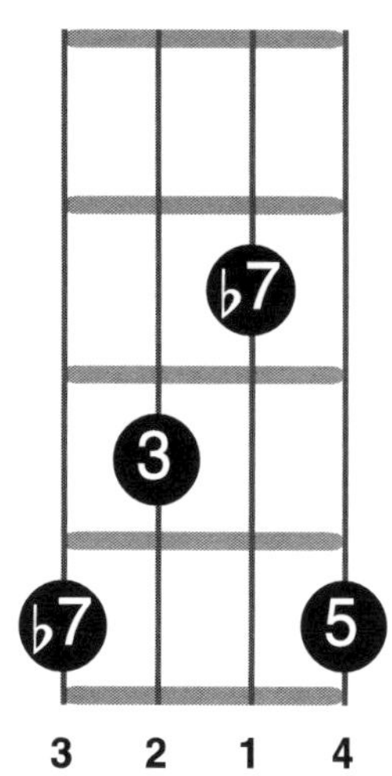

C-Shape
7th Chord
Variation 4

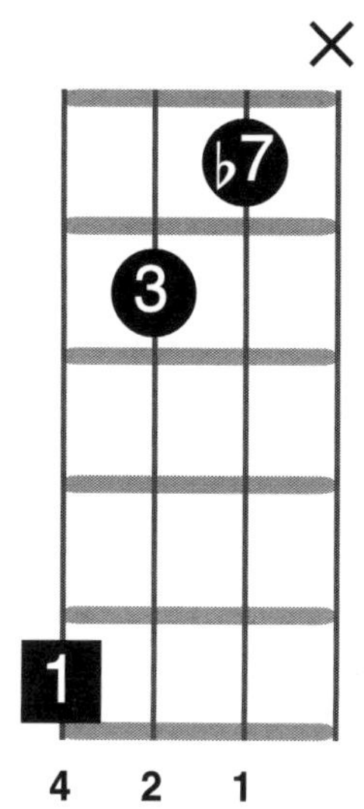

C-Shape 7th Exercise 1: This study includes chords in the pattern; when you make up your own practice patterns remember to locate and play your home chord to tie these notes into your muscle memory of fingering the chords. The second half of this exercise is fairly challenging, so it might be a good idea to start by memorizing bars 1-3, and then practice bars 4-6 before playing them all at once. Don't forget to try these patterns in other places up and down the neck.

C-Shape 7th Exercise 1

E7

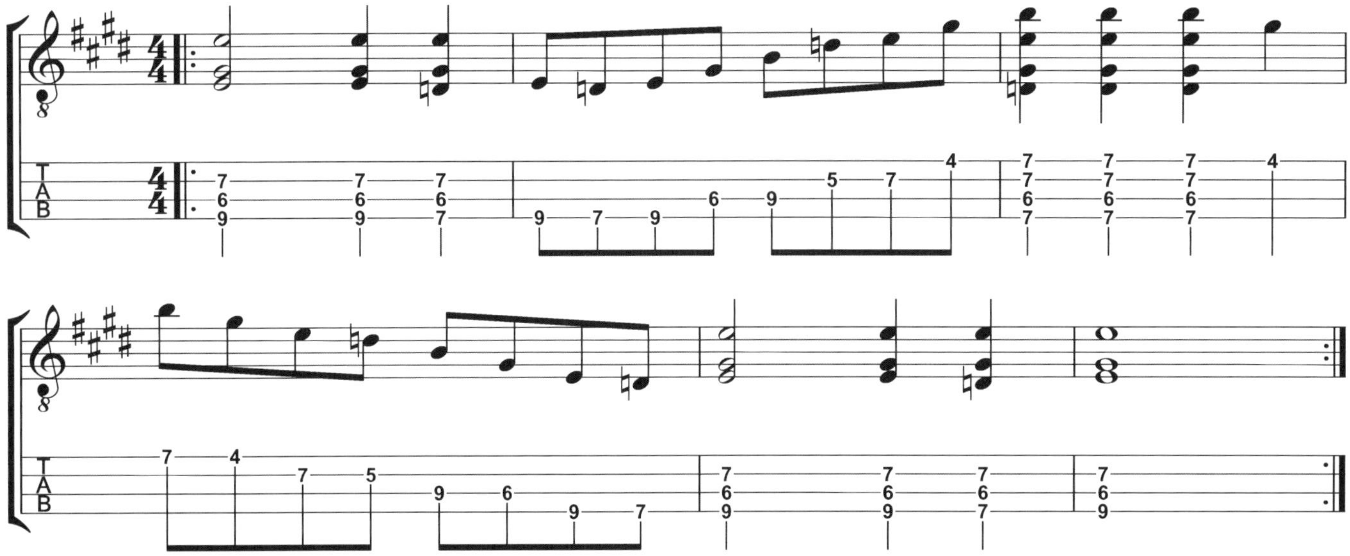

C-Shape 7th Exercise 2: This study uses an arpeggio pattern that moves forward in sequence of four notes, then starts the next four notes in order from the second note of the previous pattern, and so on.

C-Shape 7th Exercise 2

D7

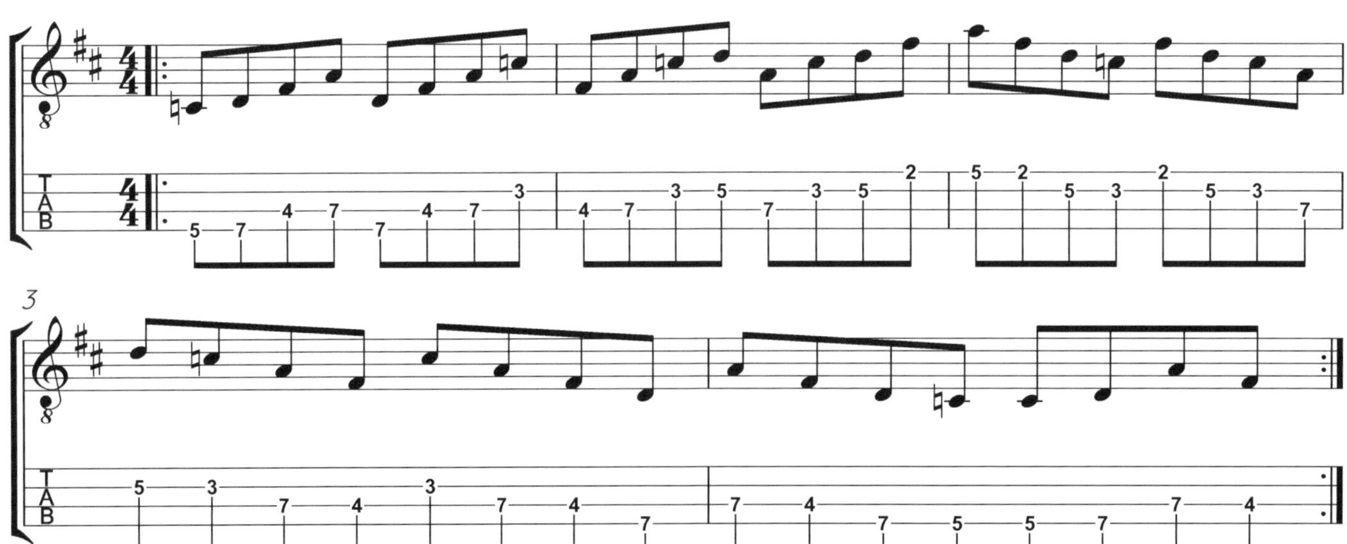

C-Shape 7th Exercise 3: The arpeggio moves from the C-shape 7th arpeggio to the C-shape minor arpeggio. Practice each bar until you can play it cleanly and then add another. There is a big position shift from bar 3 to 4. Plan your fingers out ahead of time! Notice how the arpeggios connect to each other from bar to bar.

11

C-Shape 7th Exercise 3

D7 - E minor

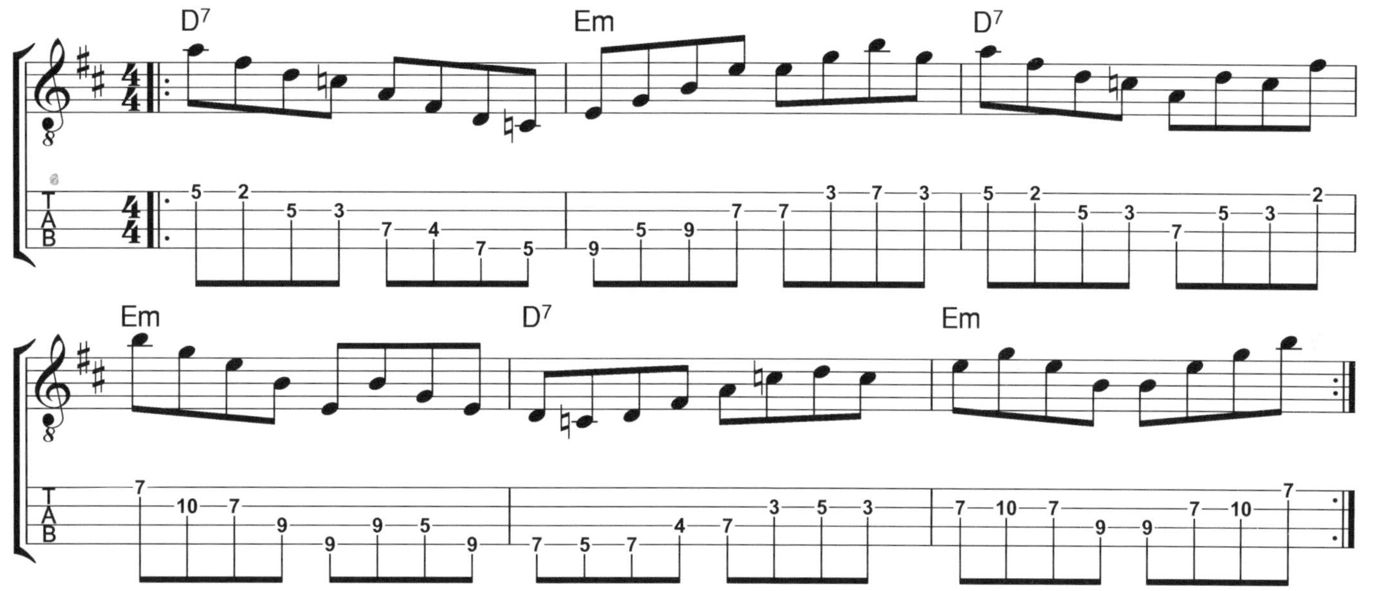

Practice Tip:

Using speakers, play along with a chord progression you already know. Then find the location of those chords on the tenor guitar, using the C-shapes that we have just learned. While the song plays, practice playing arpeggios with each chord in time with the chord changes. It's fun to fit harmonic patterns to music you know! Do this over and over and over with all the chord shapes you learn.

C-Shape 7th Exercise 4: The focus here is on the lower 3 strings. The progression follows this pattern; Em, D7, Em, D7, G, G. As you get more familiar with each of these C-shape arpeggios, create your own patterns on the higher strings moving from chord to chord, up and down the neck. And of course, you can use this strategy on your own progressions.

12

C-Shape 7th Exercise 4

E Minor - D7 - G Major

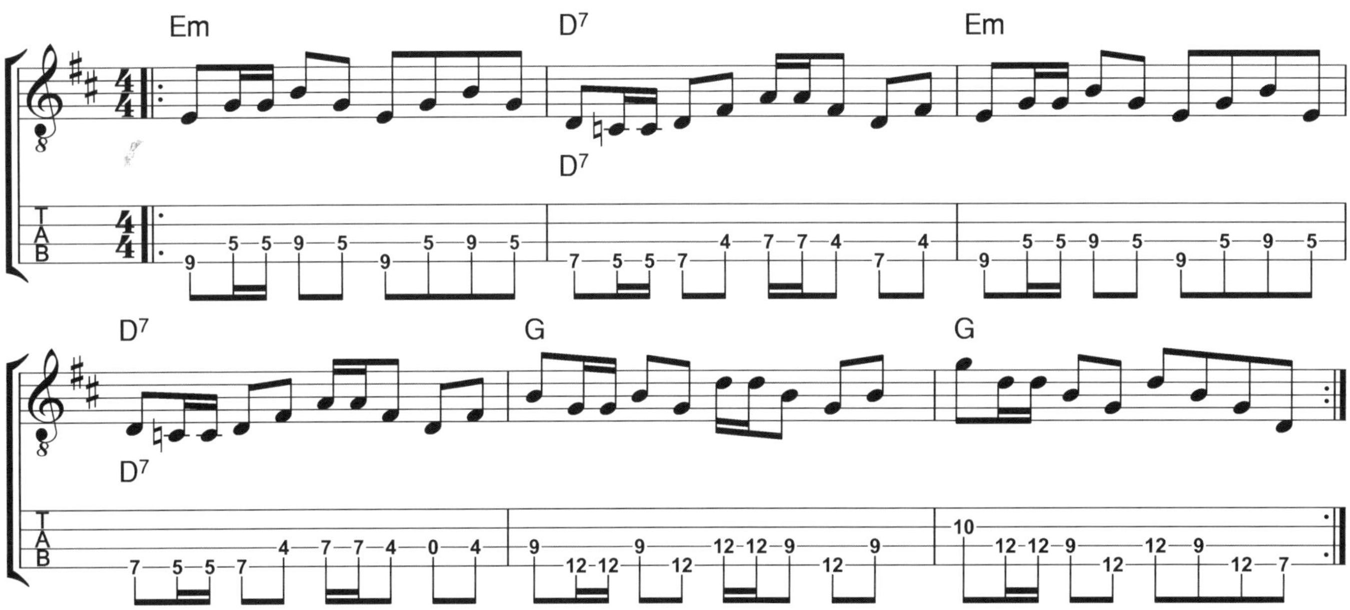

These exercises are meant to be a musical framework to build on, with the focused purpose of ingraining the location of the notes of each chord into your muscle memory. Then later, when you add other melody or rhythm notes from whatever scale or song you are using in your practice or on a song, your phrasing will sound focused, like you meant to suggest the underlying chord in your melody line.

As you practice songs with these chords, instead of just strumming add some of the key arpeggio notes. Of course, you won't want to play all the notes up and down in order because that will sound like practice. So mix up your patterns, use only a couple notes, make the patterns into riffs over chords...the possibilities are endless!

Chapter 1-4: C-Shape Melody Ideas

Let's start out with the relatively easy chord progression of C major to D major. Though there are infinite ways of approaching the creation of melodies, one way to approach this is to first consider what key we are working with. The major scale has the chord pattern of 1-major, 2-minor, 3-minor, 4-major, 5-major, 6-minor, 7-diminished, and the eighth chord takes us back to the root octave of the first chord.

So, if you notice the 4th and 5th chords are major chords side by side, like the C and D major we are about to practice. The C and D major chords occur at the 4th and 5th degrees in the key of G major in this order; G-Am-Bm-C-D-Em-F♯dim- G. This means when we create a melody over C and D major we can try notes in the G major scale (G-A-B-C-D-E,-F♯).

Let's first locate the chord forms we want to use for a section of C to D major. Then we will locate the most convenient G major scale notes to these chords. In the G major scale chart below, the gray notes are the arpeggio notes of the C and D major in the C-shape, and they are indicated by note name as well. As we play our melodies, it may be a good idea to play corresponding arpeggio notes when the chords change, and blend-in other G major scale notes to taste.

G Major Scale Near Chords

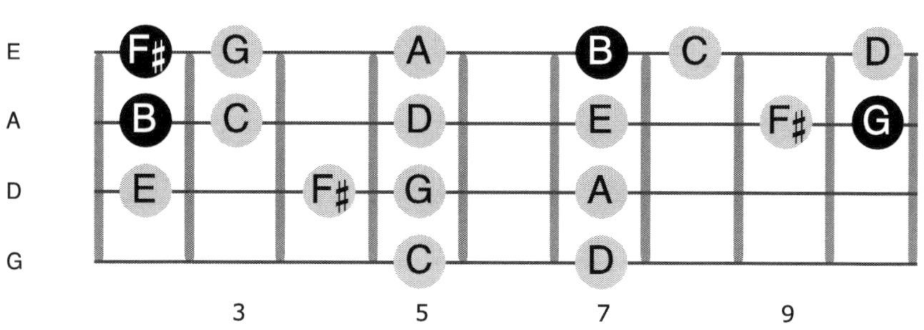

C-Shape C Major Chord

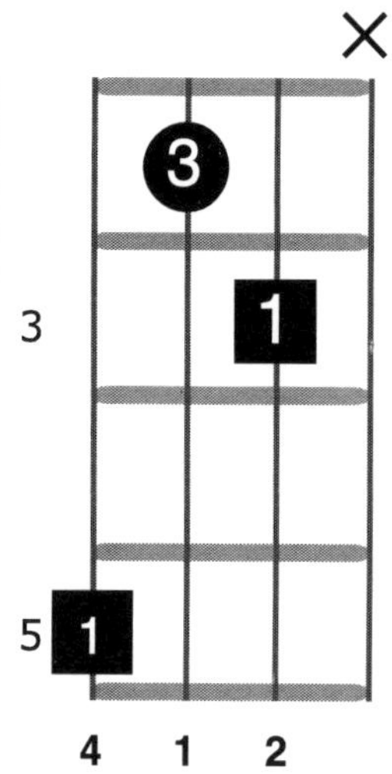

C-Shape D Major Chord

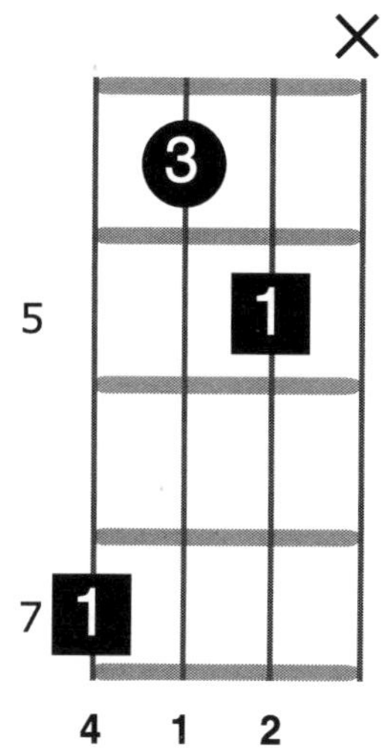

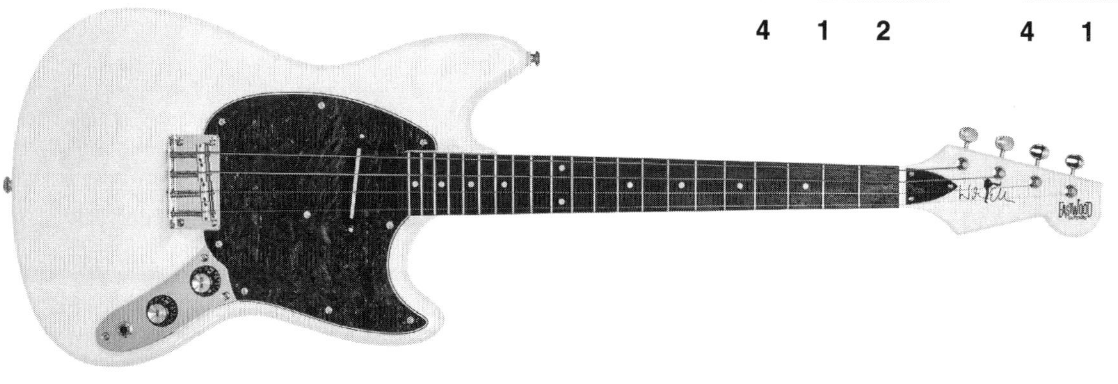

Warren Ellis Tenor Guitar by Eastwood

13

C Major to D Major Melody Exercise

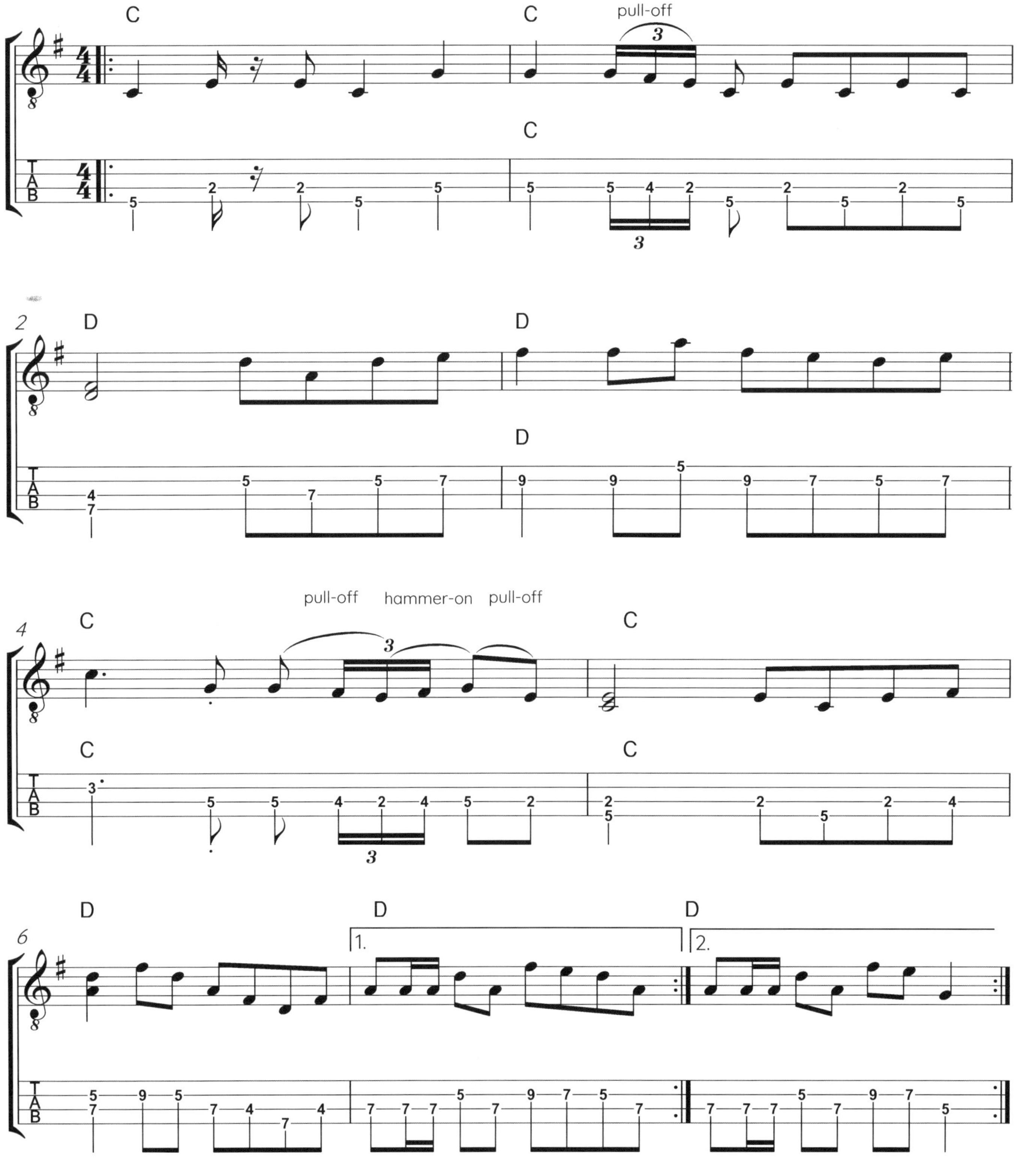

Chapter 2-1: A-Shape Major Chords and Arpeggio Exercises

A-Shape
Major Chord

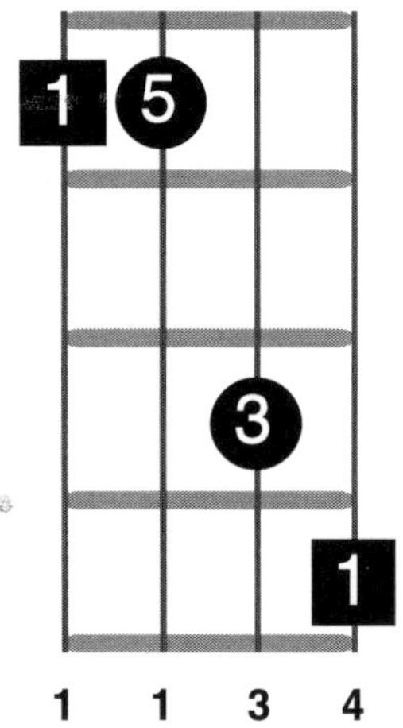

At left is the A-shape major chord. This shape has two root notes, with one on the low string and another on the high string. This gives the chord a strong fundamental root note that is clearly defined. The C-shape and the A-shape have this in common, while the other chord shapes have the root note on higher strings, which may be desirable or not- depending on the context. This chord shape is made up of the complete triad with the 1, 3, and 5 notes. To me, this shape is comparable to the bar chord on guitar.

To move this chord anywhere on the neck, just locate the note you want on the low G-string, make this shape and you have the major chord in the A-shape of that particular root note.

A-Shape
Major Arpeggio

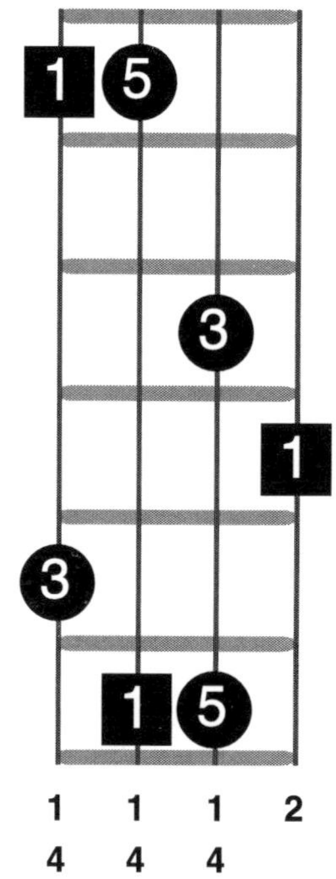

Alternative Chord Shapes

Try these alternative major chords for variety by using different combinations of the arpeggio notes. Here are 4 variations of major chords made from the A-shape major arpeggio. Try making your own using any notes from the arpeggio. You never know when you'll need a convenient chord shape to finish your musical thought.

A-Shape
Major Chord
Variation 1

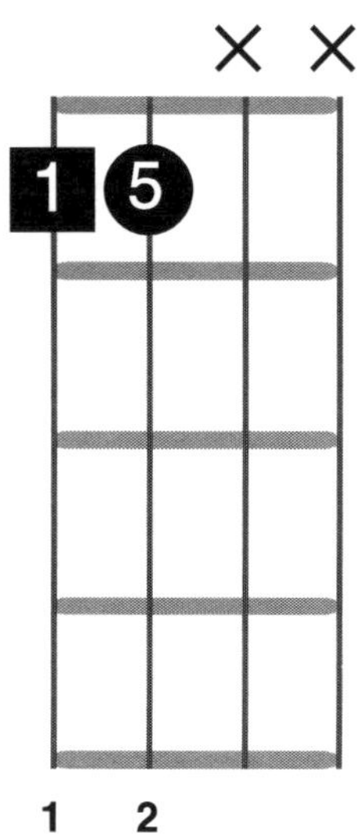

A-Shape
Major Chord
Variation 2

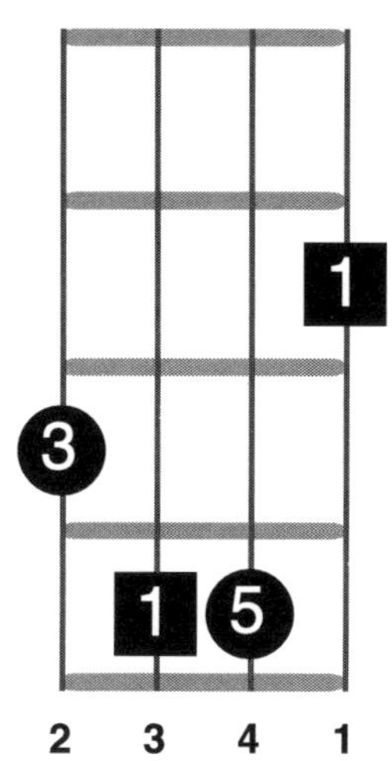

A-Shape
Major Chord
Variation 3

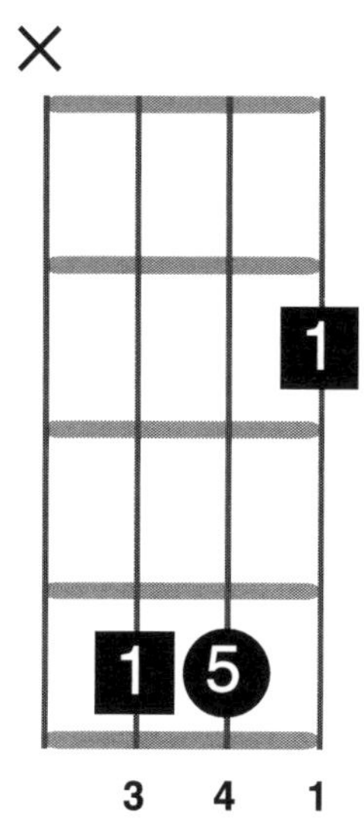

A-Shape
Major Chord
Variation 4

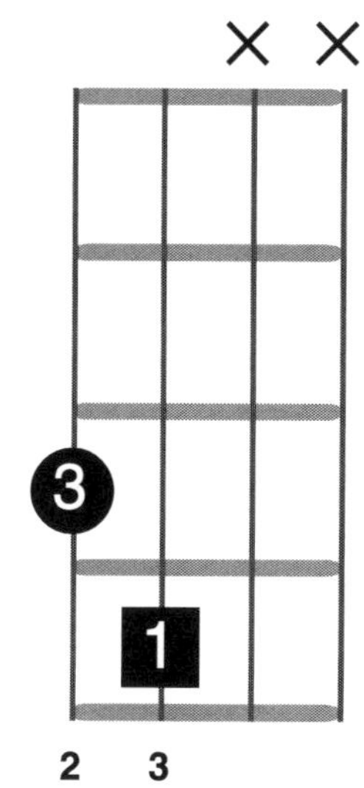

A-Shape Major Exercise 1: Strum the chord and then play the ascending and descending arpeggio until you can do it without looking. Do this over and over continuing to strum the chord periodically to memorize the fingering of these important notes as connected to the chord shape.

A-Shape Major Exercise 1

D Major

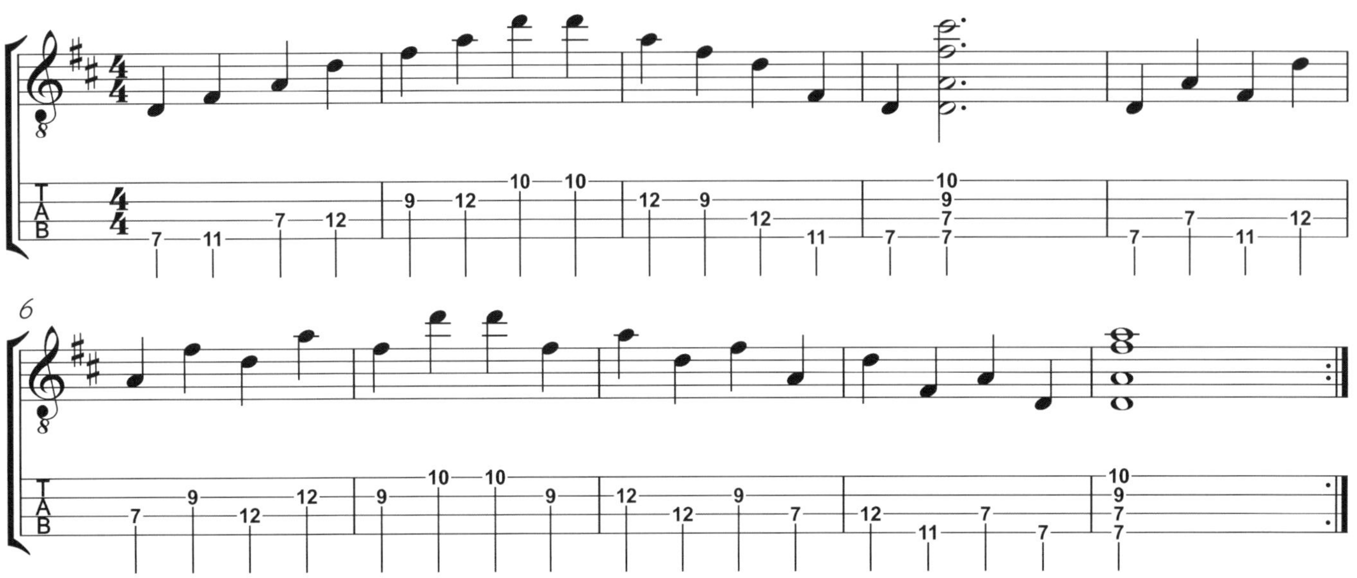

A-Shape Major Exercise 2: Practice the arpeggio notes in this pattern of playing three notes forward and then go back to the second note, and then play the next three forward and so on.

A-Shape Major Exercise 2

D Major

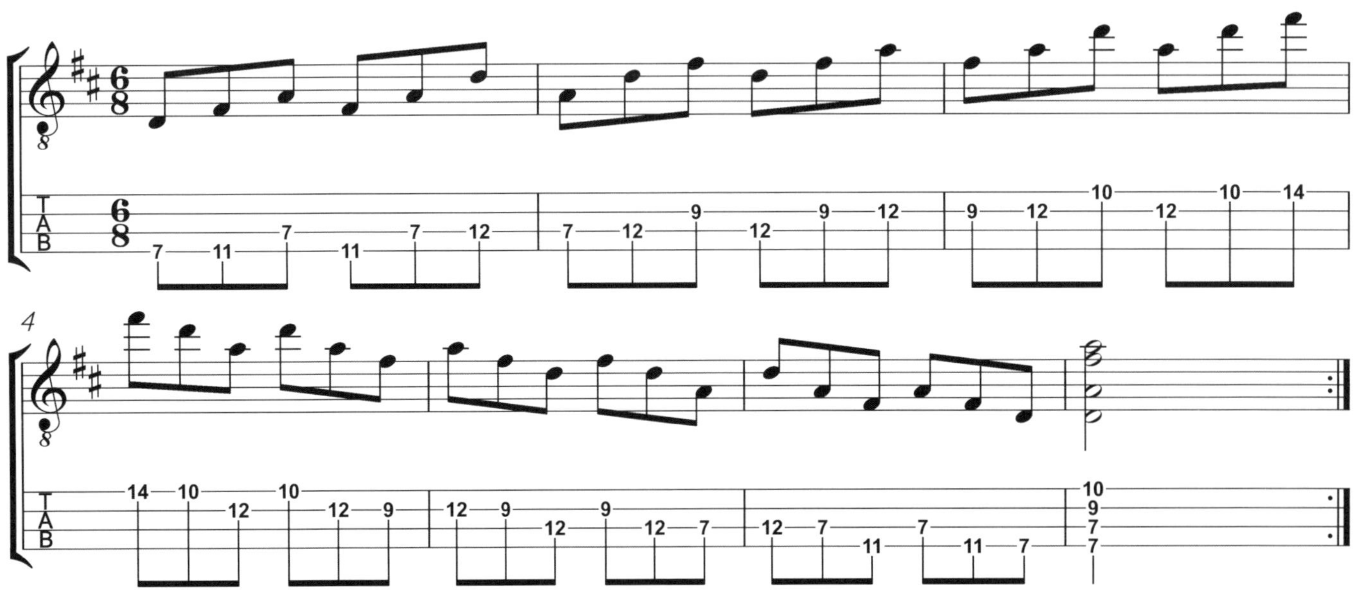

A-Shape Major Exercise 3: Practice the A-shape arpeggio at C major and practice changing directions. Set a tempo where you can play each note cleanly and then speed up slowly.

16

A-Shape Major Exercise 3

C Major

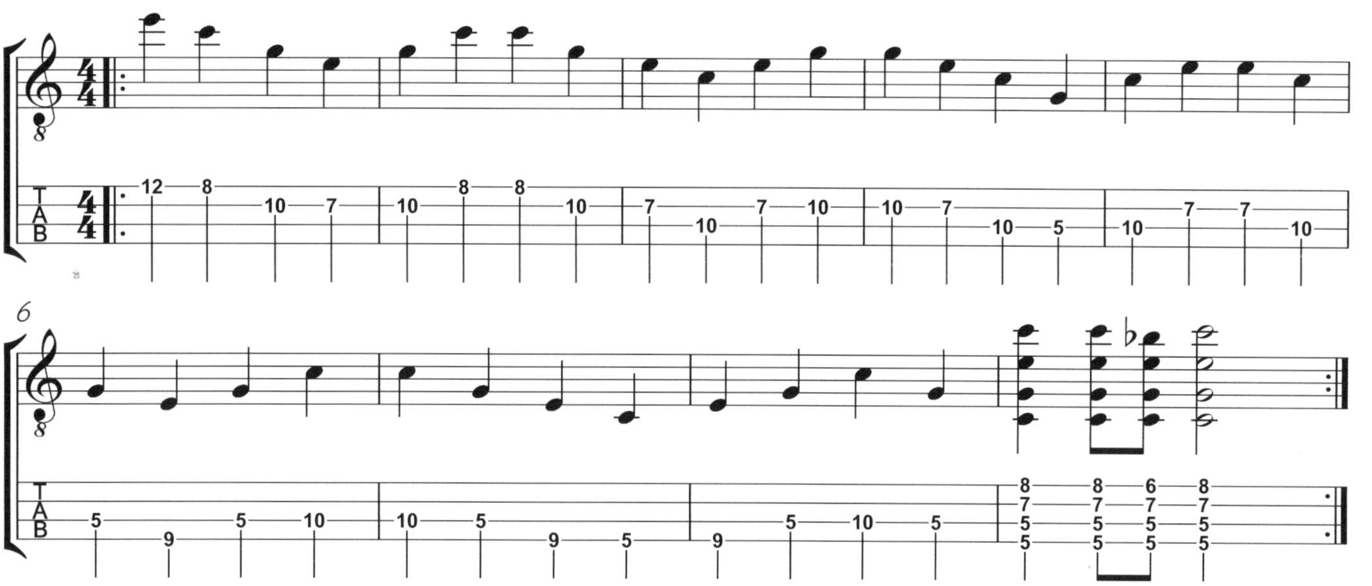

A-Shape Major Exercise 4: Practice moving between the A-shape and C-shape major arpeggios. This one requires long finger stretches and hand position shifts. Practice short segments as needed. Try not to slide unintentionally in bar 6, unless you want to!

17

A-Shape Major Exercise 4

D Major in 2 Shapes

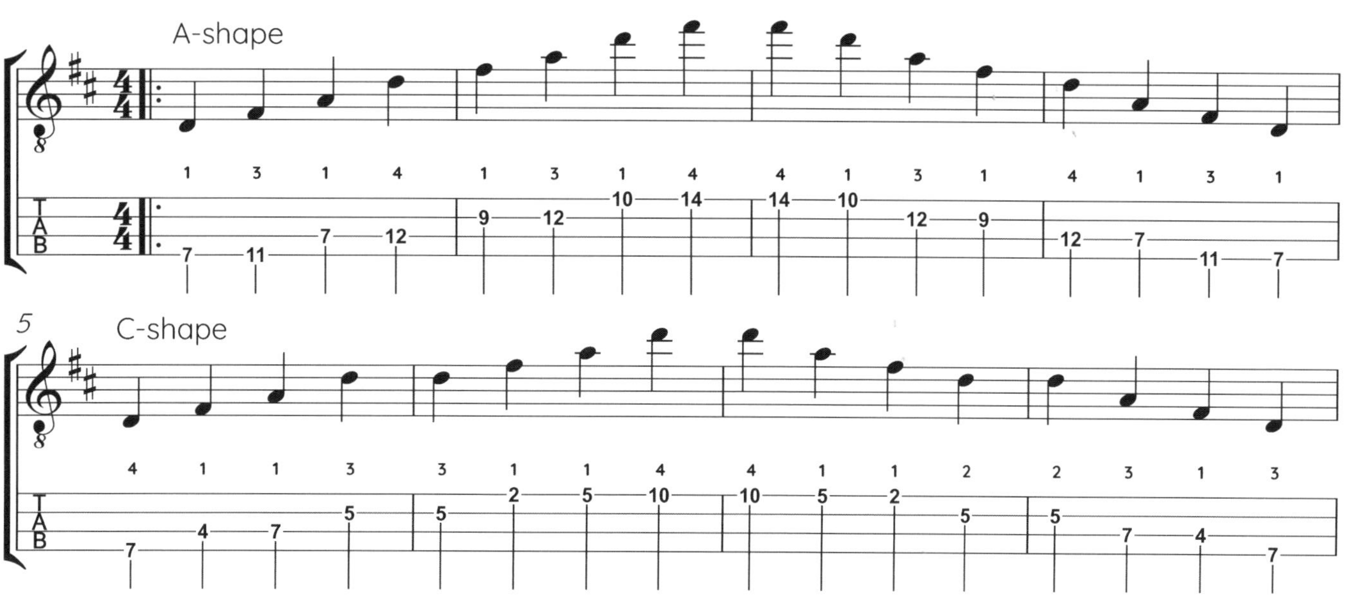

Chapter 2-2: A-Shape Minor Chords and Arpeggio Exercises

A-Shape
Minor Chord

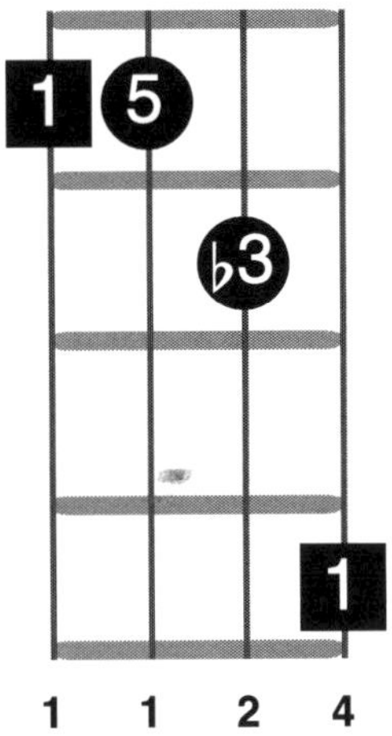

On the left is the A-shape minor chord. This shape has two root notes, with one of them falling on the lowest string. This shape can be compared to a bar chord on a regular guitar, with the root note being on the low and high strings. It uses all four strings, includes the 1, 3, and 5 notes and is easy to locate by the 1 note on the low string. It has a strong fundamental root note that is clearly defined. The only difference between the minor and major chords is that the 3 note moves down one half-step.

Before you try the finger exercises below, practice this arpeggio up and back, many times while looking at the chart to aid visual memory; and until you can play it without thinking too much or looking at your fingers.

A-Shape
Minor Arpeggio

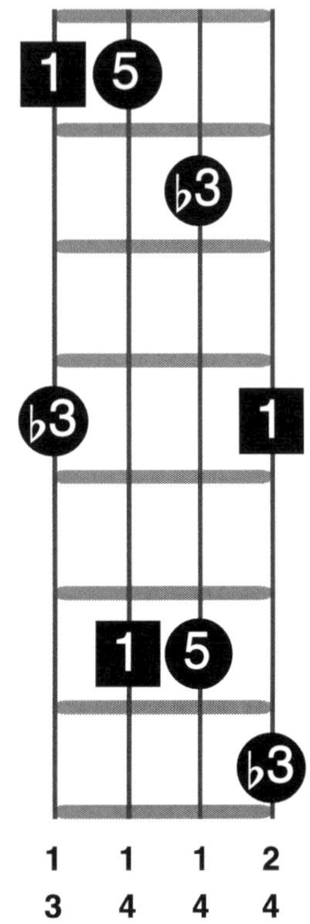

Alternative Chord Variations

These minor chord variations are built from the arpeggio notes of the A-shape minor arpeggio. Variation 1 can be used as a minor or major chord. In variation 2, you can mute the third and first string by rotating your fretting fingers over a little bit to stop those strings from sounding.

A-Shape
Minor Chord
Variation 1

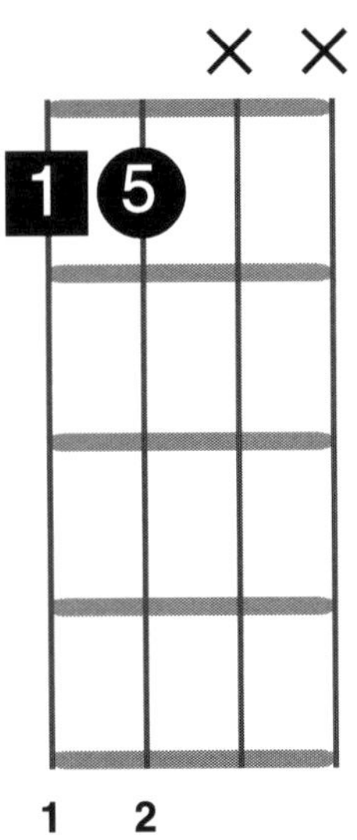

A-Shape
Minor Chord
Variation 2

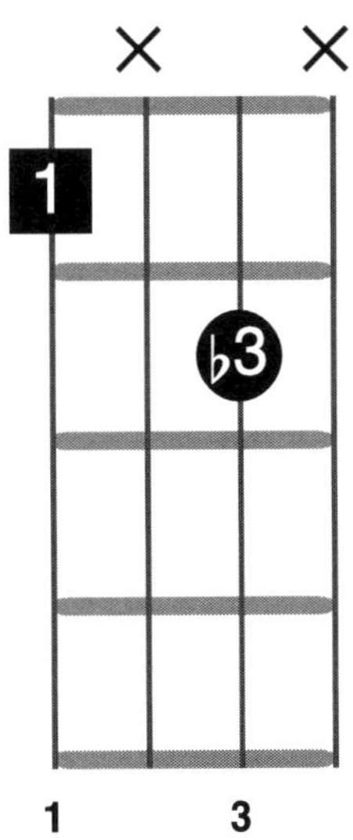

A-Shape
Minor Chord
Variation 3

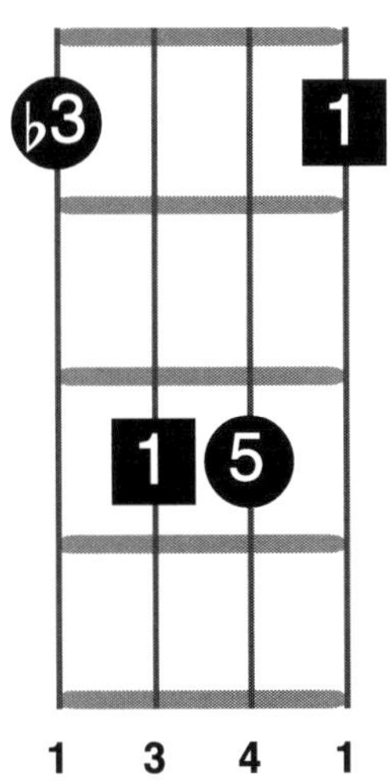

A-Shape
Minor Chord
Variation 4

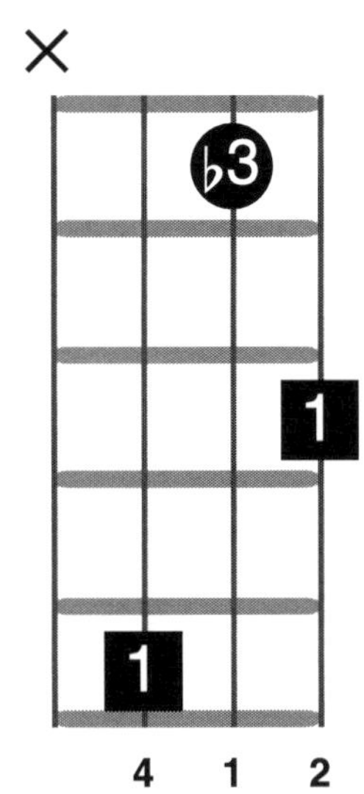

Practice Tip: Break 'em apart and experiment!

It's good to learn to play each practice pattern until it's easy to play in time and so that you can find those key notes automatically without thinking, and as connected to the chord shape. The real fun and creativity happen when you are not just doing exercises, but making music. For example, take a bar, or half of a bar and experiment with it. Treat short phrases as starting ideas to new riffs or melodic sections in tunes you are learning. Change the time signature or add ornamentation. Then move it to different locations around the neck. **A-Shape Minor Exercise 1:** Practice one of my tunes, "Misty Shore-Break" that uses the minor arpeggio with a swinging jig time in Exercise 1.

18

A-Shape Minor Exercise 1

"Misty Shore-Break"

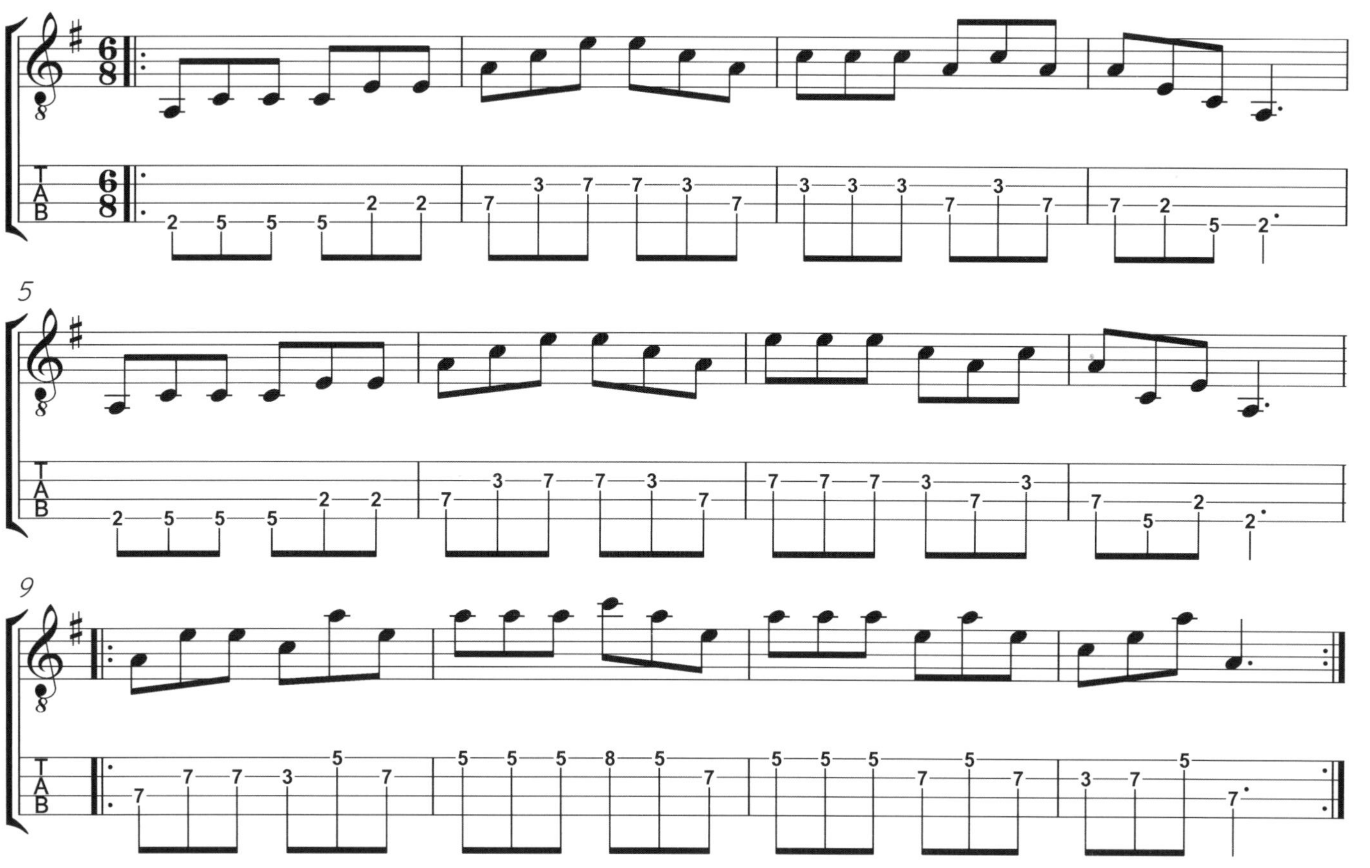

A-Shape Minor Exercise 2: It is more challenging to take parts of the A-shape minor arpeggio and move them between two chords. Repeat each bar, or pair of bars, until you can move between sections smoothly.

19

A-Shape Minor Exercise 2

E Minor to D Minor

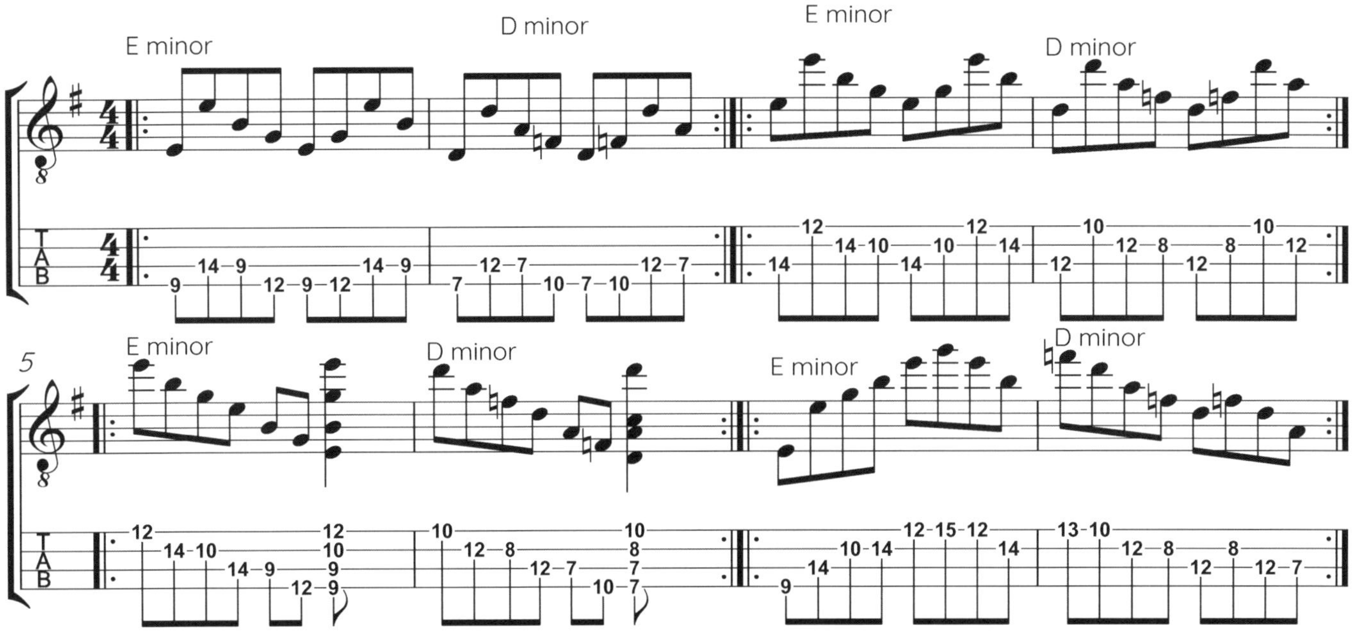

A-Shape Minor Exercise 3: Practice shifting between the two minor chord shape arpeggios that we have learned so far, C-shape and now the A-shape. This one will cover a wide fret span and some good finger stretches. Practice shifting hand positions until they are smooth.

20

A-Shape Minor Exercise 3

E Minor A-Shape to C-Shape

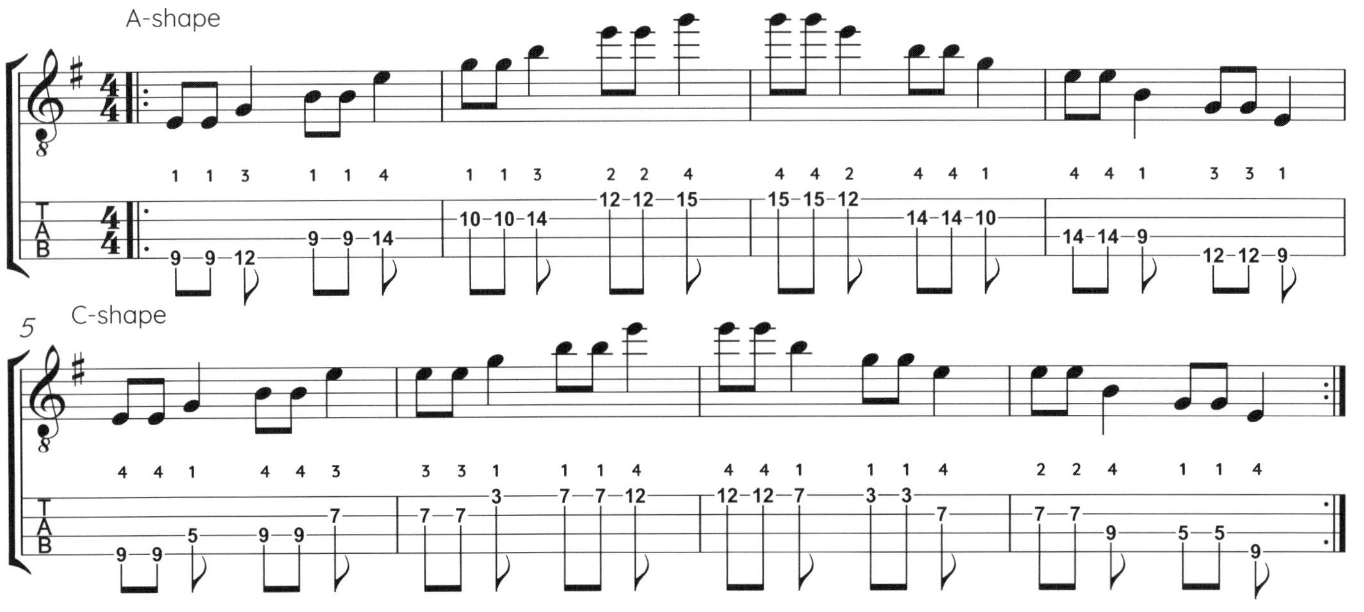

A-Shape Minor Exercise 4: Combine 3 different arpeggios in a II-V7-I progression (Em, A7, and D), with the Em (9th fret) and D (7th fret) from the A-shape, and the A7 from the C-shape (11th fret). It is always a good idea to me to learn various arpeggios notes using shapes that overlap within progressions so that all the handy notes are right under your fingers where you are already fingering those corresponding chords.

21

A-Shape Minor Exercise 4

E Minor - A7 - D Major

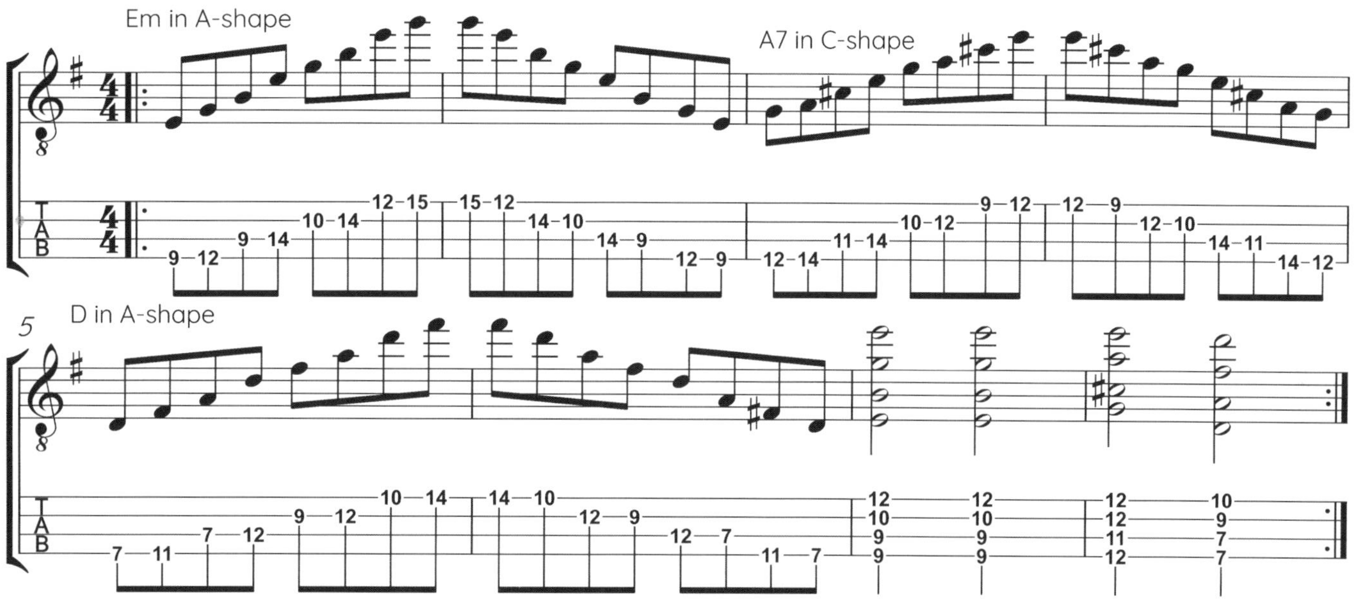

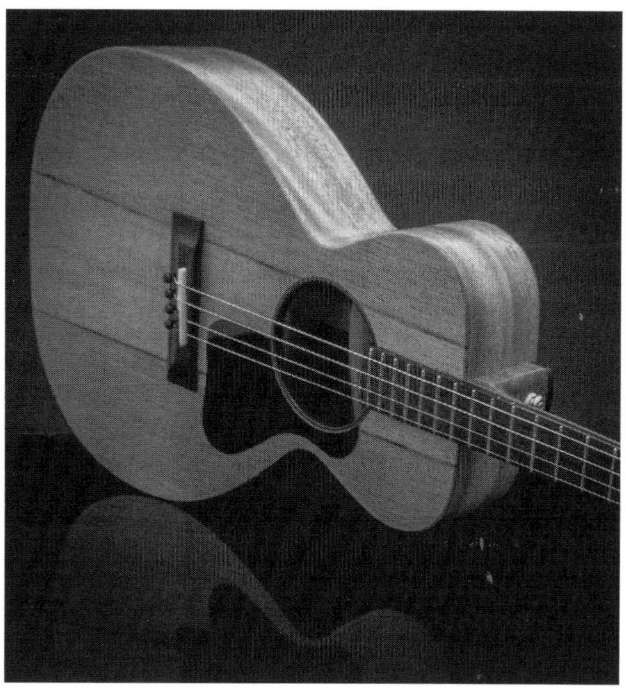

Parlour King tenor by Nigel Forster

Chapter 2-3: A-Shape 7th Chord and Arpeggio Exercises

A-Shape
7th Chord

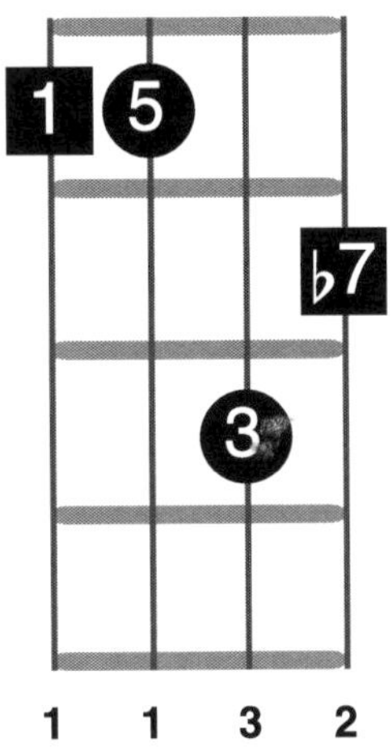

As stated in chapter 1, the 7th shape emphasizes the flatted 7th note one step down from the root note of the chord. At left, on the chord chart the higher octave root note is two frets above the ♭7 note. See location of the root notes at right. Knowing where this other 1 note is located helps one to find the ♭7 note easily in this A-shape 7th chord.

The seventh chord in the A-shape has a solid root note on the lowest string that is clearly defined, and it uses all four strings. Maybe, this is the "best" 7th chord to rely on since it's easy to finger and to place by the low string note. To find where to play this chord, just find any root note on the low-string note, make this A-shape seventh chord and that's the 7th chord at that note.

A-Shape
7th Arpeggio

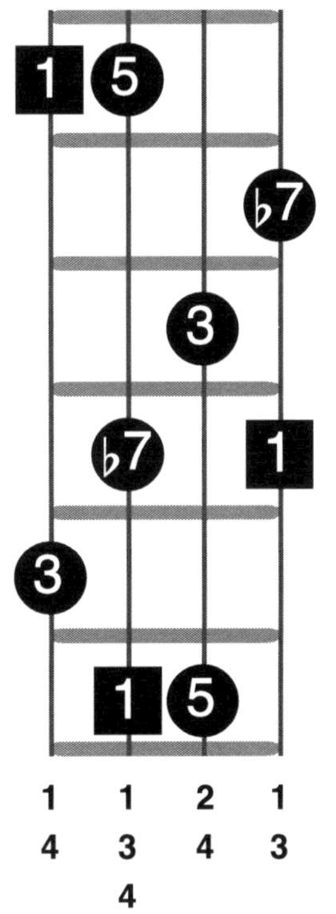

A-Shape 7th Chord Variations

Variation 1 uses just 2 notes. It's handy to know 2-note chords on the low strings for all chords. Variation 2 sounds very full and well-defined with the 2 root notes, but is slightly more difficult to finger quickly. Variation 3 is built from the 7th arpeggio but doesn't have the root note. The root note is indicated to help place the chord on the fretboard. And variation 4 is a long stretch. Try these different voicings and/or make up your own!

A-Shape
7th Chord
Variation 1

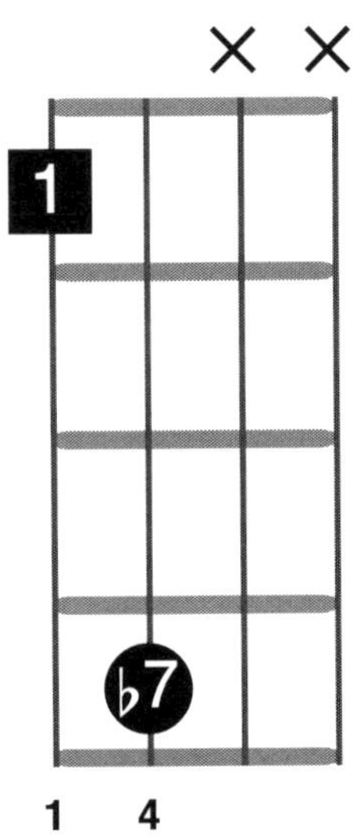

A-Shape
7th Chord
Variation 2

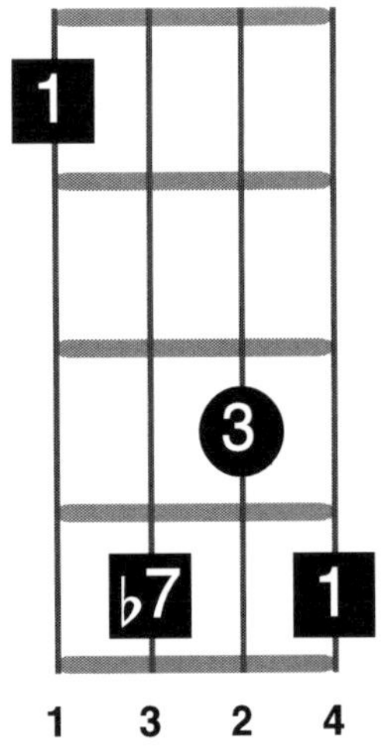

A-Shape
7th Chord
Variation 3

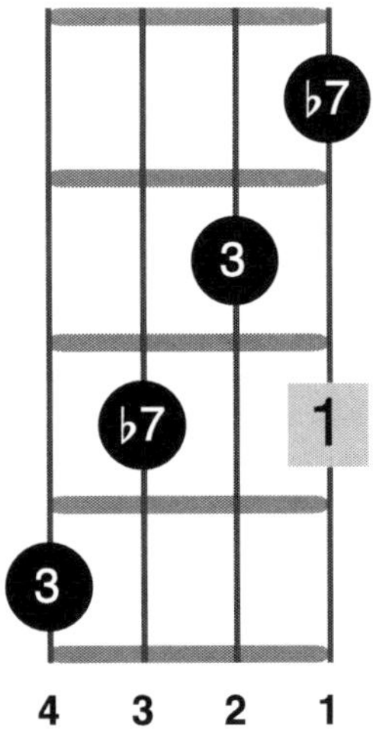

A-Shape
7th Chord
Variation 4

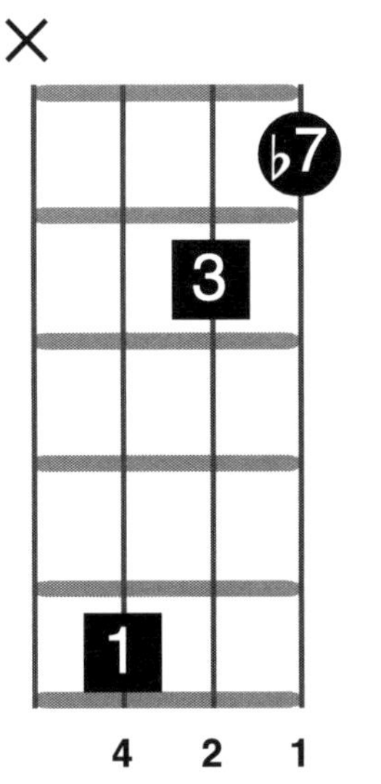

A-Shape 7th Exercise 1: Let's get familiar with this arpeggio pattern playing the notes ascending and descending in an overlapping pattern. After you get familiar with these notes, try making up riffs with any 4-notes while intermittently strumming a C7 chord rhythm.

22

A-Shape 7th Exercise 1

C7

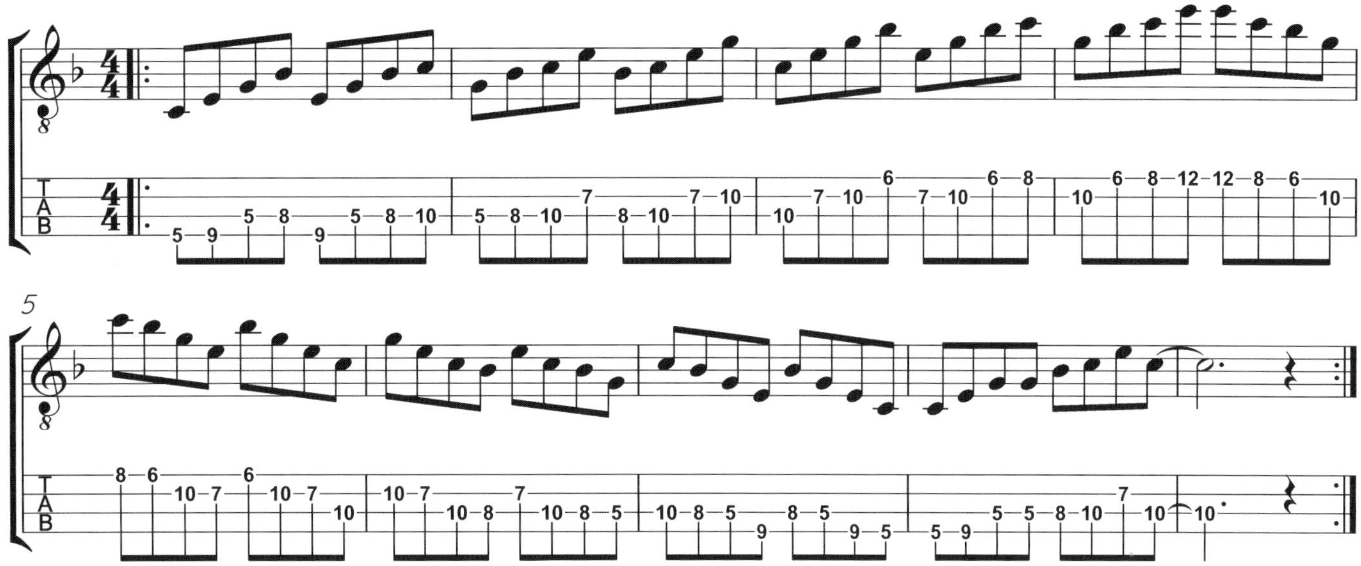

A-Shape 7th Exercise 2: Practice this arpeggio as a jig. It's always more fun to make practice more musical. Compose your own tunes with any and all arpeggios that you learn!

23

A-Shape 7th Exercise 2

A7

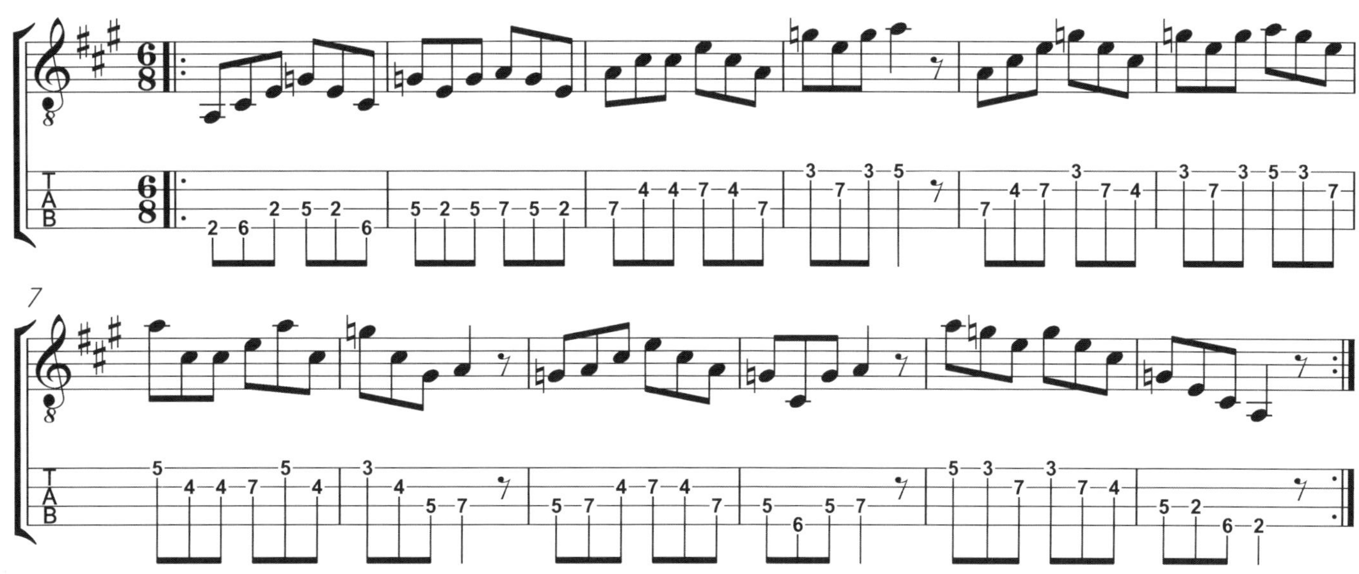

A-Shape 7th Exercise 3: Ingrain these 7th arpeggios in a 12-bar progression using B7 (A-shape at 4th fret), E7 (C-shape at 6th fret), and F♯7 (C-shape 8th fret). Try to play it with a swing-8th shuffle rhythm, and then make up your own melodies.

24

A-Shape 7th Exercise 3

B7 - E7

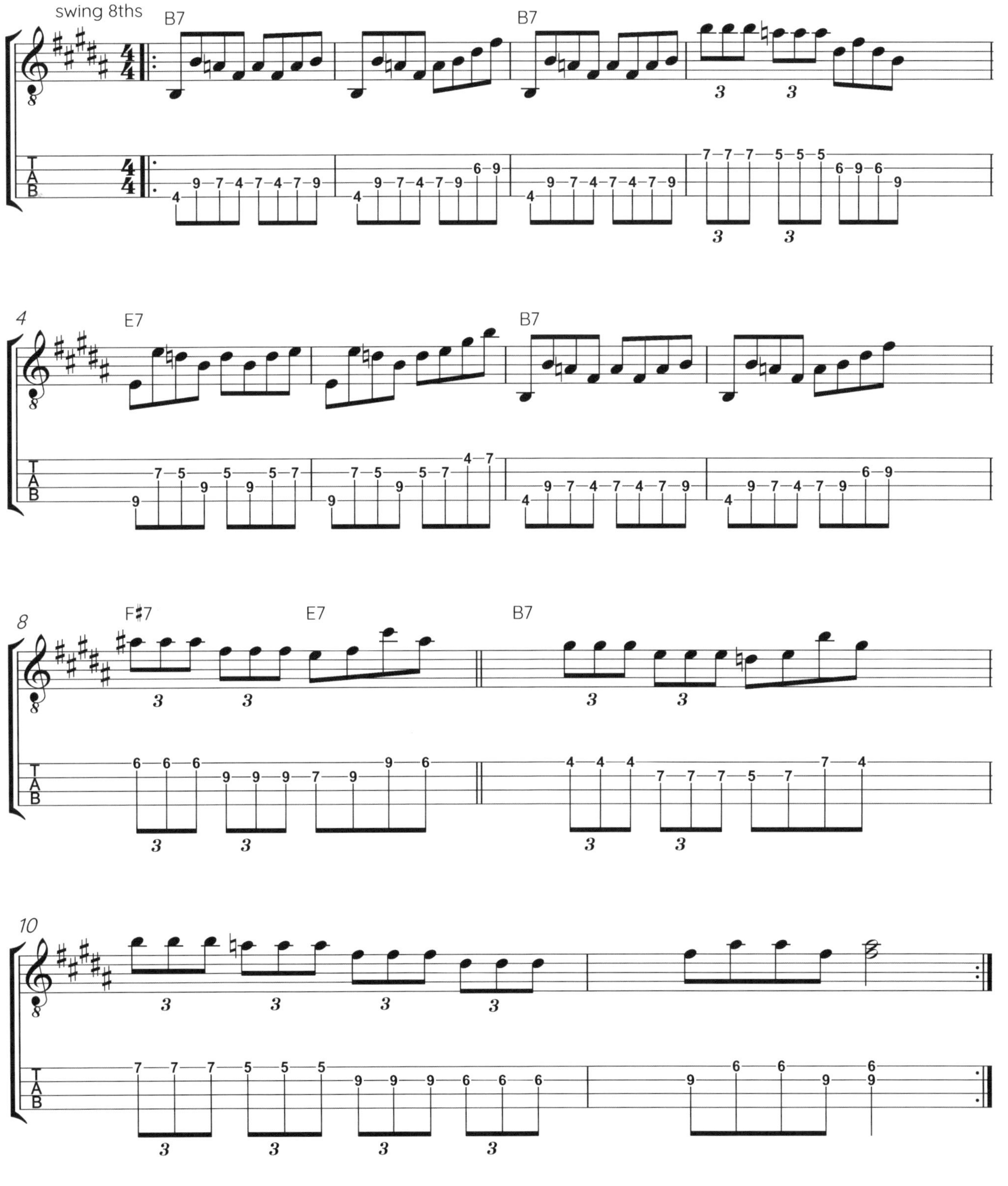

A-Shape 7th Exercise 4: Practice moving arpeggios through a chord progression; 2-5-1-6. In the key of C, this means the 2nd chord is a D minor, the 5th chord is a G7, the 1st chord is a C major, and 6th chord is an A minor. Let's use the chord shapes we have learned so far, the D minor and C major in the C-shape, the G7 chord and A minor in the A-shape.

C-Shape
D Minor Chord

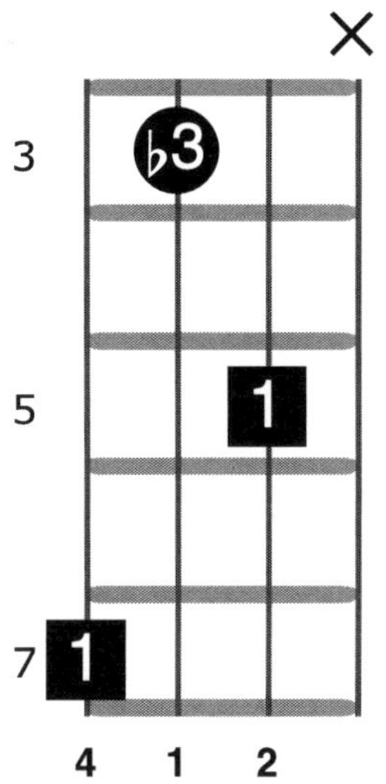

A-Shape
G7 Chord

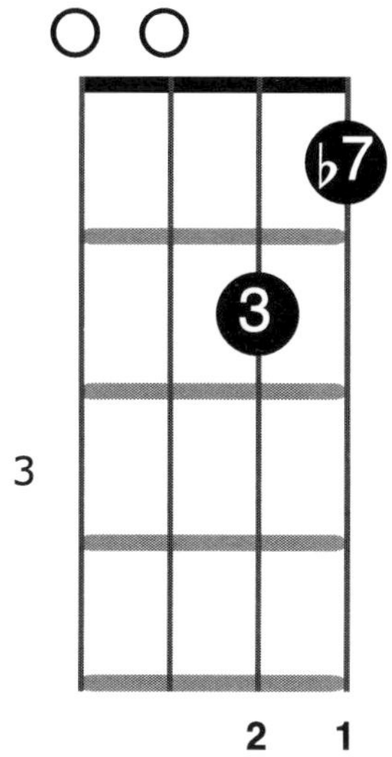

C-Shape
C Major Chord

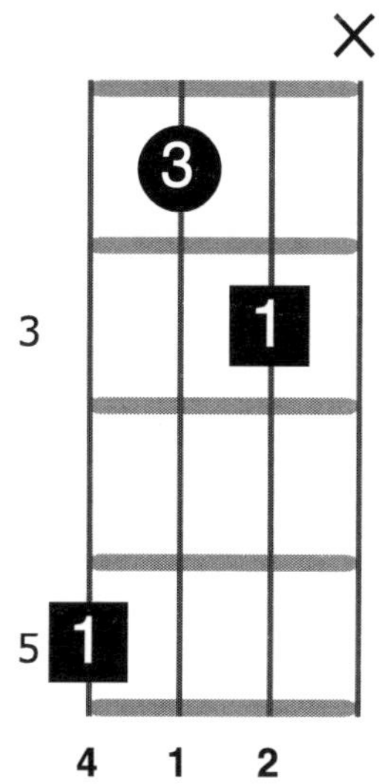

A-Shape
A Minor Chord

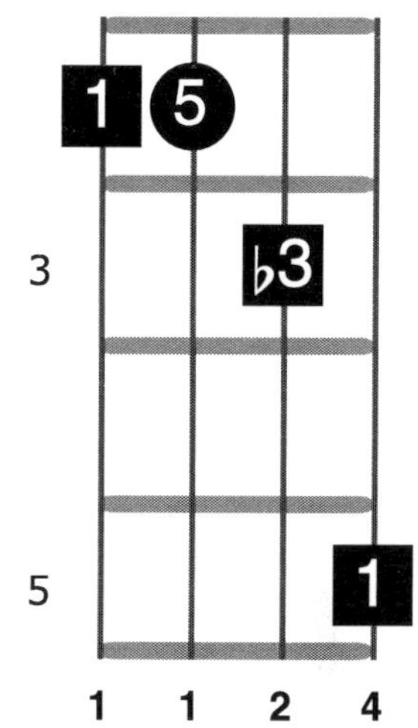

A-Shape 7th Exercise 4: Here are the corresponding arpeggios for Exercise 4. After learning this lesson, try making up your own patterns using the arpeggio notes for each chord.

C-Shape
D Minor Arpeggio

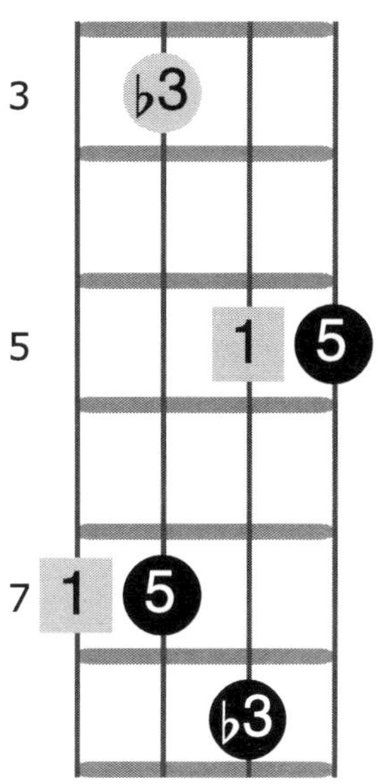

A-Shape
G7 Arpeggio

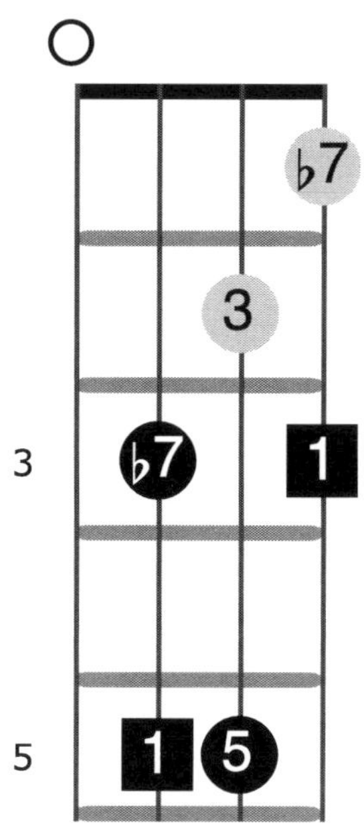

C-Shape
C Major Arpeggio

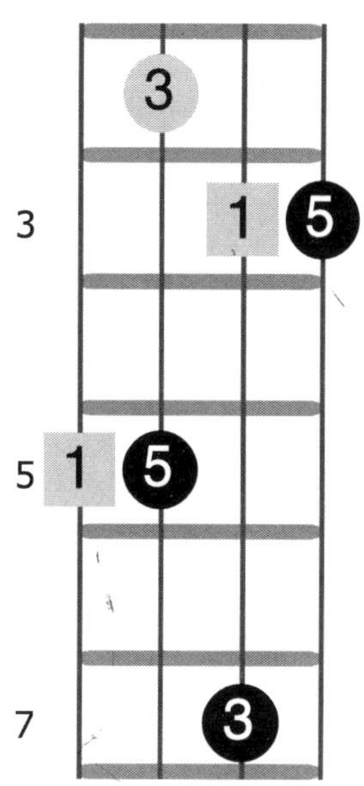

A-Shape
A Minor Arpeggio

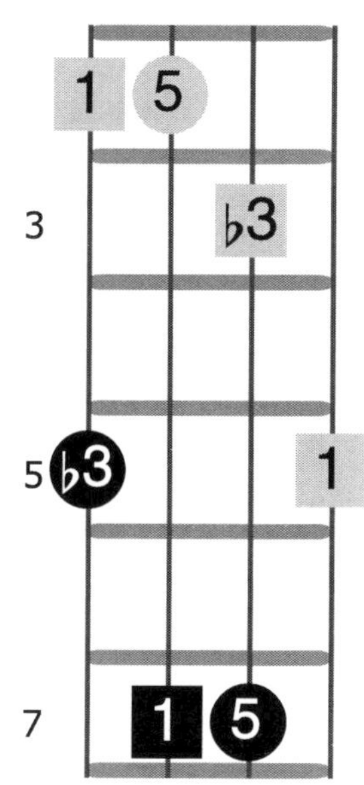

25

A-Shape 7th Exercise 4

Dm - G7 - C - Am

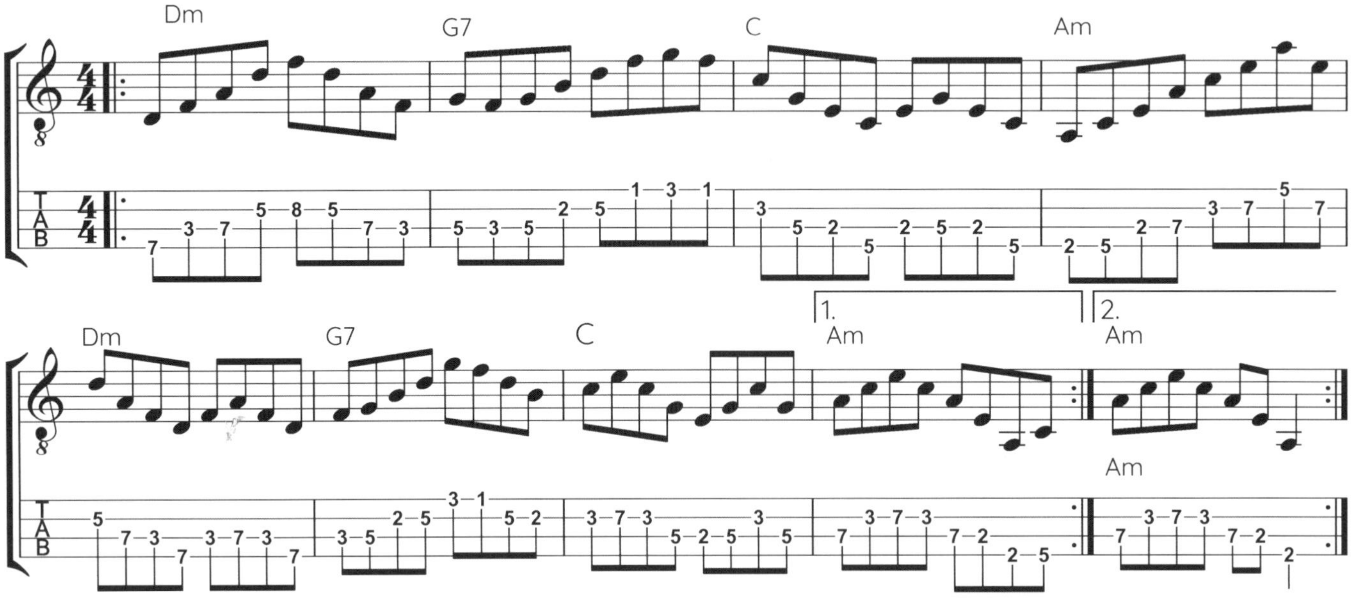

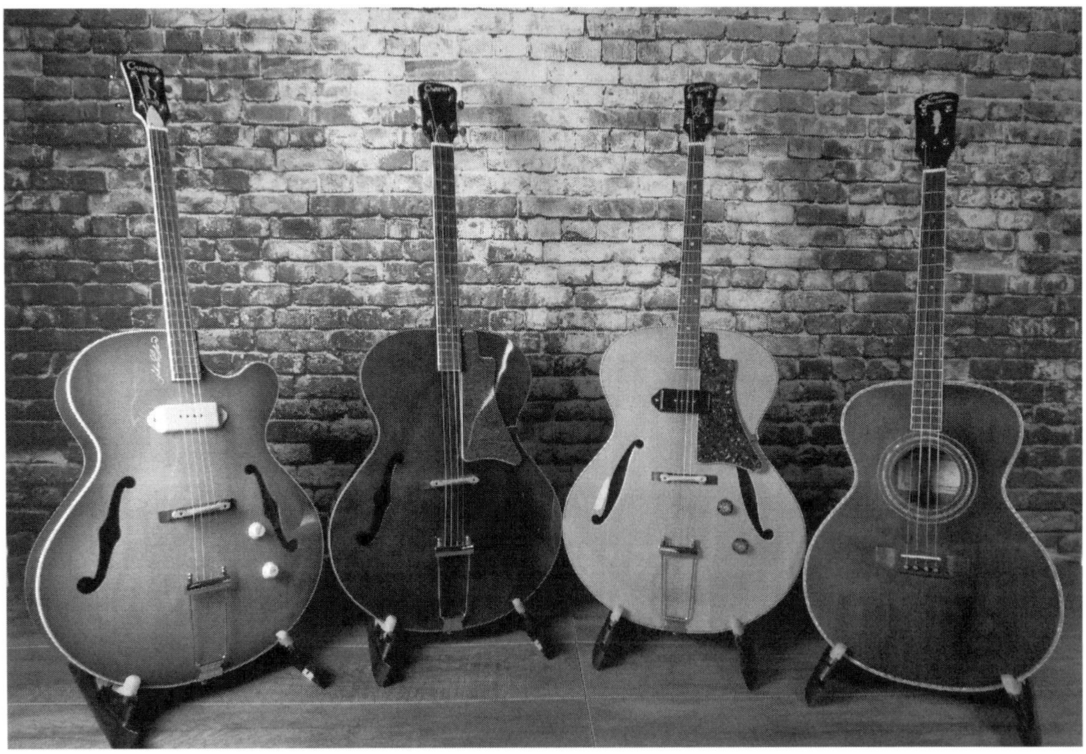

Craven tenor guitars

Chapter 2-4: A-Shape Melody Ideas

The next tune to practice is part of one of my compositions called, "Wind on Water". We will practice over the verse section that uses D minor 7, C major 7, B♭ major 7 and A minor 7 in the A-shape. Try these jazzier chord shapes.

D Minor 7

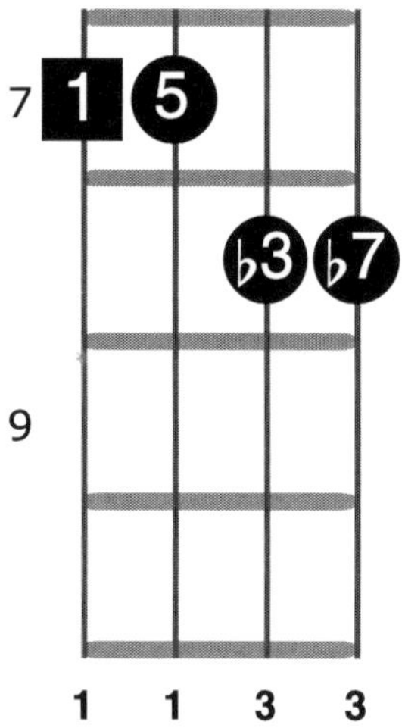

C Major 7

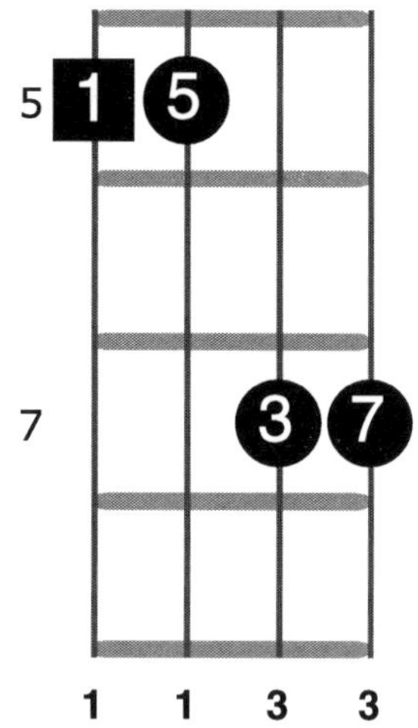

B♭ Major 7

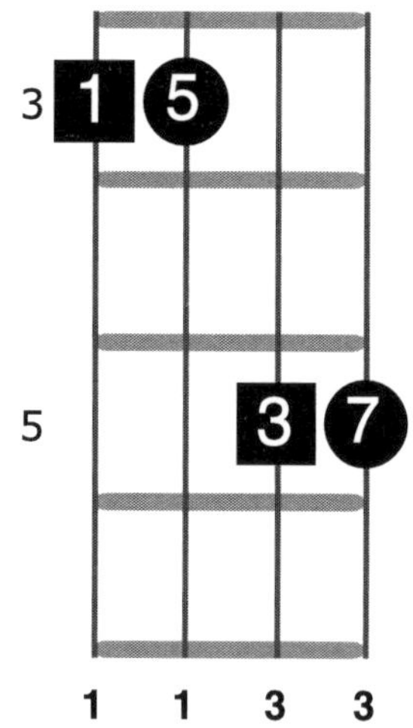

A Minor 7

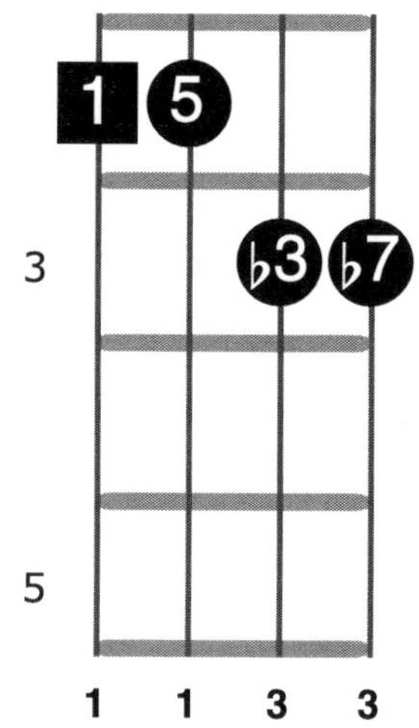

Wind on the Water

Strumming Rhythm

by Todd Montgomery

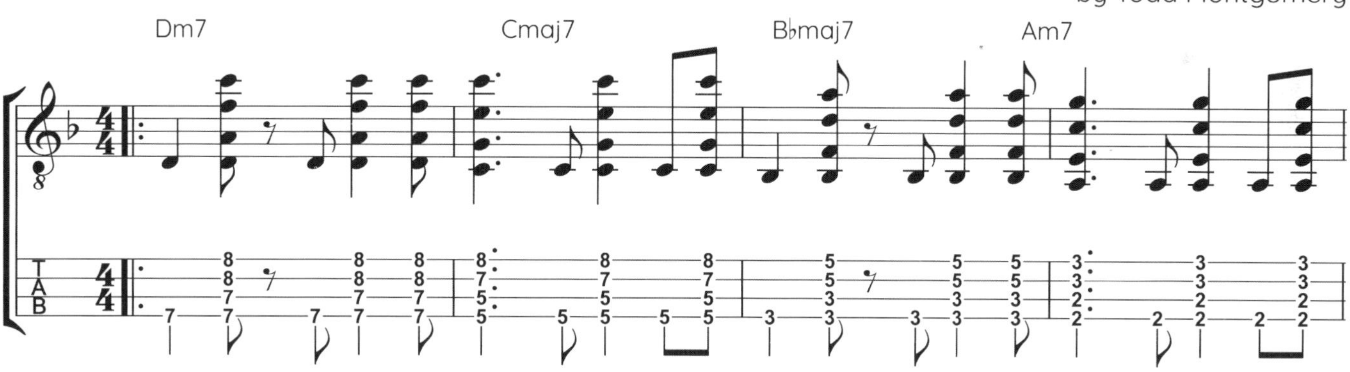

This tune is in the key of F, so we can use the notes of the F major scale but remembering to focus on arpeggio notes. In bars 1-4, we'll use the 3rds of each chord as our focal point. In bars 5-8, we'll use the F major scale notes on the low 3 strings from frets 3-7 making sure to land on root notes. In bars 9-12, we move to the G-shape chords and arpeggio notes starting with the D minor on the 9th fret and adding notes of the F major scale again and adding some chords as well. In bars 13-16, we will use double stops on the low strings to kick off each bar. The double stops are created from using the low two notes from the C-shape D minor chord, and the A-shape C major, B♭ major, and A minor chords. As you can see, we are using melodic phrases built around the different chord shapes and using a kind of parallel structure where the rhythm is echoed with slight variations from bar to bar to give cohesion.

27

Wind on the Water

Melody Ideas

by Todd Montgomery

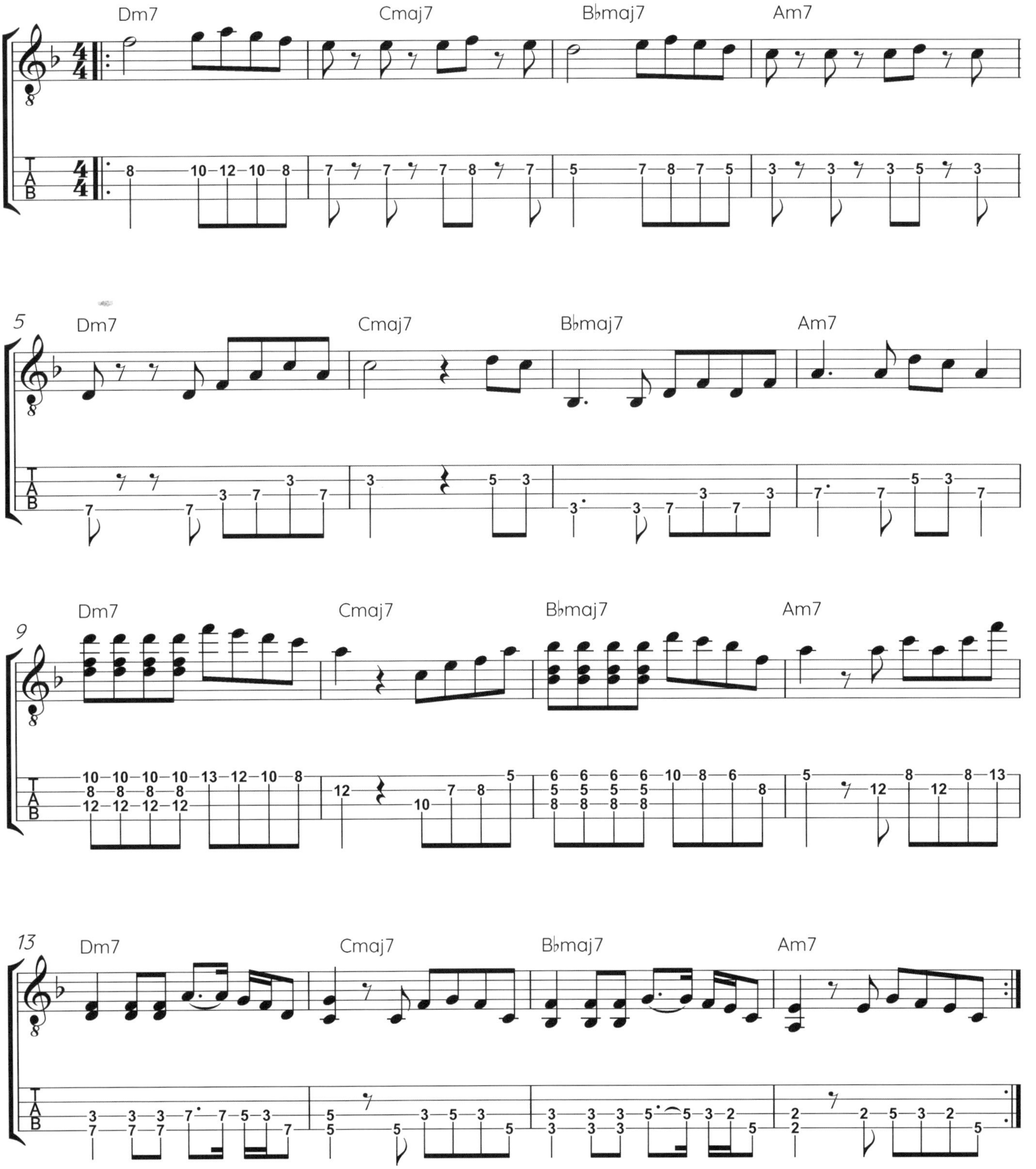

Chapter 3-1: G-Shape Major Chords and Arpeggio Exercises

G-Shape
Major Chord

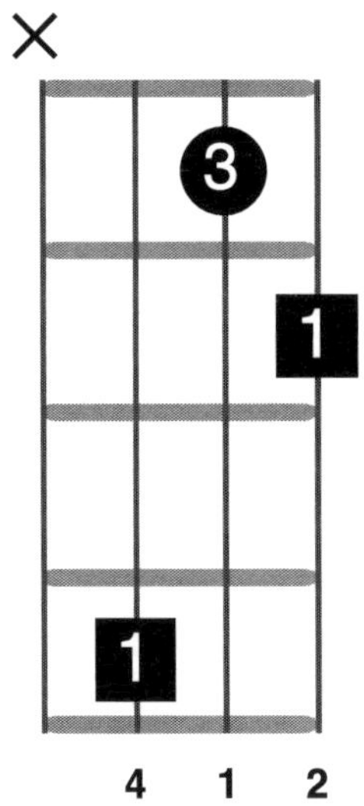

Here is the G-shape major chord. This shape has the same fingering as the C-shape, just moved over one string higher. It also has two root notes, with one of them falling D-string. This chord shape is made up only the 1 and 3 chord tones. Be aware that you will often have to mute the low string when it is not part of the chord. This is probably most easily done with your thumb around the back of the neck. However, It's okay to play the open G note with any chord containing a G natural.

To move this chord anywhere on the neck, just locate the note you want on the D string, make this shape and you have the major chord in the G-shape of that particular root note.

Finger the G-shape major chord and then practice running this arpeggio up and down until you can play it smoothly with a metronome. You may need to shift your hand position to reach the high note on the E-string.

G-Shape
Major Arpeggio

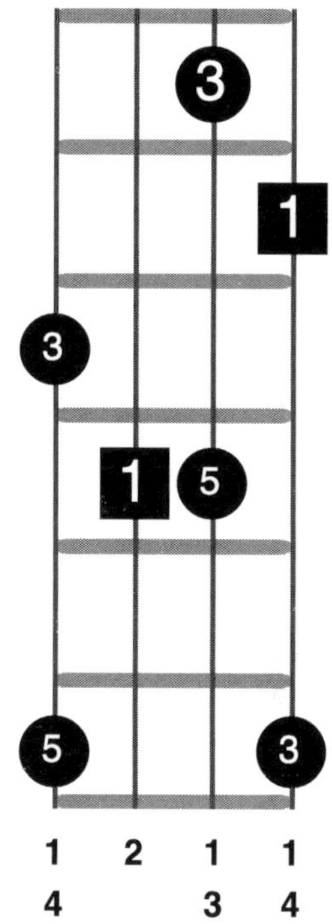

Alternative Chord Shapes

Here are four variations of major chords made from the G-shape major arpeggio. Variation 1 emphasizes the 5, while variation 2 has the complete triad, but with the 3rd note on the bottom. Variation 3 is a quick and easy double stop major chord form. Variation 4 also has the full triad but emphasizes the major 3rd. Try making your own variations using any notes from the arpeggio.

G-Shape
Major Chord
Variation 1

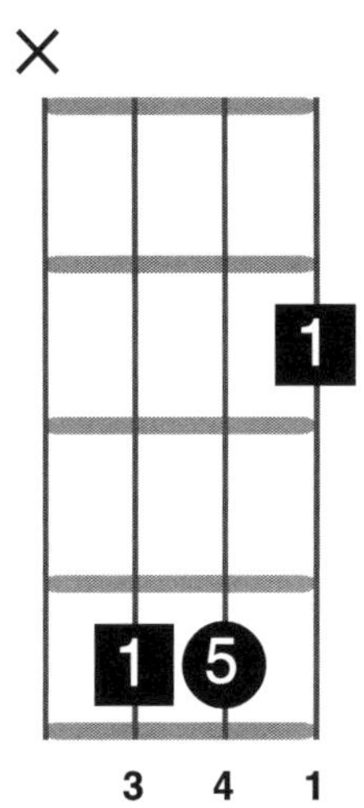

G-Shape
Major Chord
Variation 2

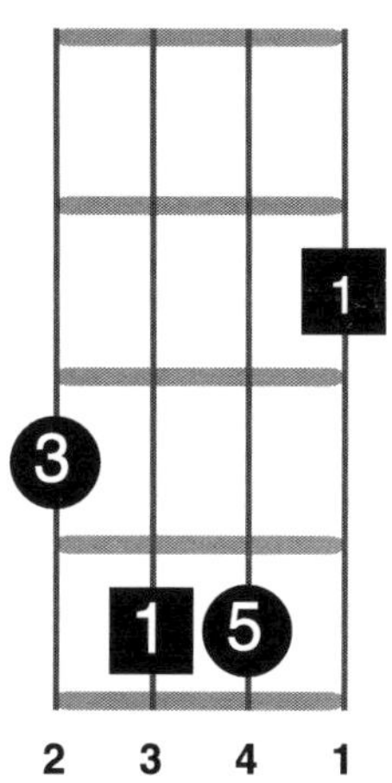

G-Shape
Major Chord
Variation 3

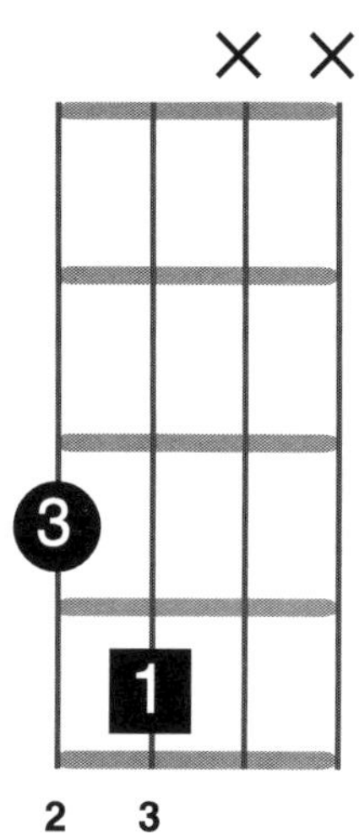

G-Shape
Major Chord
Variation 4

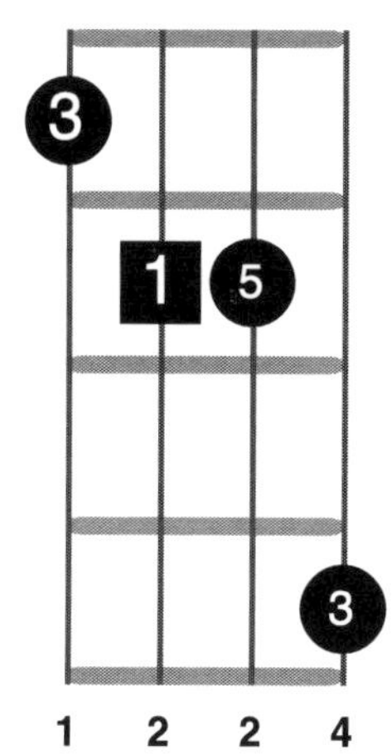

G-Shape Major Exercise 1: Let's keep it simple and get used to smoothly fingering the arpeggio up and down the fretboard. It may take some practice to cleanly play the stretched fingering on the high string. Remember to go as slowly as you need to in order to play it effortlessly with each note ringing until you pluck the next.

28

G-Shape Major Exercise 1

A Major

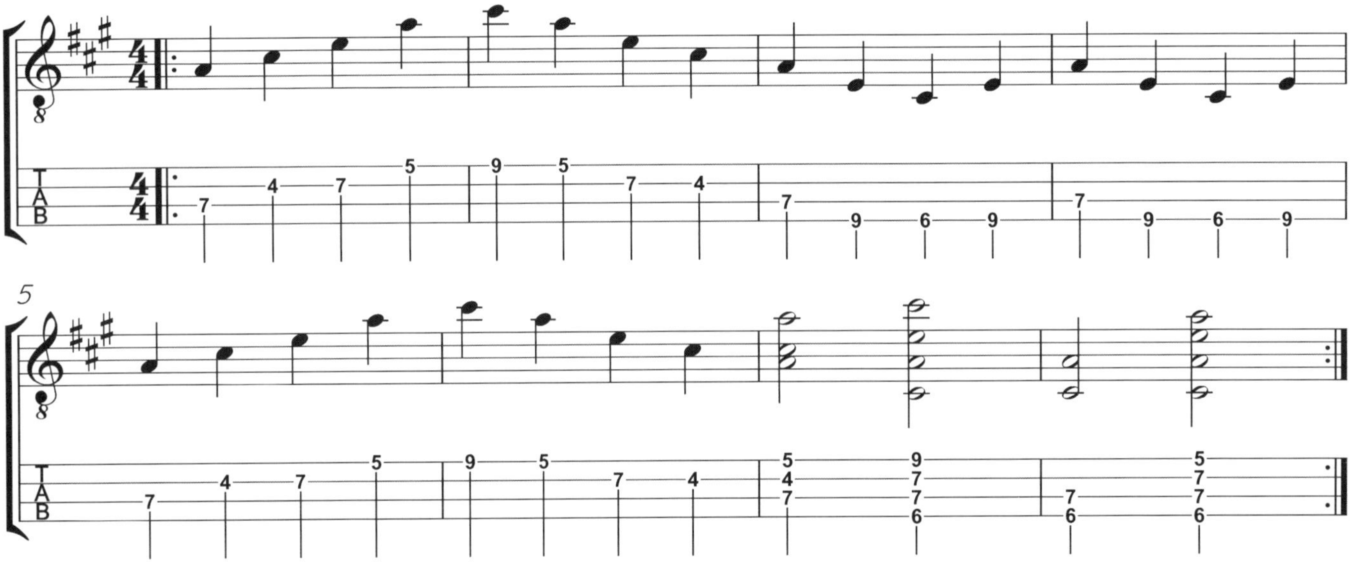

G-Shape Major Exercise 2: Move from G-shape, A major arpeggio to D major arpeggio, entering either arpeggio from the low end and then from the high end.

29

G-Shape Major Exercise 2

A Major - D Major

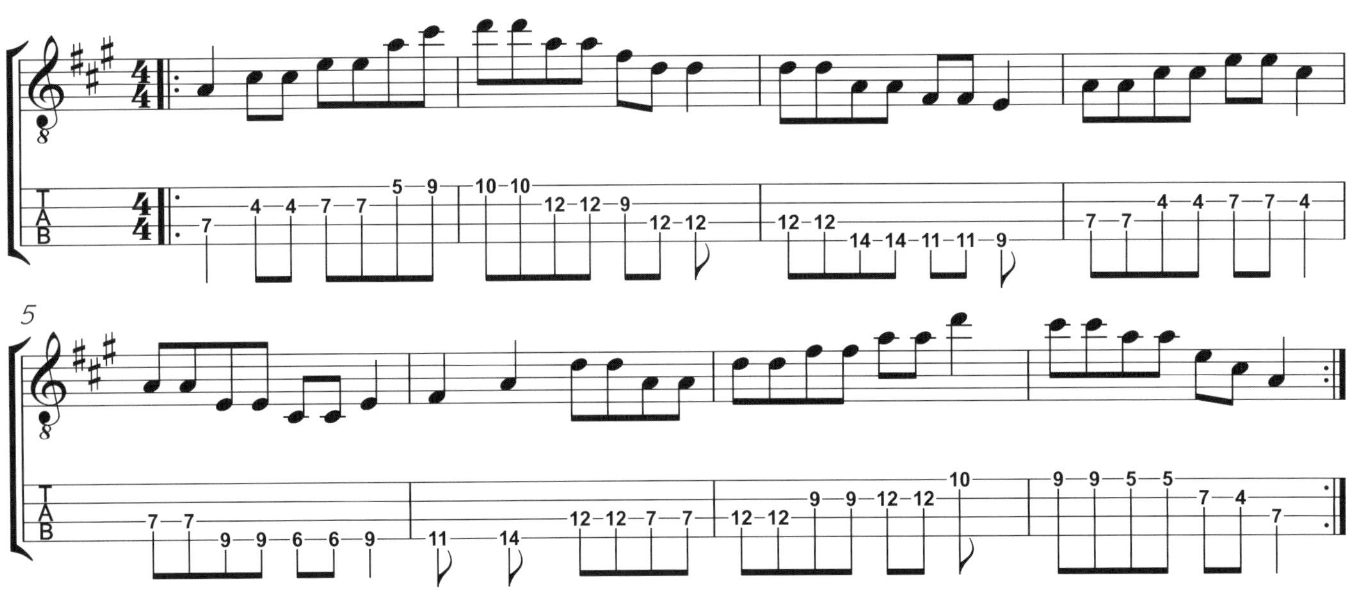

G-Shape Major Exercise 3: Practice the G-shape major arpeggios in a more uncommon chord progression (C-B-D-C♯m). It starts with a one-fret descent from C to B major in the G-shape, then goes up to D major on the 9th fret, also in the G-shape, and the last chord is C♯m in the A-shape at the 6th fret. Once you have memorized the arpeggios and can move them around fluidly, practice playing more freely and melodically using select notes of each arpeggio in varying patterns and directions.

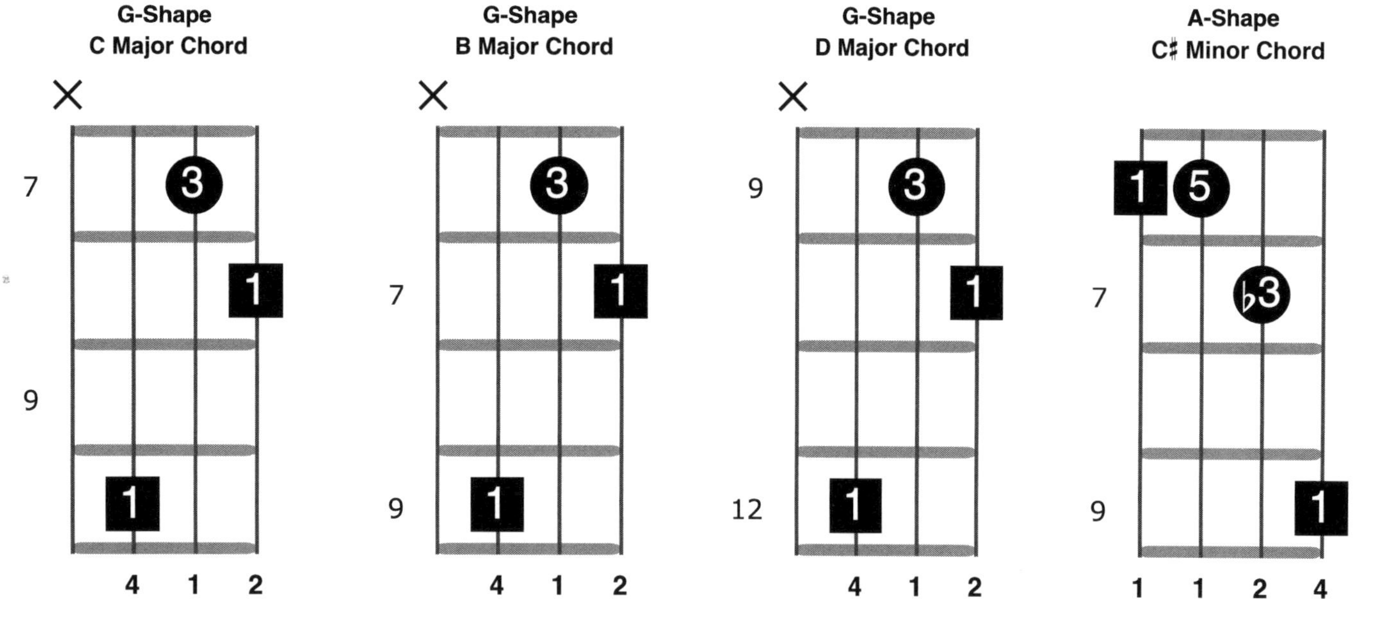

30

G-Shape Major Exercise 3

C - B - D Major in G-shape - C♯ Minor in A-shape

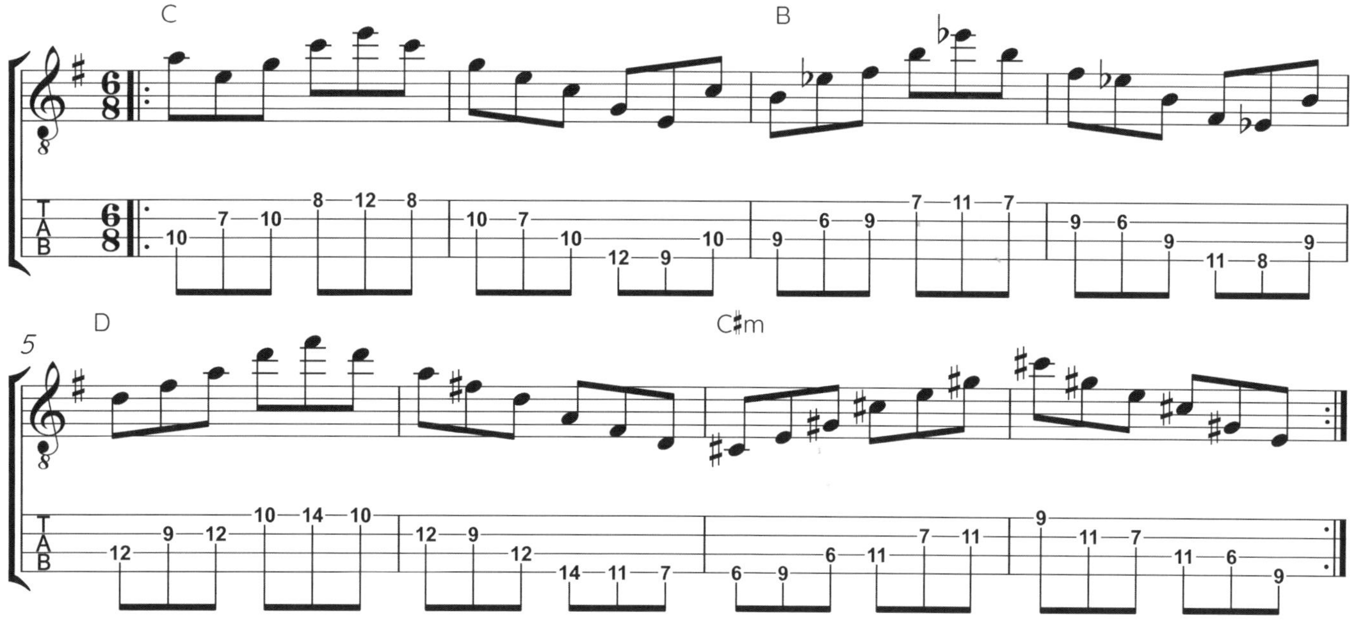

Chapter 3-2: G-Shape Minor Chords and Arpeggio Exercises

G-Shape
Minor Chord

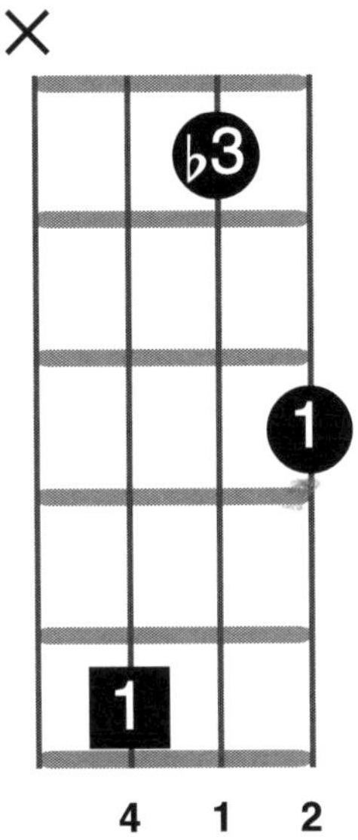

Here is the G-shape minor chord. Like the major chord, this shape has two root notes, with one of them falling on the D-string. This chord shape is made up of just the 1 note and the minor third note. The only difference between the minor and major chords is that the third note moves down one half-step (one fret) from the major third to the minor third interval. This chord shape and arpeggio require a pretty big finger stretch.

As always, before you try the finger exercises below, practice this arpeggio up and back many times while looking at the diagram to aid visual memory, and until you can play it without thinking too much or looking at your fingers.

G-Shape
Minor Arpeggio

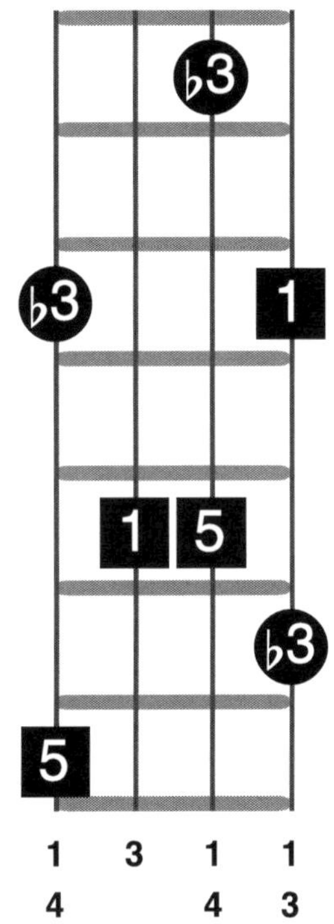

Alternative Chord Shapes

Here are four variations of minor chords made from the G-shape minor arpeggio. Variations 1 and 2 contain the complete triad, but sound quite different from each other. Variation 1 sounds a bit more neutral while 2 sounds more like a minor chord. Variation 3 can be played as a minor or major chord. Variation 4 is a handy double stop.

G-Shape
Minor Chord
Variation 1

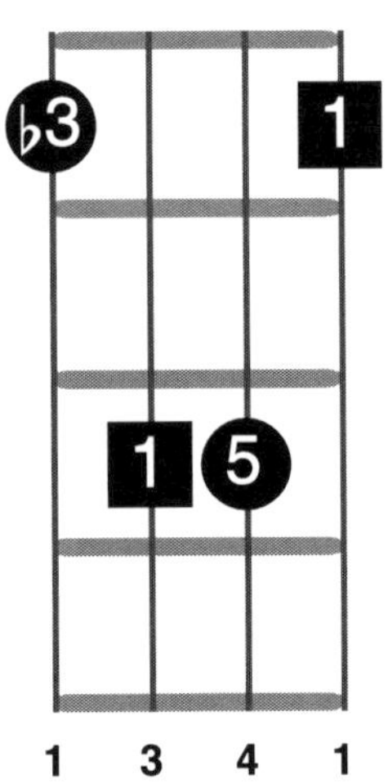

G-Shape
Minor Chord
Variation 2

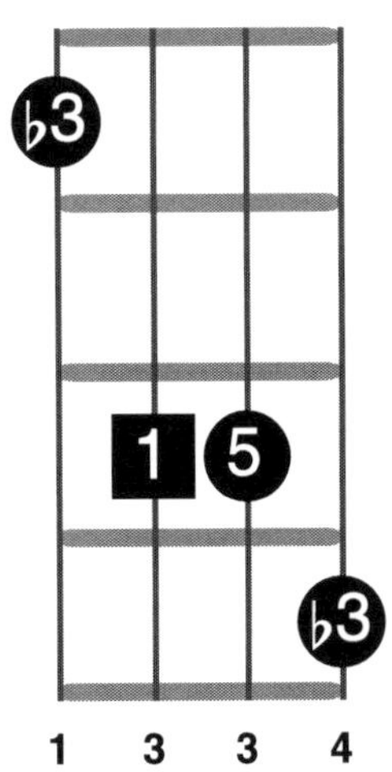

G-Shape
Minor Chord
Variation 3

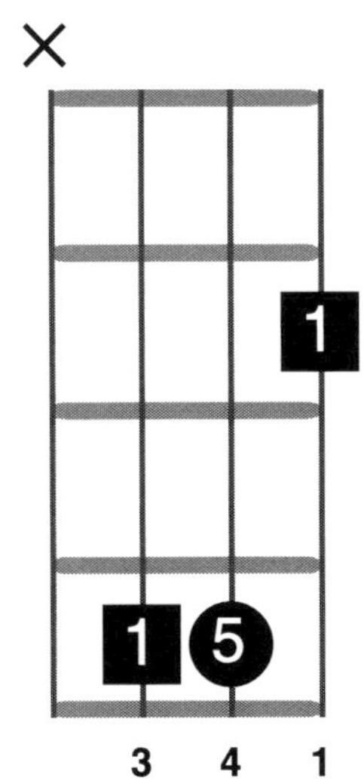

G-Shape
Minor Chord
Variation 4

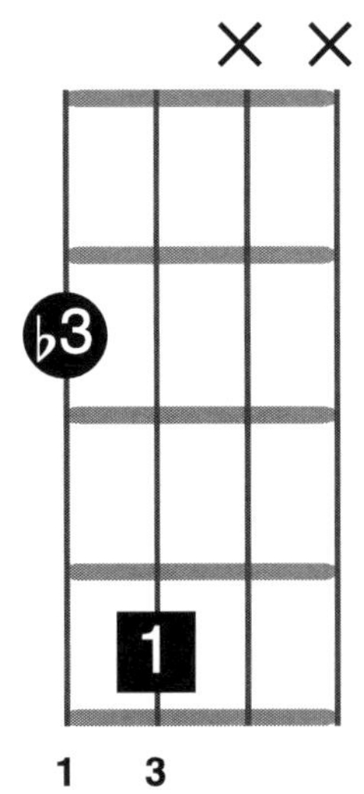

G-Shape Minor Exercise 1: Practice the G-shape minor arpeggio high up the neck in E minor from the E note at the 14th fret.

31

G-Shape Minor Exercise 1

E Minor

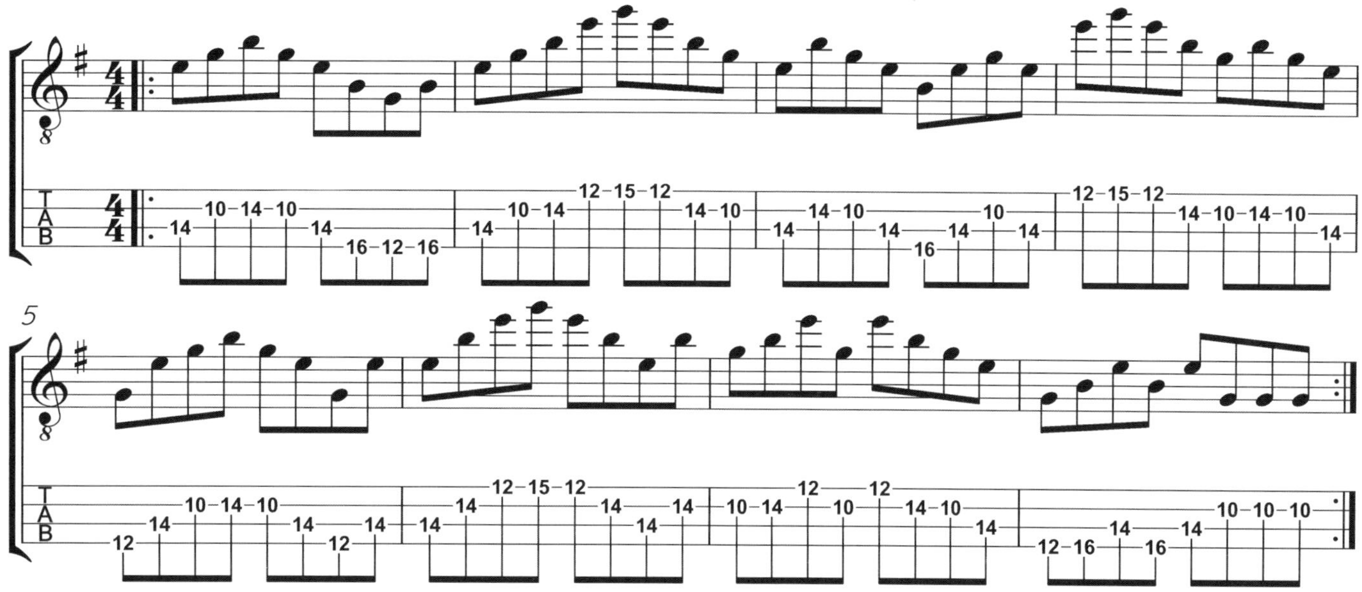

G-Shape Minor Exercise 2: Get used to playing the G-shape minor arpeggio with chord variations.

32

G-Shape Minor Exercise 2

B Minor

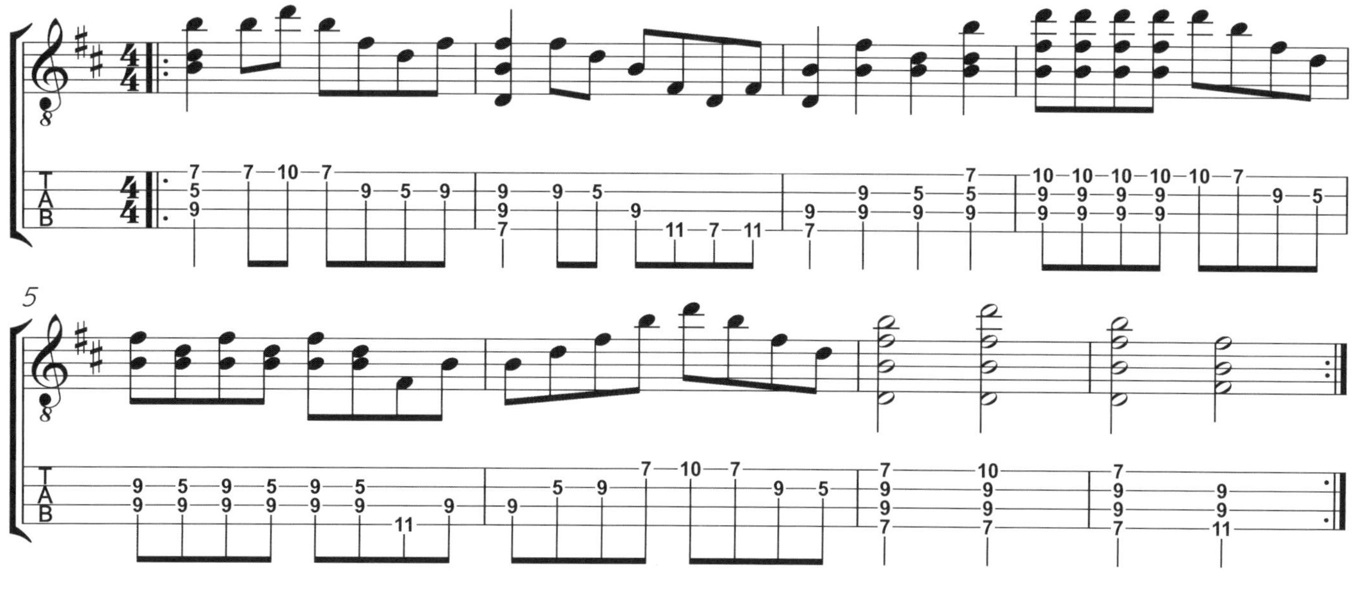

G-Shape Minor Exercise 3: Move this G-shape minor chord through a 1-4-5 progression.

33

G-Shape Minor Exercise 3

Dm - Gm - Am

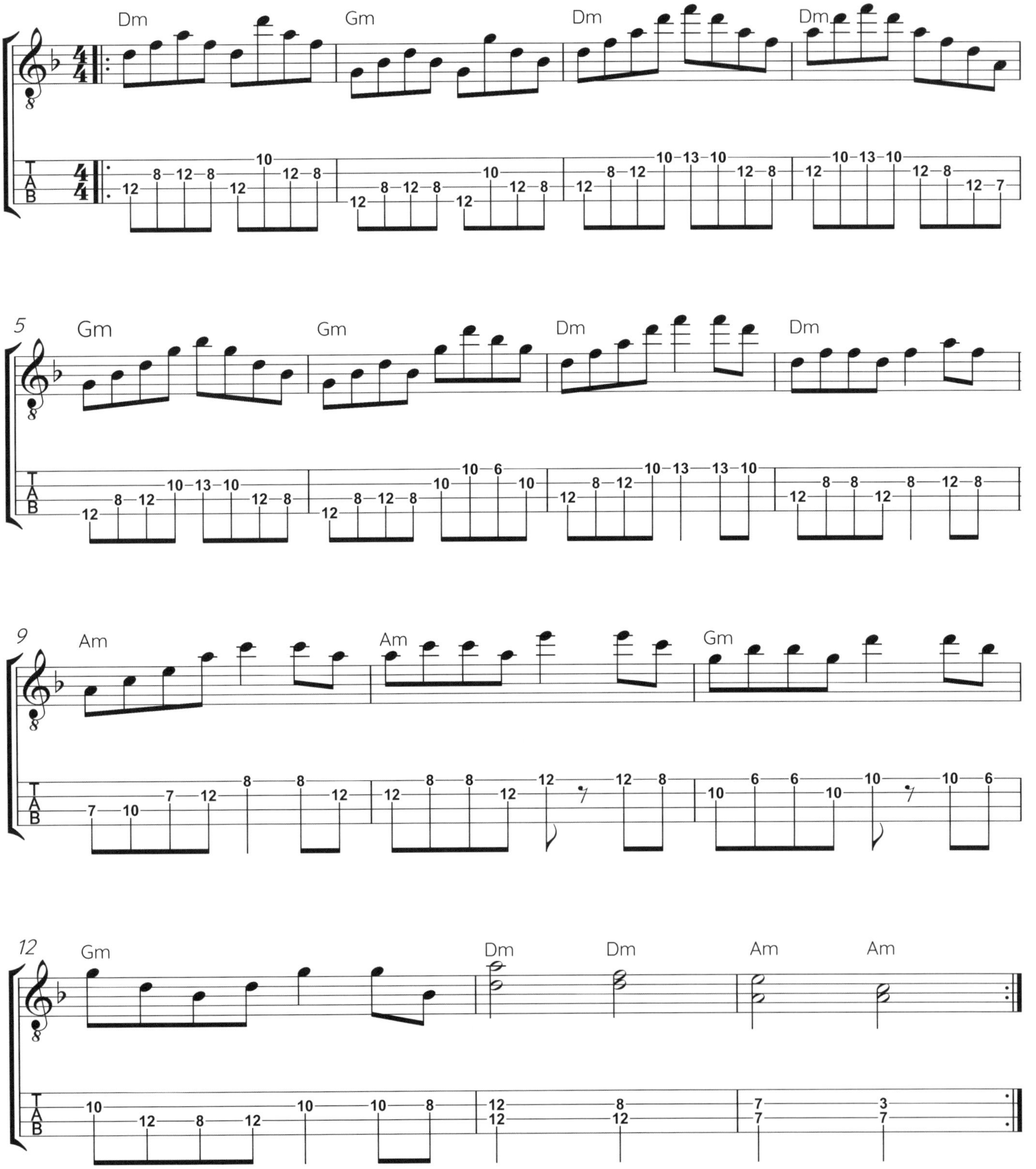

Chapter 3-3: G-Shape 7th Chords and Arpeggio Exercises

G-Shape
7th Chord

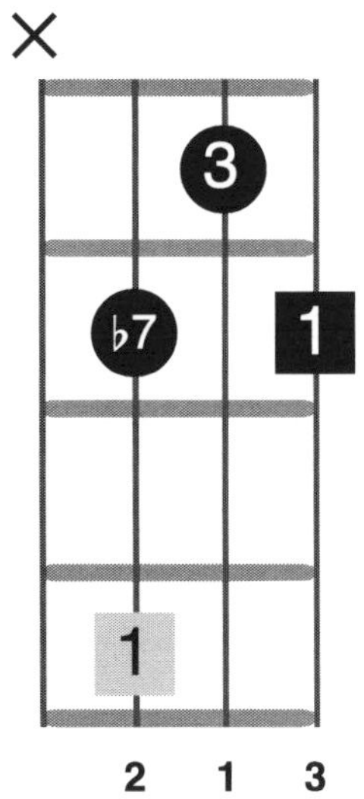

As stated in chapter 1, the 7th shape emphasizes the note one step down from the root note, the flatted 7th note, somewhere in the chord. The seventh chord in the G-shape doesn't really have a solid root note in this 3-finger shape. Therefore, sometimes it's helpful to include the root note above the flat-7. To find where to play this chord, make a G-shape major chord then slide the low 1 note, indicated in gray, down one step to the ♭7 note.

Notice again how the arpeggio pattern on the lower two strings repeats on the two high strings, slid 2 frets toward the nut.

G-Shape
7th Arpeggio

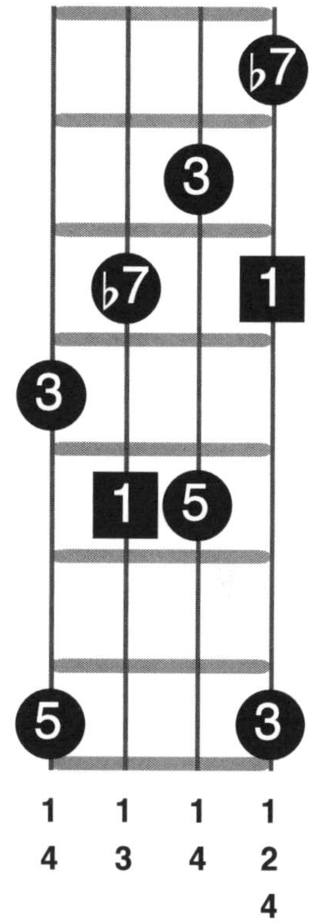

Alternative Chord Shapes

Variation 1 requires a good stretch and is maybe better for use higher up the neck. Variation 2 does not have the root note, which can be appealing in certain situations (indicated in gray to locate the chord position). Variation 3 has uses all four strings, but with the flat-7 on the bottom. And variation 4 again has no root note, but you can strum all four strings. Try these different inversions and/or make up your own.

G-Shape
7th Chord
Variation 1

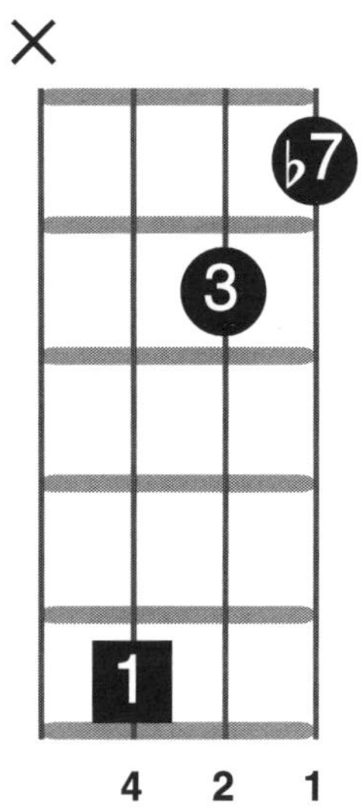

G-Shape
7th Chord
Variation 2

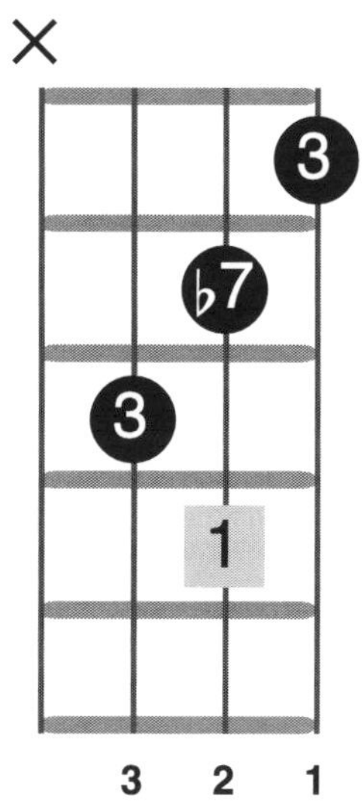

G-Shape
7th Chord
Variation 3

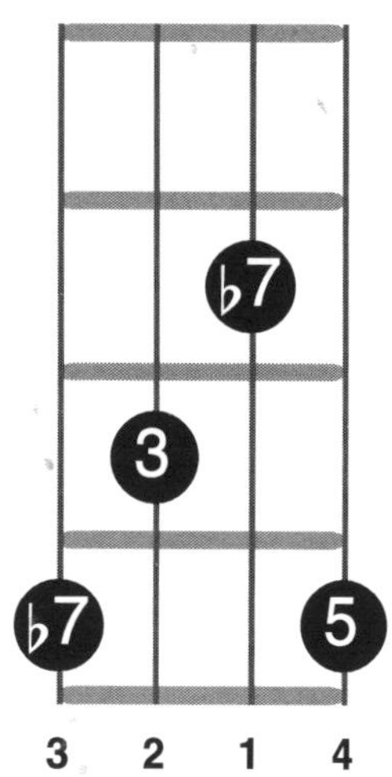

G-Shape
7th Chord
Variation 4

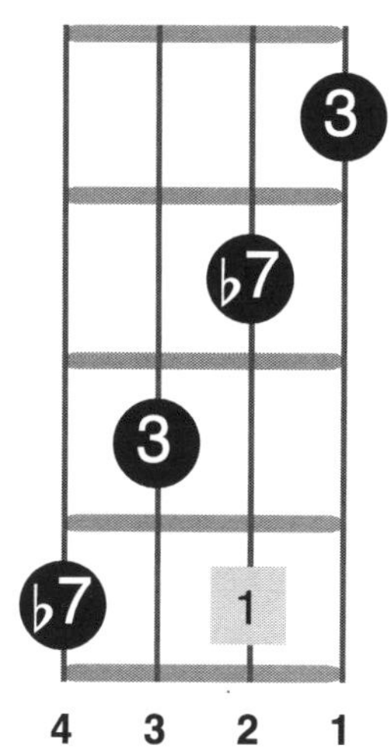

G-Shape 7th Exercise 1: Let's practice running the G-shape 7th arpeggio up and down the fretboard for Exercise 1. On the last 4 bars hold your first 3 fingers in place while fretting the 7th chord with just lifting your pinky on and off of the root note on the 7th fret.

34

G-Shape 7th Exercise 1

A7

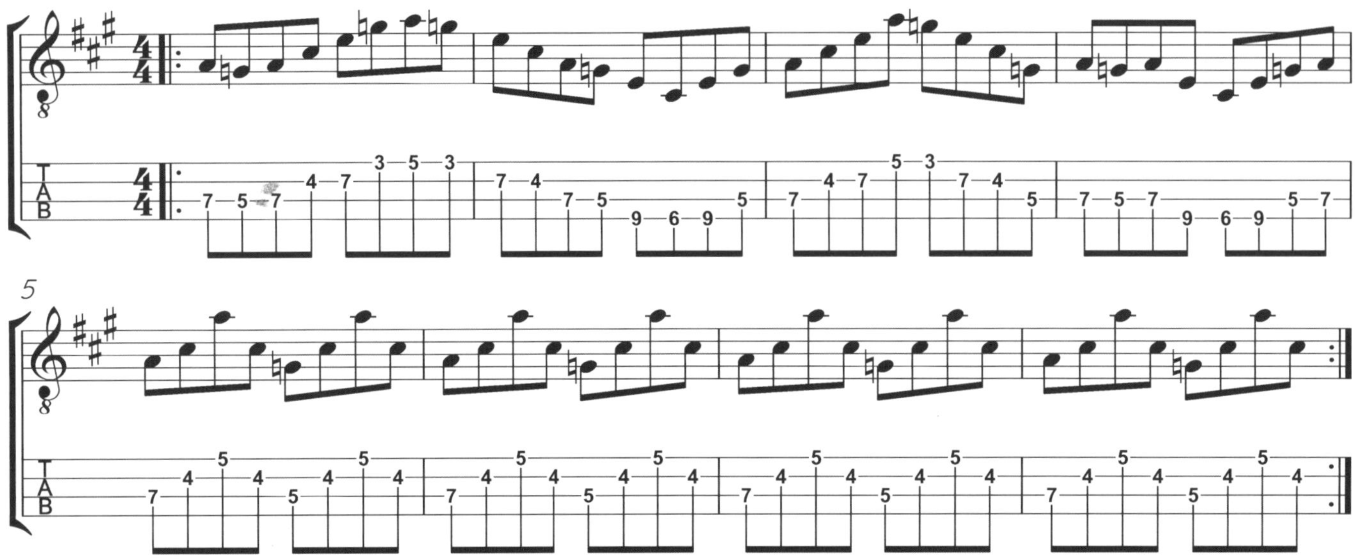

Before you try the next exercise, get warmed up with these notes of the G7 arpeggio. Notice the open G-string indicated on the chart. This is to remind you to have fun plucking that open string while you experiment with riffs and melodies with these notes. It's easier to find melodic ideas if you are practicing with a drum track or metronome. Try choosing three notes and create melodic phrases. Go back and forth rhythmically between two notes and then add the 3rd in for spice. Keep it simple and grooving. If you want to fret notes on the low string, the B at the 4th fret and the D at the 7th fret are part of this arpeggio. I think you'll find that it's very easy and satisfying to make up melodic phrases in this setting with these notes of the G7 arpeggio.

G-Shape
G7 Arpeggio

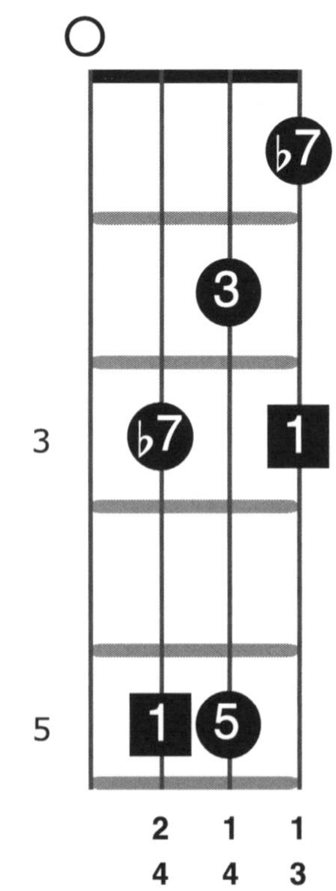

G-Shape 7th Exercise 2: The focus is on the G7 arpeggio notes over the open G note. Play this jig with an exaggerated swing feel.

G-Shape 7th Exercise 2

G7

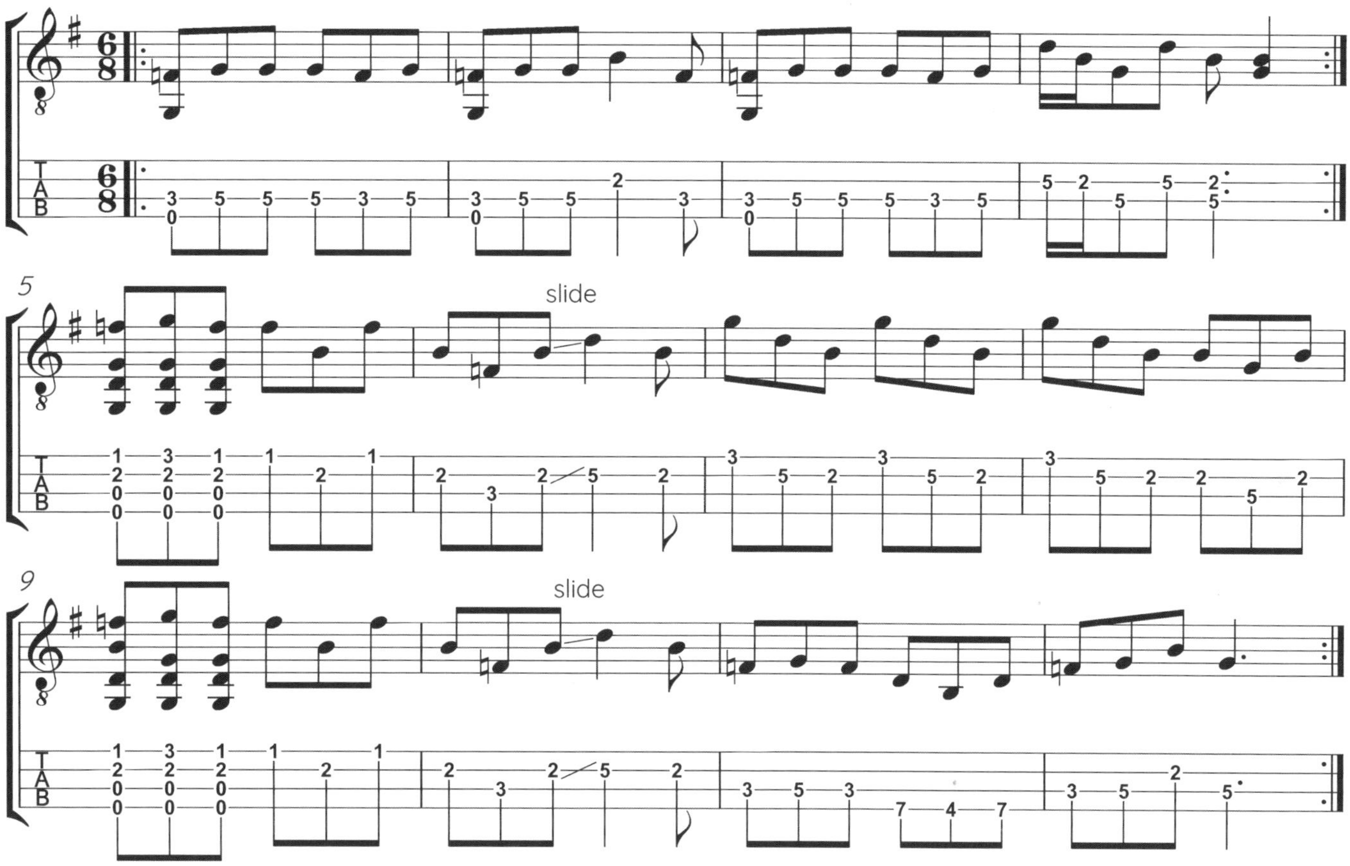

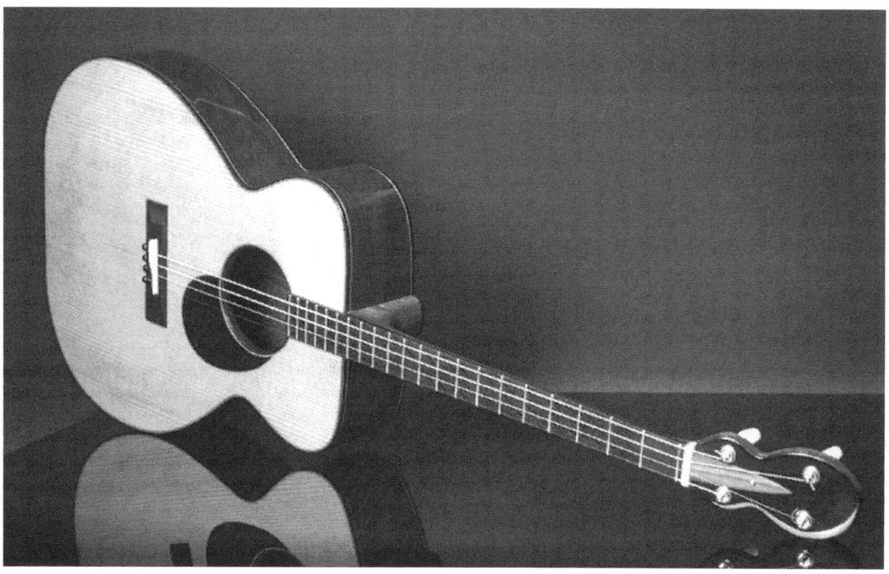

Shallow Session King Tenor by Nigel Forster

G-Shape 7th Exercise 3: Let's begin playing higher up the neck, and break up the order of the notes in the arpeggios while playing through a chord progression E minor, A minor, C7 and B7. We use E minor in the G-shape at the 10th fret, A minor in the C-shape at the 10th fret, with C7 and B7 in the C-shape at the 14th and 13th frets respectively. Instead of strumming these chords we will use the arpeggio notes that will suggest a melody while going around the chord changes. This demonstrates a starting idea of how to create a solo that moves with the progression. At first, play the exercise as notated, but as you get familiar with where your choice notes are, play it looser-make up melody lines and riffs and mix in chords too.

On the arpeggio charts below the chords are indicated by gray notes. It might be a good idea to start by playing these chords around the progression. Then run each arpeggio up and down a few times and then try the exercise.

G-Shape
E Minor Chord

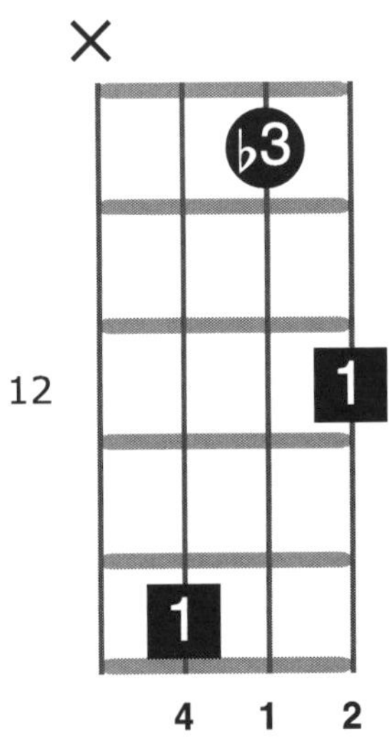

C-Shape
A Minor Chord

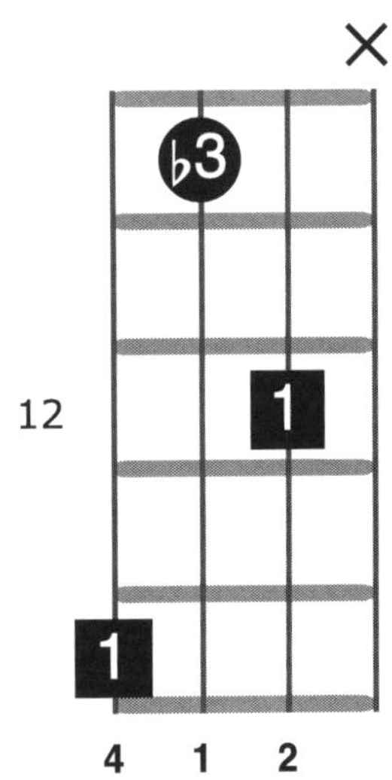

C-Shape
C7 Chord

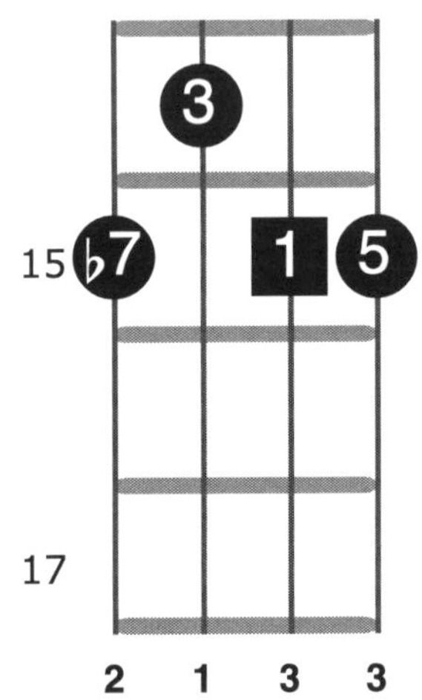

C-Shape
B7 Chord

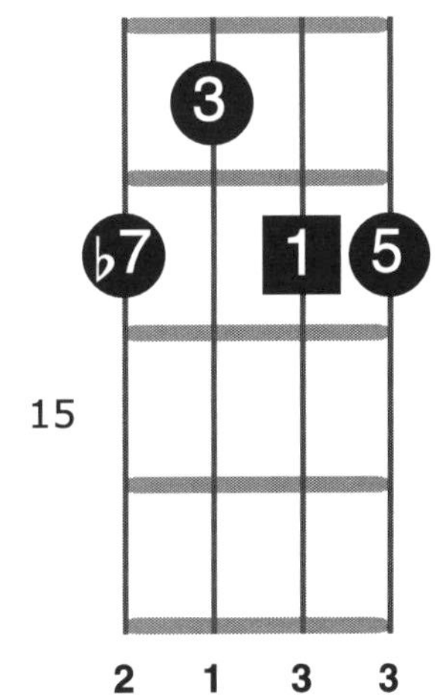

G-Shape
Em Arpeggio

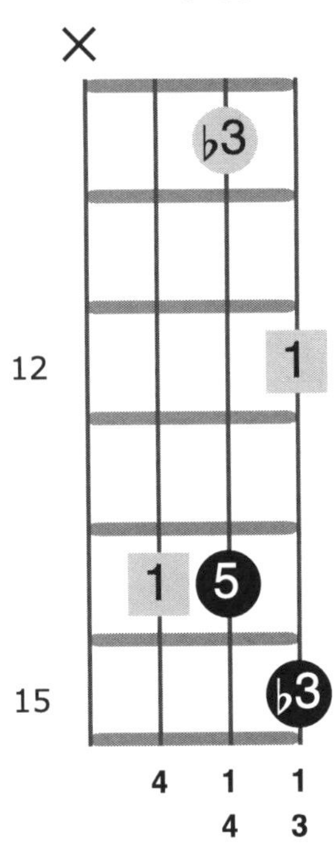

C-Shape
Am Arpeggio

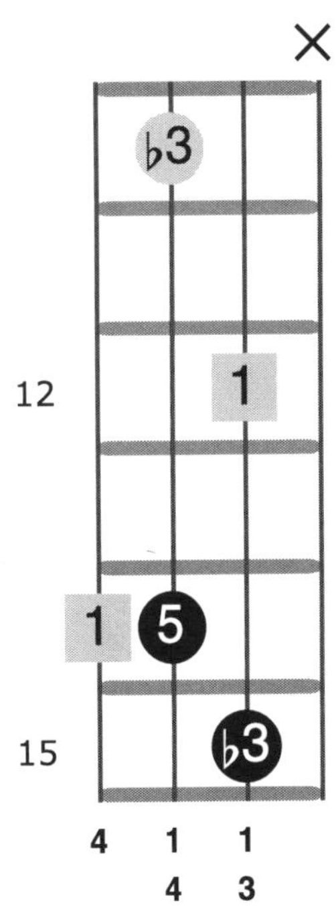

C-Shape
C7 Arpeggio

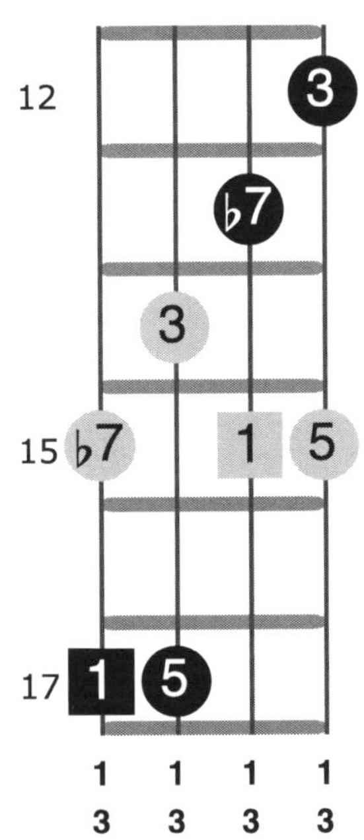

C-Shape
B7 Arpeggio

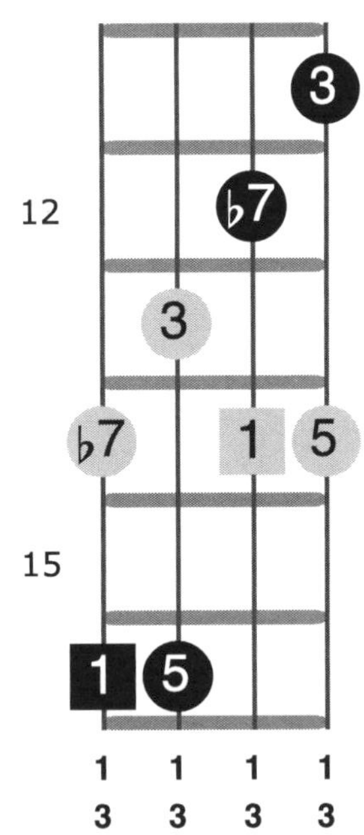

36

G-Shape 7th Exercise 3

Em - Am - C7 - B7

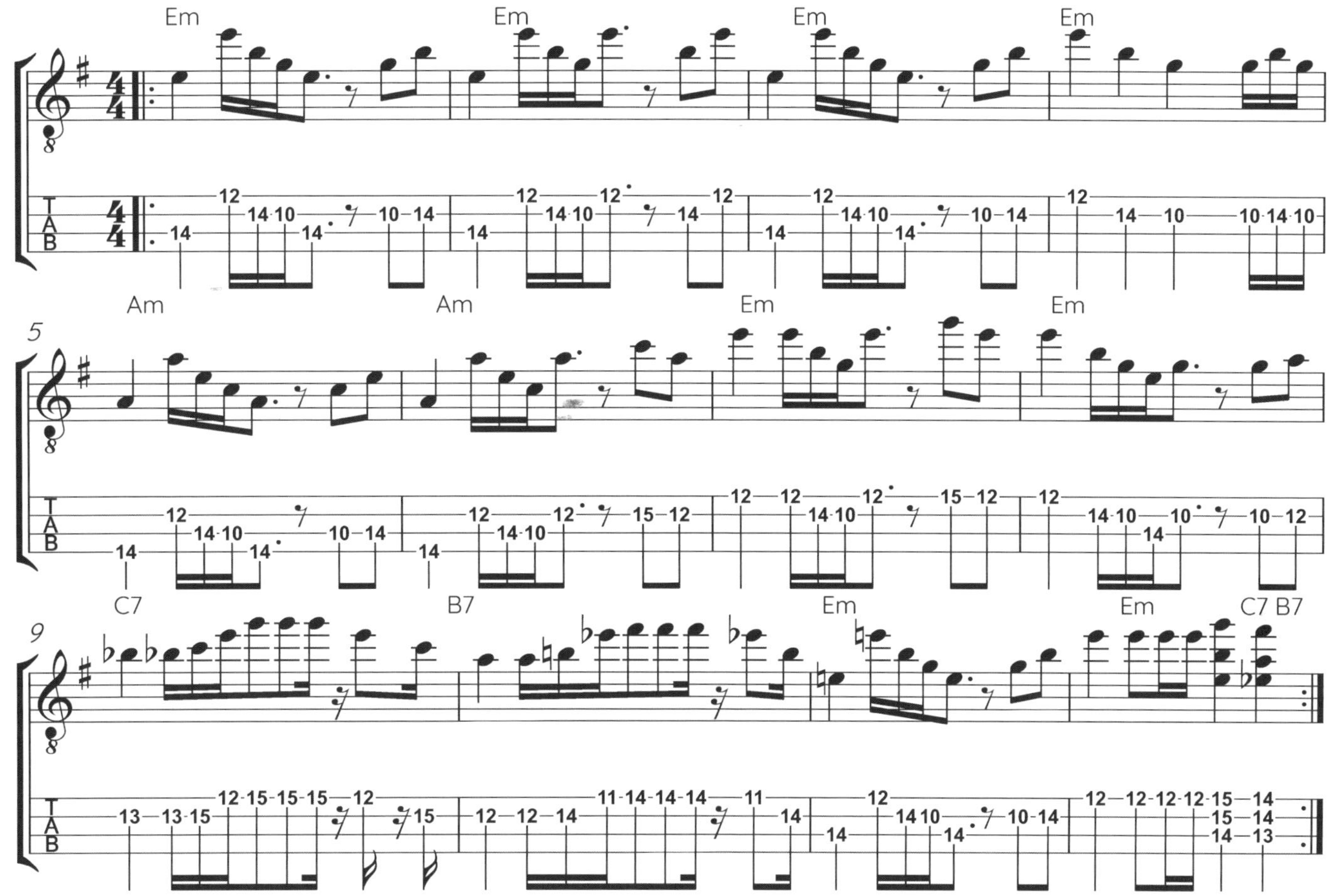

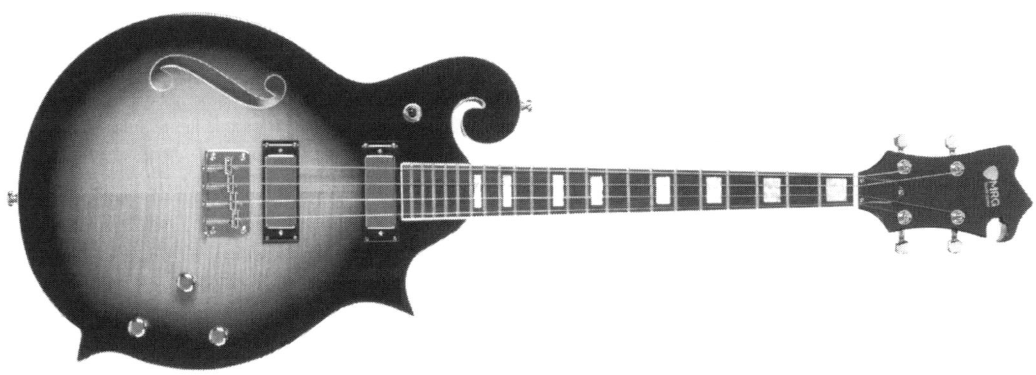

MRG Tenor Guitar by Eastwood

Chapter 3-4: G-Shape Melody Ideas

Now that you have practiced the G-shape arpeggios in the previous exercises, let's apply that knowledge to making a melody line over a chord progression. We are still going to focus on the arpeggio notes for each chord, but we will choose only a few arpeggios notes for each chord while concentrating on the musical flow from one chord to the next. The notes of the related major scale (G major scale in this case) are often used to transition between chords or to vary the phrases so that we are not only using arpeggio notes, but other elements as well.

The next melody-chord exercise (Track 37) addresses a progression consisting of G-shaped A minor, G major, and C-shape D major chords. It also uses an E-shape E minor chord (more on this shape next chapter) for this progression: Am, G, Em, D. The melody notes are intentionally chosen to be within these particular chord positions, so that as you become used to thinking in chord shapes while you play, these notes are readily available so you can easily play and mix in chords with melodic phrases. At bar 9, the notes might be easier to use under an E-shape A minor chord at the 7th fret.

G-Shape A Minor | **G-Shape G Major** | **E-Shape E Minor** | **C-Shape D Major** | **E-Shape A Minor**

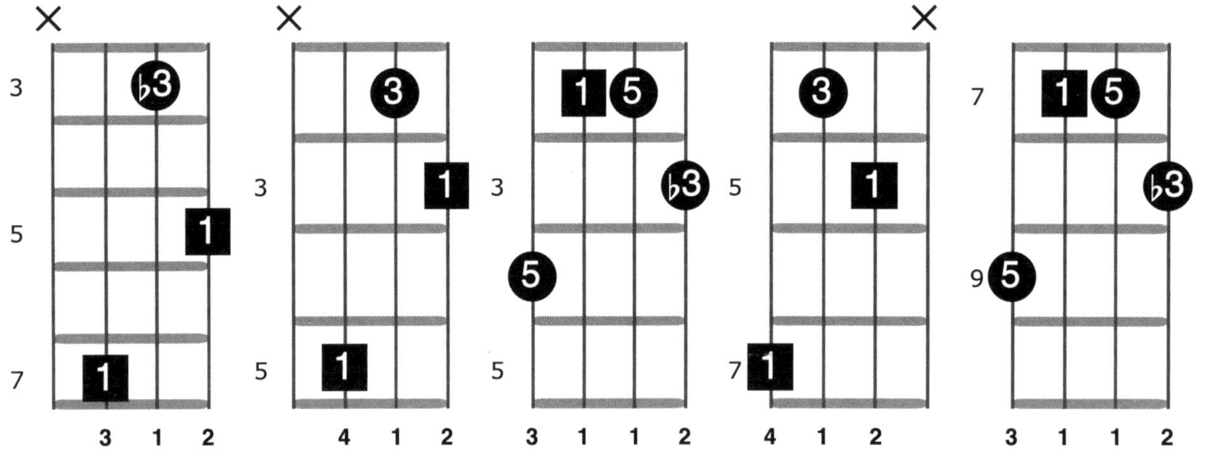

G-Shape A Minor Arpeggio | **G-Shape G Major Arpeggio** | **E-Shape E Minor Arpeggio** | **C-Shape D Major Arpeggio** | **G Major Scale**

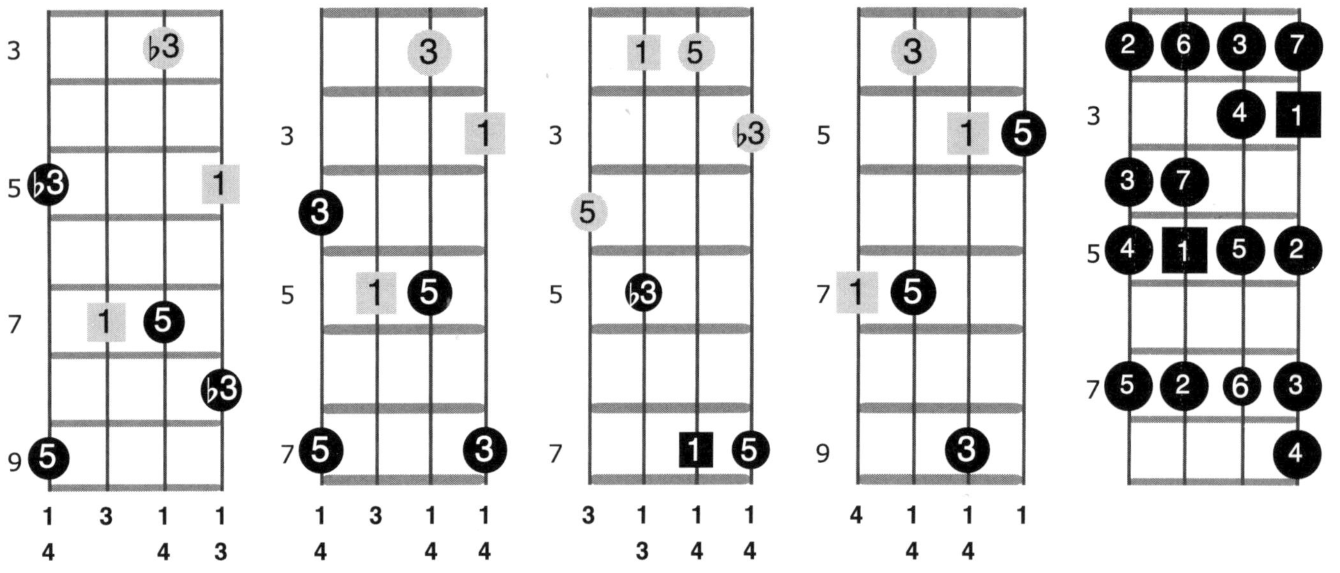

37

G-Shape Melody Ideas Application

Am - G - Em - D and G Major Scale

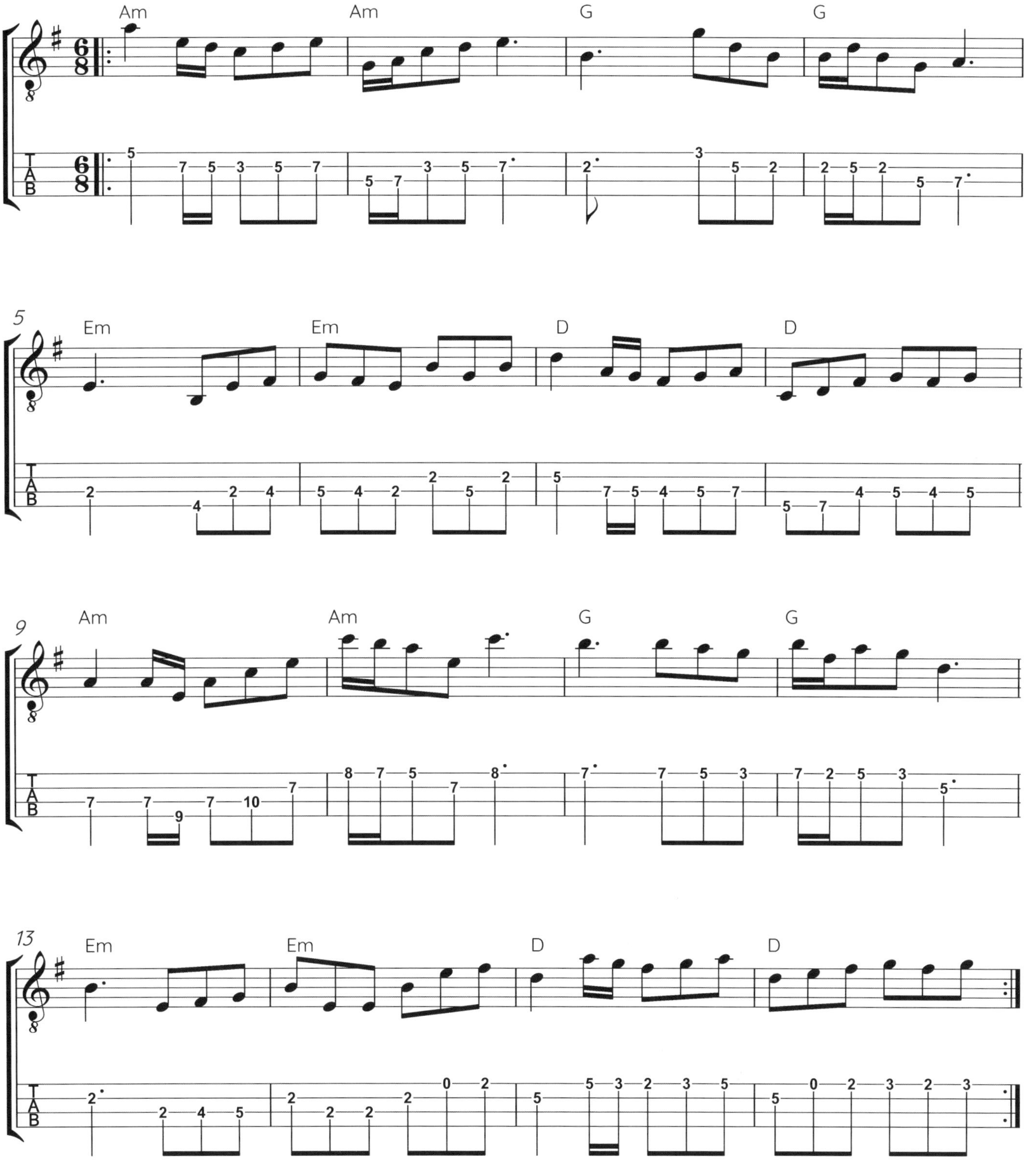

Chapter 4-1: E-Shape Major Chords and Arpeggio Exercises

E-Shape
Major Chord

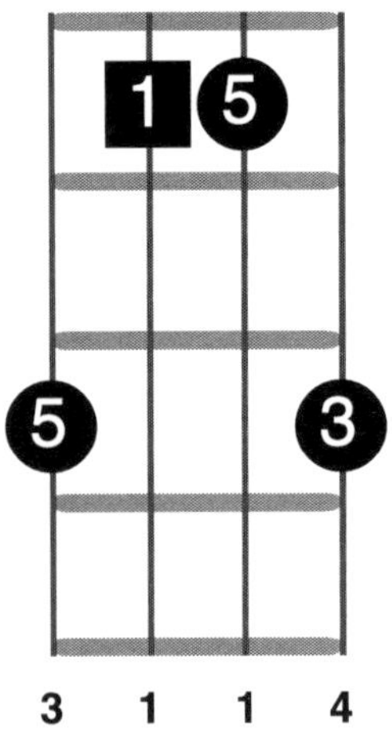

Here is the E-shape major chord. This shape uses all 4 strings so we don't have to worry about muting any strings, but be aware that the root note of the chord is on the D-string with the lowest note being the 5th of the chord. This chord shape is made up of the complete triad with the 1, 3, and 5 notes.

To move this chord noting the position of the 1 note anywhere on the neck, just locate the note you want on the D string, make this shape and you have the major chord in the E-shape of that particular root note.

Finger the E-shape major chord and then practice running this arpeggio up and down until you can play it smoothly with a metronome.

E-Shape
Major Arpeggio

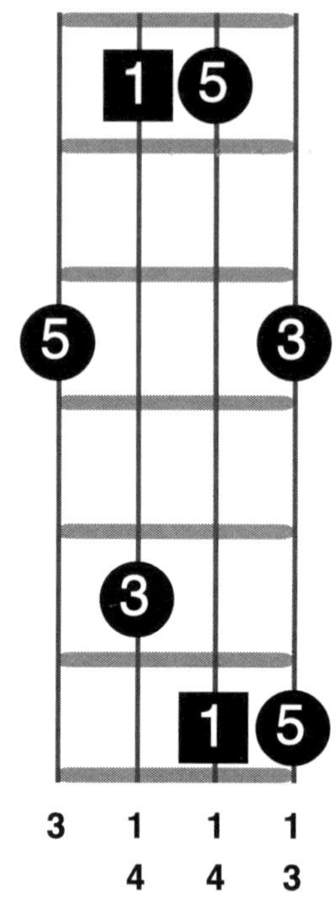

Alternative Chord Shapes

Here are 4 variations of major chords made from the E-shape major arpeggio. Variation 1 is our handy double stop chord for this shape. Variation 2 has the complete triad, but emphasizes the high strings. Variation 3 may seem less defined as the root note is on the A-string. Variation 4 is for folks with long fingers (or for playing higher up the neck) when you want to play octaves in one chord.

E-Shape
Major Chord
Variation 1

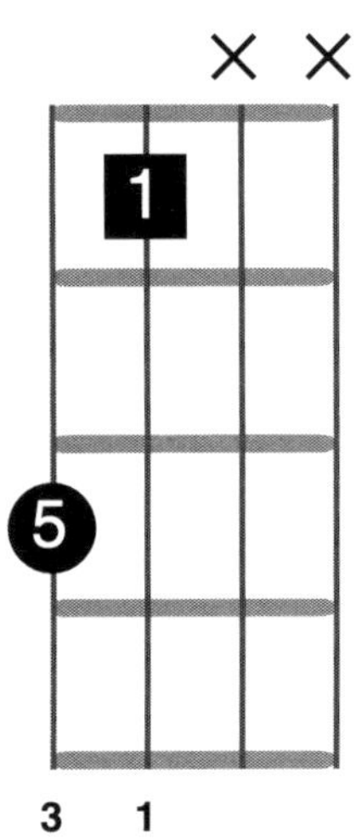

E-Shape
Major Chord
Variation 2

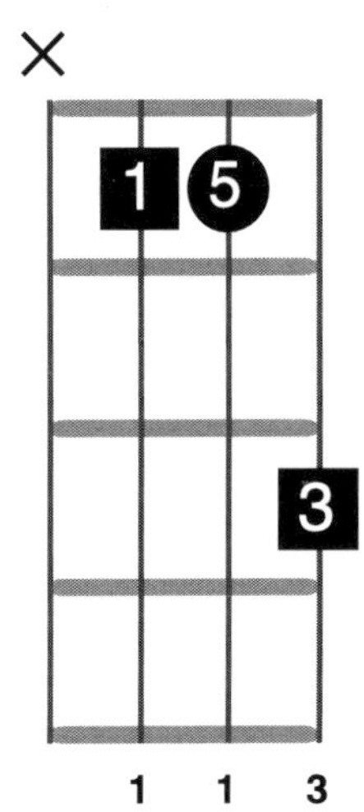

E-Shape
Major Chord
Variation 3

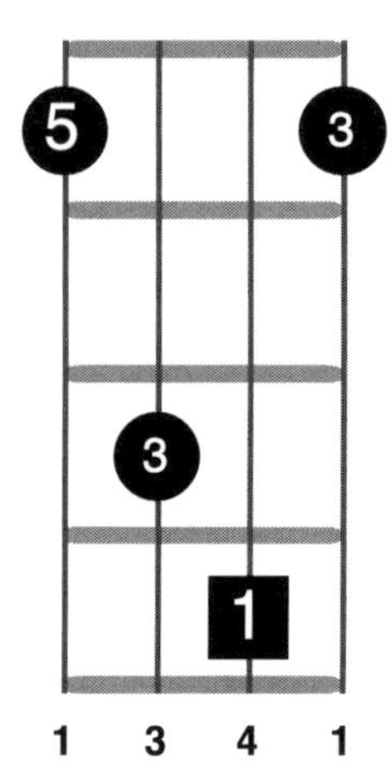

E-Shape
Major Chord
Variation 4

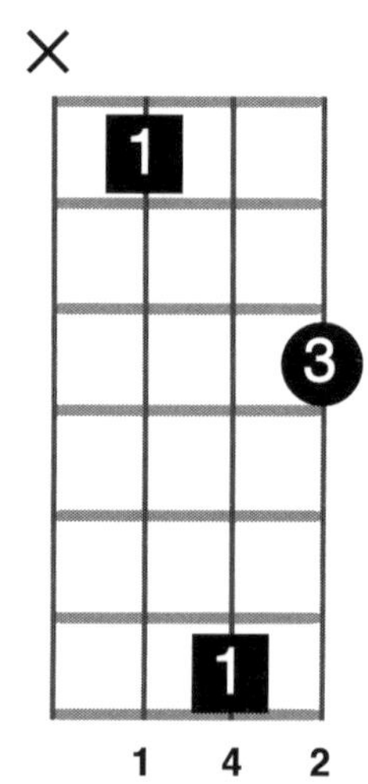

E-Shape Major Exercise 1: Let's keep it simple playing the arpeggio notes mostly in order concentrating on making the long finger stretches. Try to let each note ring out until the next note is plucked. We are building finger strength and flexibility. This exercise is based on the E-shape, G major chord at the 5th fret.

38

E-Shape Major Exercise 1

G Major

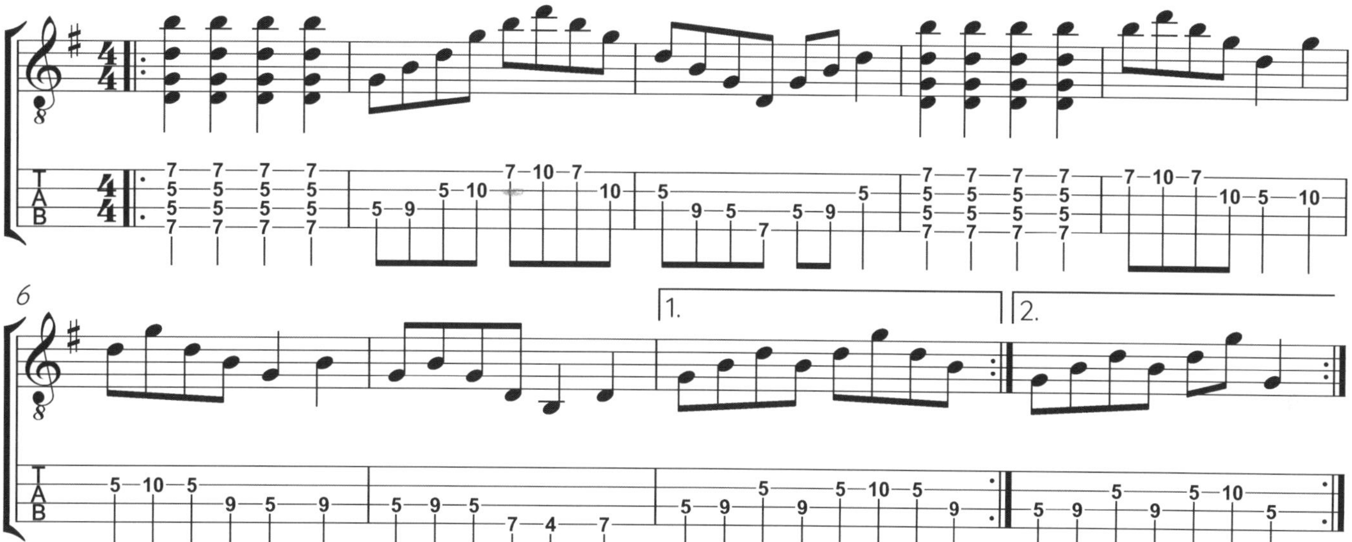

E-Shape Major Exercise 2: Practice moving the E-shape major arpeggio from A to G. Once you have memorized this exercise, try using a similar rhythmic pattern with different chords.

39

E-Shape Major Exercise 2

A Major - G Major

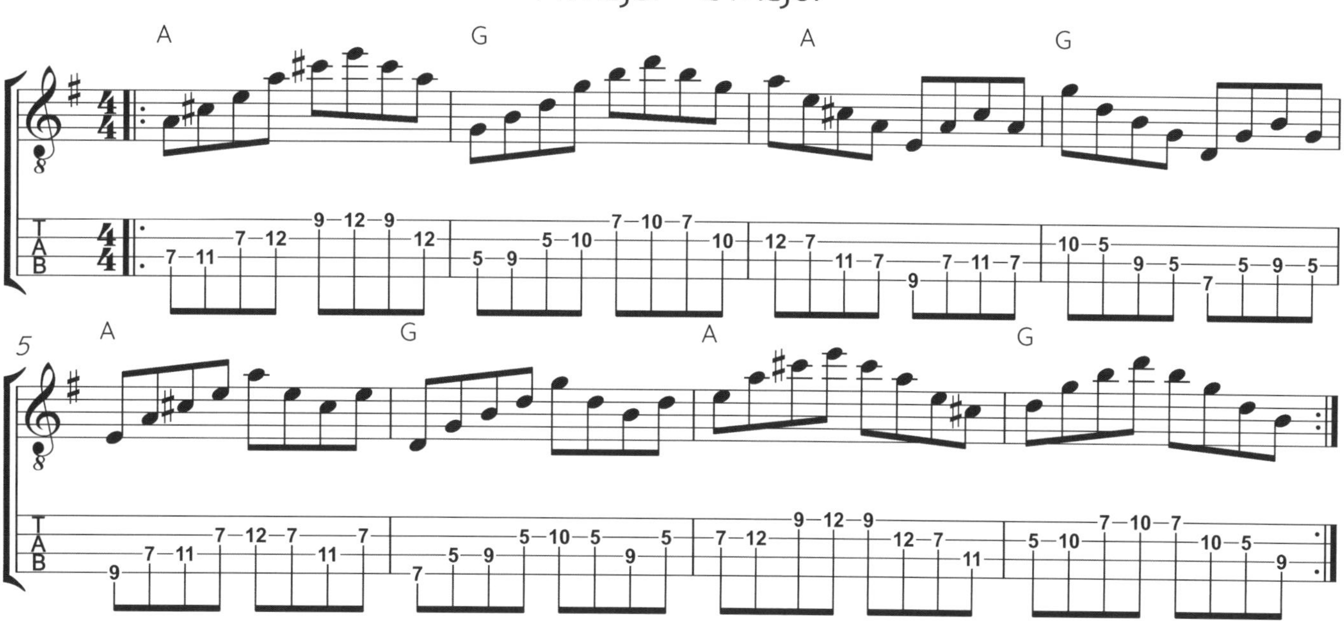

When choosing which shape to use often it makes sense to find shapes that overlap, or are generally near each other. **E-Shape Major Exercise 3:** We will use the C-shape for E major and A-shape for C♯m at the 6th fret, then back to E-shape for A major and B major at the 7th and 9th frets respectively. The basic chord shapes are indicated by the gray tones in the following diagrams.

C-Shape E Major Arpeggio | **A-Shape C♯ Minor Arpeggio** | **E-Shape A Major Arpeggio** | **E-Shape B Major Arpeggio**

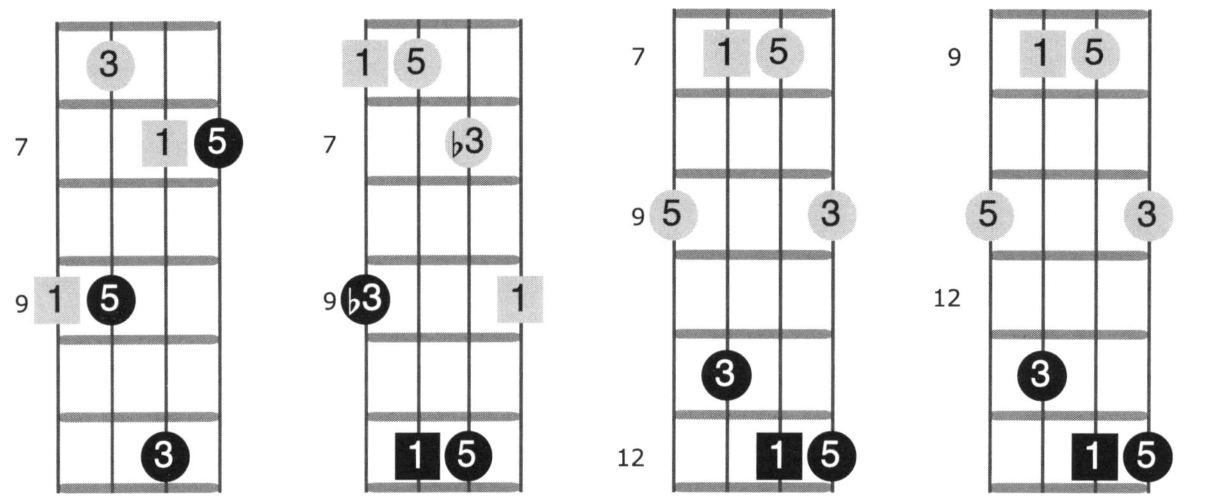

E-Shape Major Exercise 3

E - C♯m - A - B

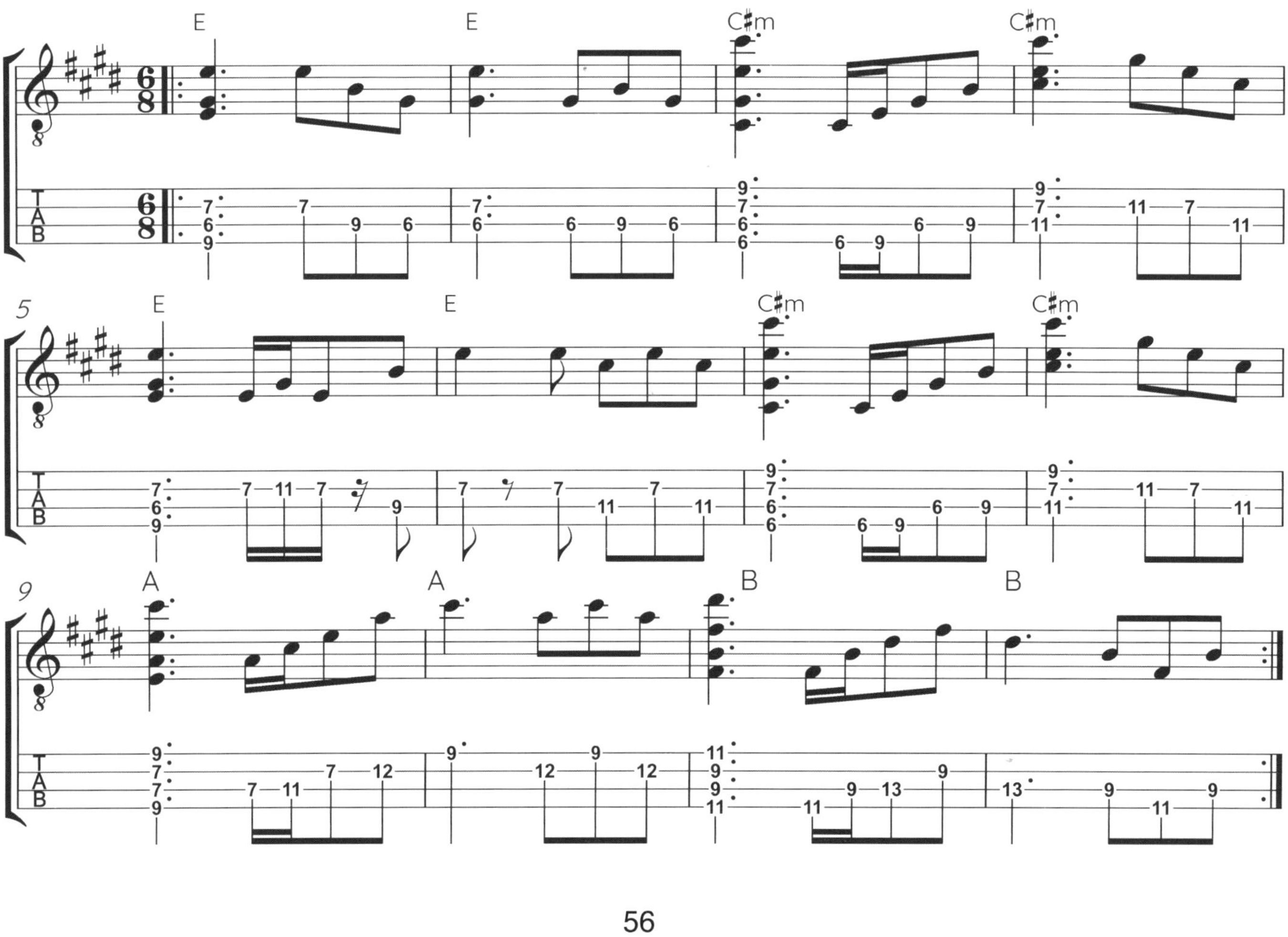

Chapter 4-2: E-Shape Minor Chords and Arpeggio Exercises

E-Shape
Minor Chord

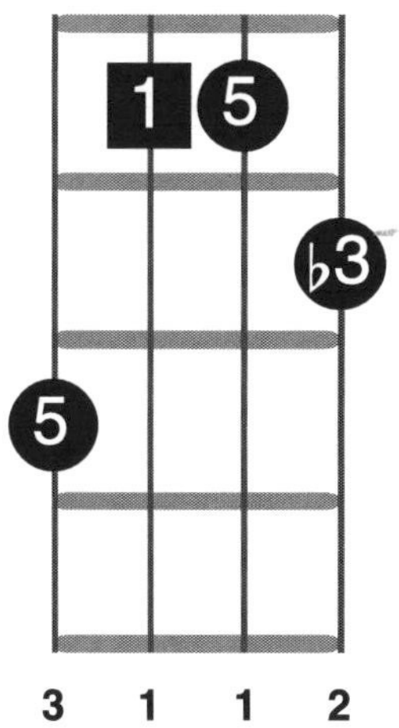

Here is the E-shape minor chord. Like the E-shape major chord, this shape has the root note on the D-string. As you may have noticed, each different shape emphasizes different notes. This time, the 5-note gets two voices within the chord. Remember, the only difference between the minor and major triads is that the interval of a major third note moves down one half-step (one fret) from the major third to the flat third. This arpeggio does require a pretty big finger stretch and is obviously easier to apply higher up the neck until you get used to long stretches.

As always, before you try the finger exercises below, practice this arpeggio up and down many times while looking at the chart to aid visual memory-until you can play it without thinking too much or looking at your fingers.

E-Shape
Minor Arpeggio

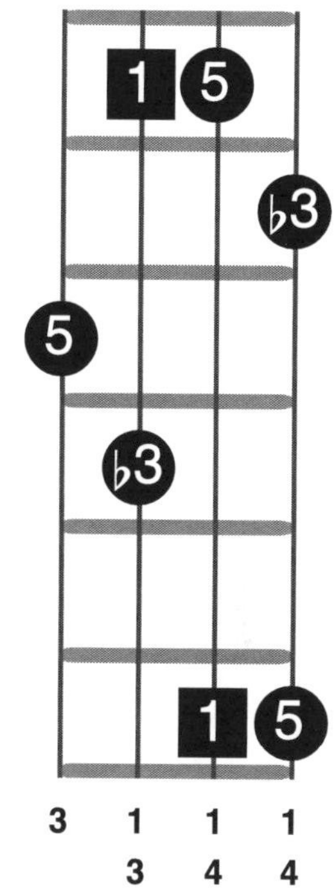

Alternative Chord Inversions

Variations 1 and 2 are similar except that Variation 2 only has the essential 1 and ♭3. With a little practice, it's easy to mute those 2 strings on Variation 2 by using your thumb around the back to mute the low string, and have the first finger fretting the 1 note lay over a little bit to mute the A-string. Variations 3 and 4 are two double stop options that are always useful to add power to a melody line by hitting chords sprinkled in with your single-note lines.

E-Shape
Minor Chord
Variation 1

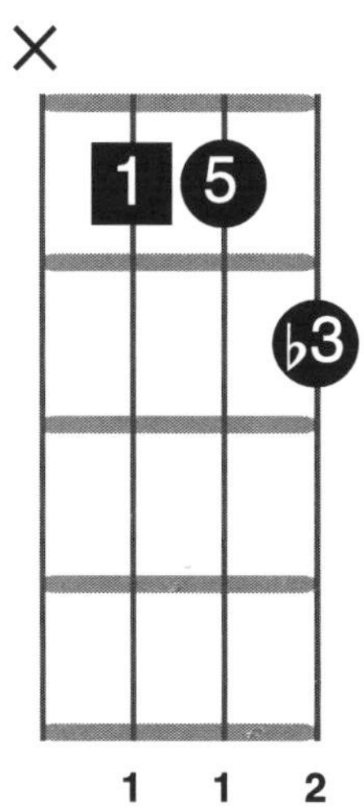

E-Shape
Minor Chord
Variation 2

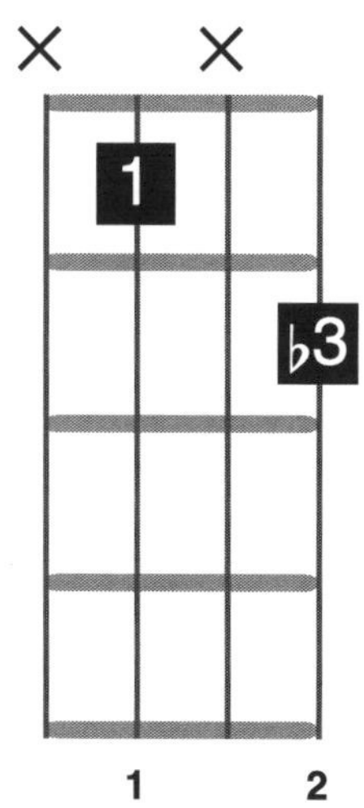

E-Shape
Minor Chord
Variation 3

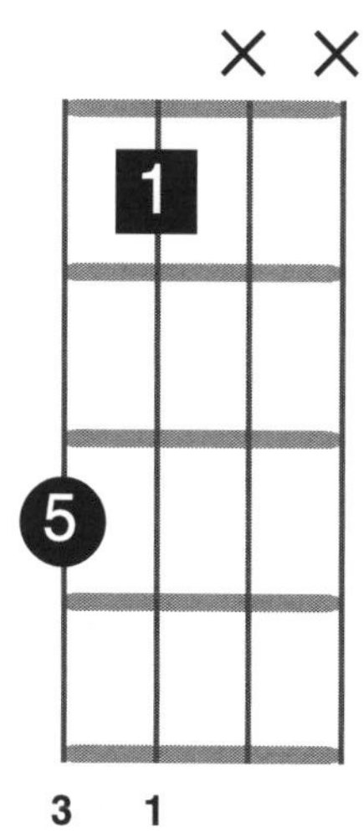

E-Shape
Minor Chord
Variation 4

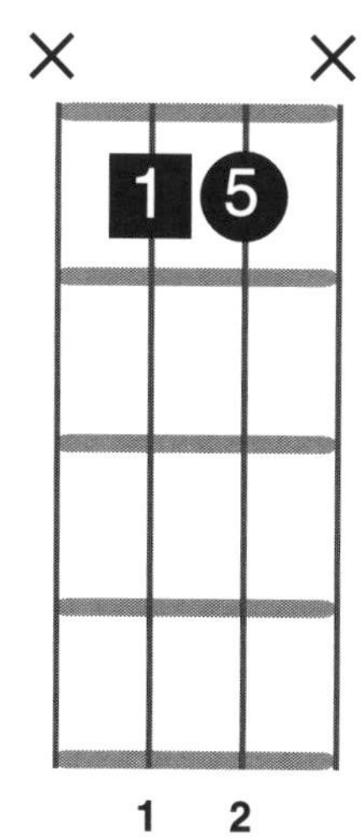

E-Shape Minor Exercise 1: Practice the E-shape minor arpeggio in A minor. In bars 1, 4, and 7 fret the chord shape and pluck each individual note. Remember, we want to memorize these key notes as they are related to each chord shape.

41

E-Shape Minor Exercise 1

A Minor

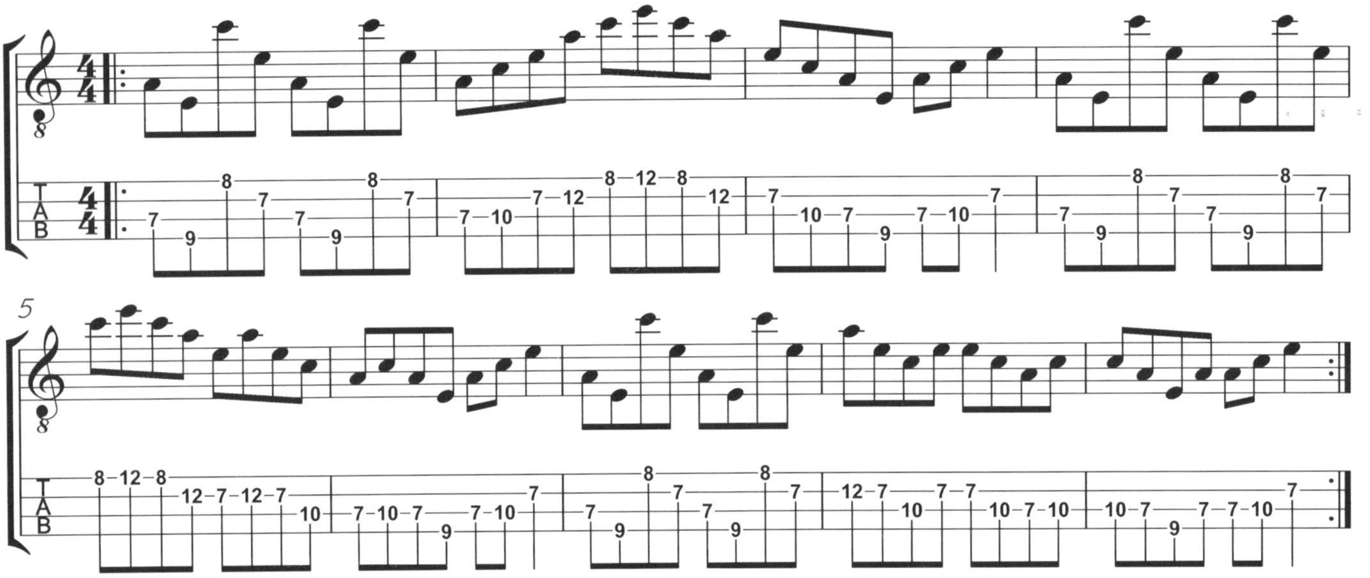

E-Shape Minor Exercise 2: Practice moving from the E-shape minor to A-shape minor arpeggios. Let's use the E-shape, A minor chord at the 7th fret, the A-shape, D minor at the 7th fret, and the A-shape, E minor at the 9th fret.

42

E-Shape Minor Exercise 2

Am - Dm - Em

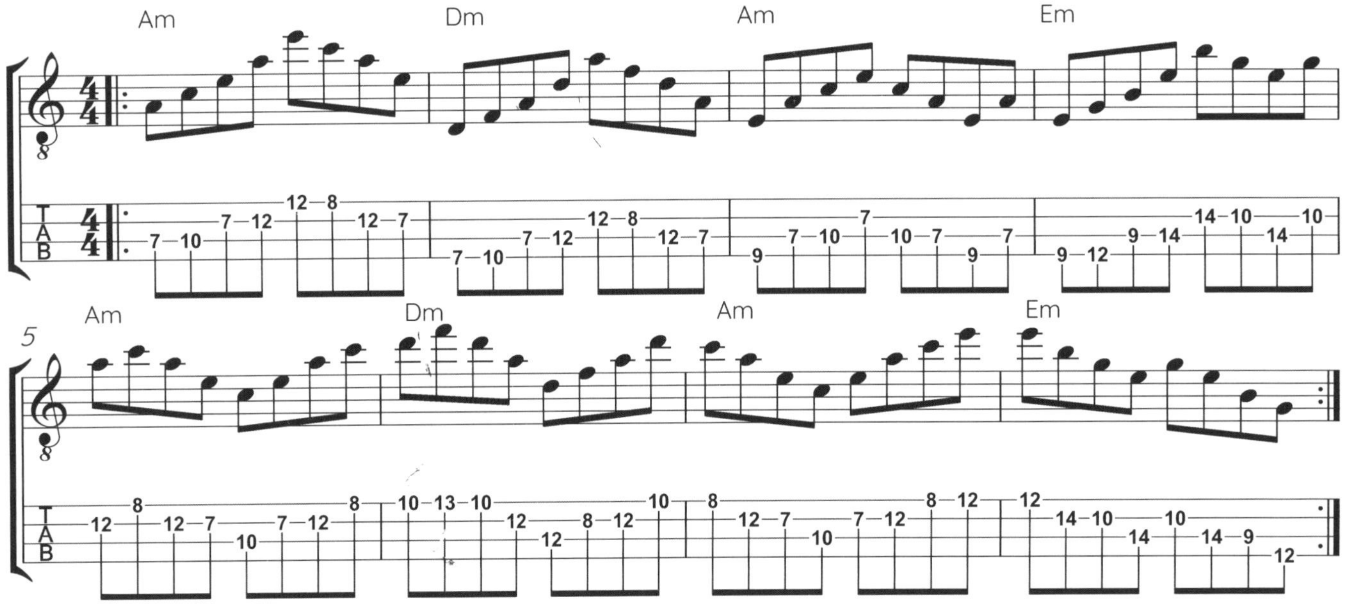

Now that you have been working on the specific chord shape arpeggios for a while (hopefully!), let's think of more strategies to create solos. The really useful thing about knowing all your chord shape arpeggios is that if you want to create a melody line over a progression, and if you only use arpeggio notes over the changes, that it will sound in key and harmonically appropriate.

At some point, however, you may want to include other notes, in addition to the arpeggio notes. One strategy is to add in notes of the scale of the song, or section. I like to start from the perspective of the major scale. For example in F major, the chords of the scale are F, Gm, Am, B♭, C(7), Dm, E dim, and back to F. Those are the 1st, 2nd, 3rd, 4th, 5th, 6th, 7th, and 8 degrees of the scale.

E-Shape Minor Exercise 3: The chords of this progression are D minor, C major, B♭ major, and A minor. These are the 6, 5, 4, and 3 chords of the F major scale. To create a melody line or solo over this progression, we can focus on hitting the arpeggio notes for each chord, but also add in notes from the F major scale. Here are the E-shape chords for this progression.

E-Shape
D Minor Chord

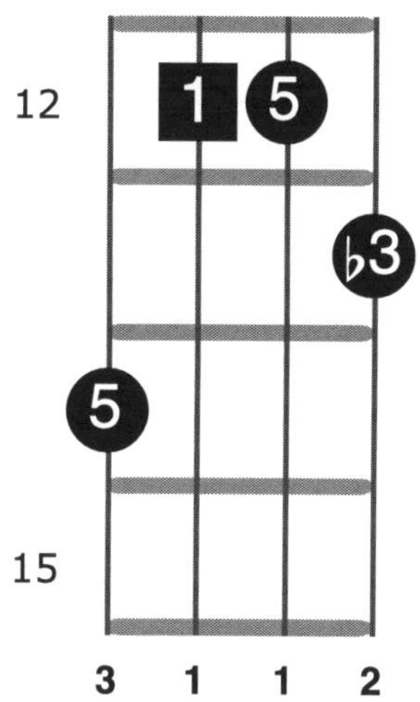

E-Shape
C Major Chord

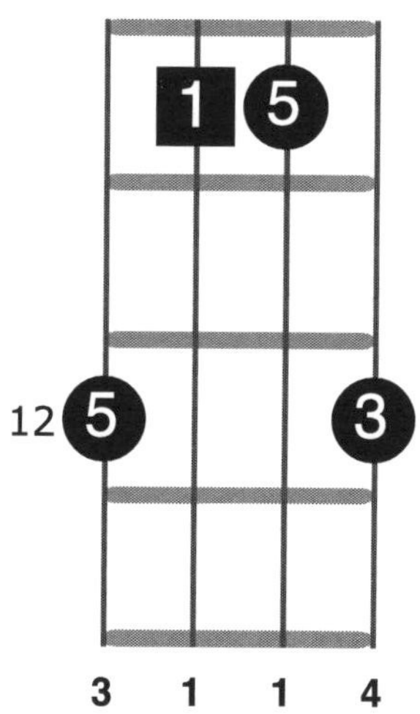

E-Shape
B♭ Major Chord

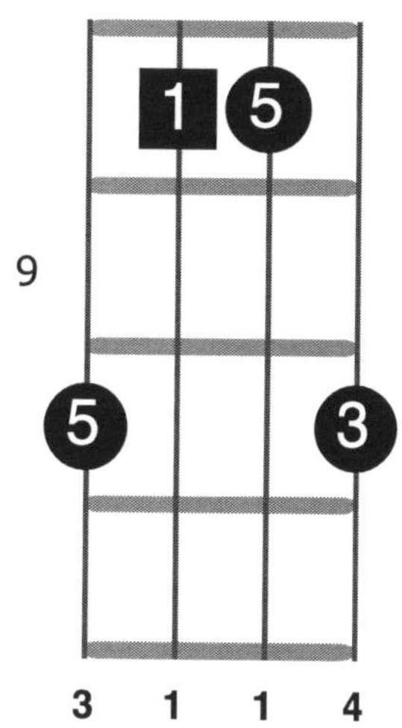

E-Shape
A Minor Chord

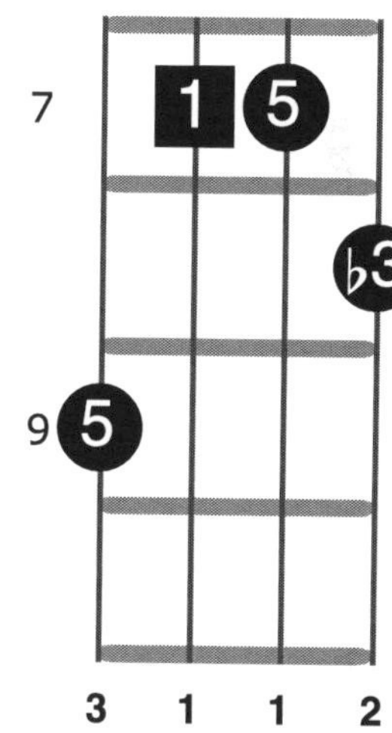

Since these chords span from the 12th to the 7th fret, let's keep our melody practice in that same area on the fretboard. Below is the F major scale pattern from the 7th fret. Run up and down this scale numerous times to get warmed up. Notice that you can clearly see the root notes of the progression here in the scale.

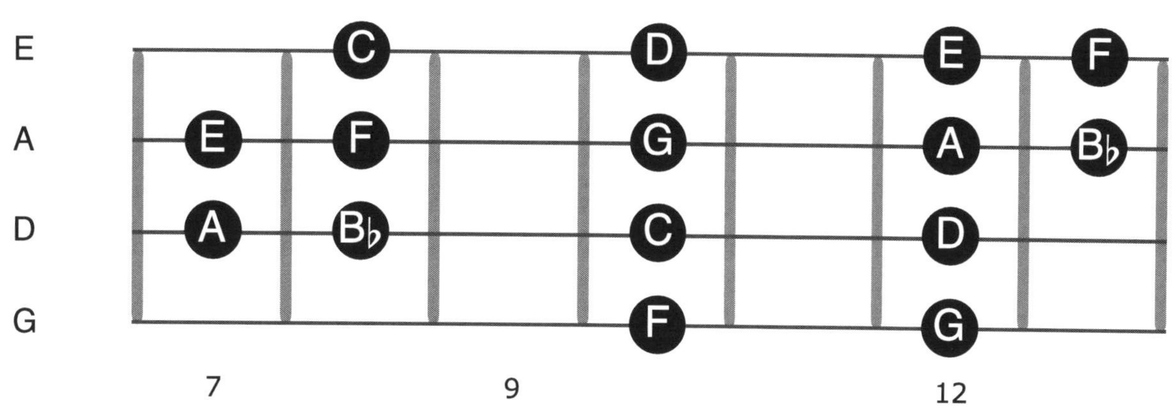

With the basic chord shapes indicated in gray, here are the most convenient chord arpeggios in this region.

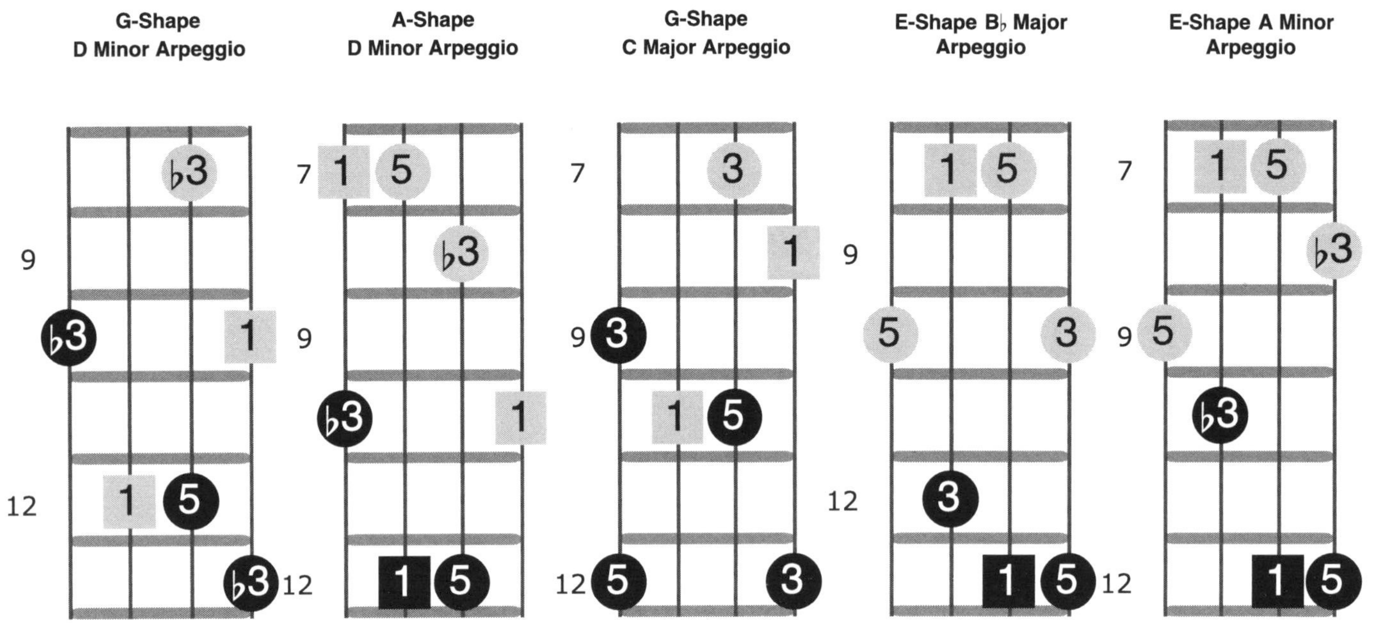

Now, I know this seems like a lot of info to keep in mind with all of these charts, chord shapes and arpeggios. We need to simplify our thinking. Often, less is more. **Melody Strategy Exercise 1:** Start out with the simple idea of focusing mostly on the root notes as the chords descend, but keep the rhythm interesting.

43

Melody Strategy Exercise 1

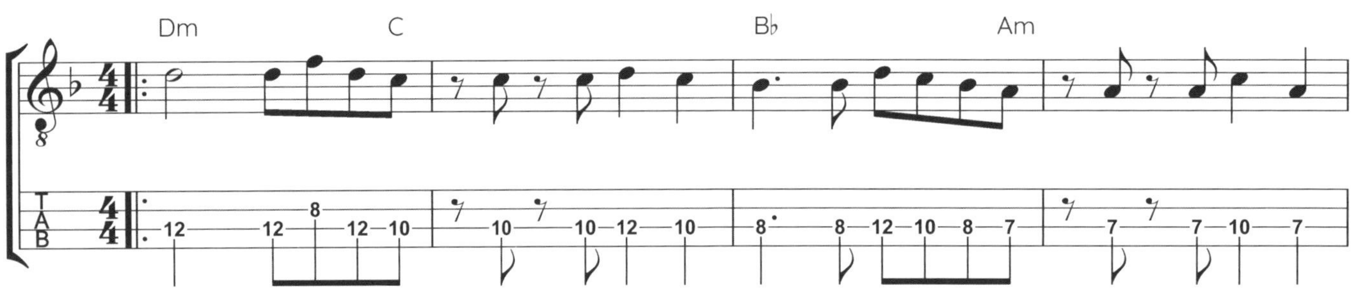

Melody Strategy Exercise 2: Now find other key notes and make up your own rhythmic line. Make some phrases more dense with notes than others. The groove is what you want to focus on first. Then add your notes. In "Melody Strategy Exercise 2", we will use only arpeggio notes.

44

Melody Strategy Exercise 2

Arpeggio Notes

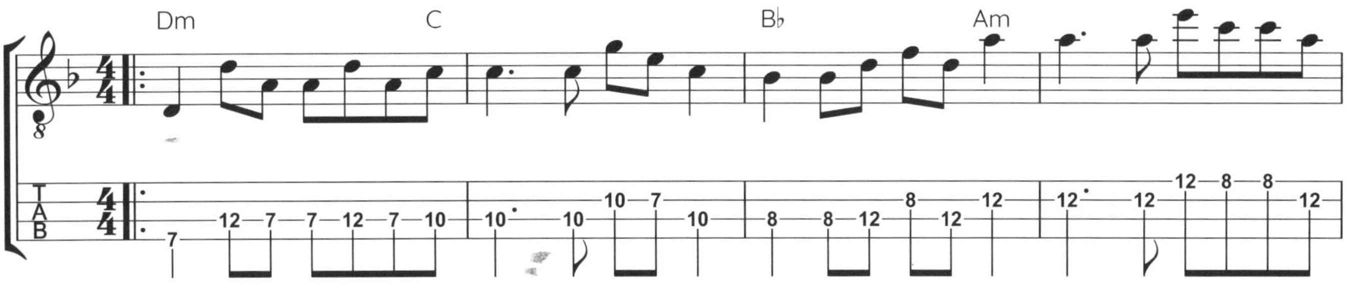

Melody Strategy Exercise 3: This time, the focus is on the various arpeggio notes, rather than simple placing the root tone at the start of each bar and we will add in some notes of the F major scale.

45

Melody Strategy Exercise 3

Arpeggio and F Major Scale Notes

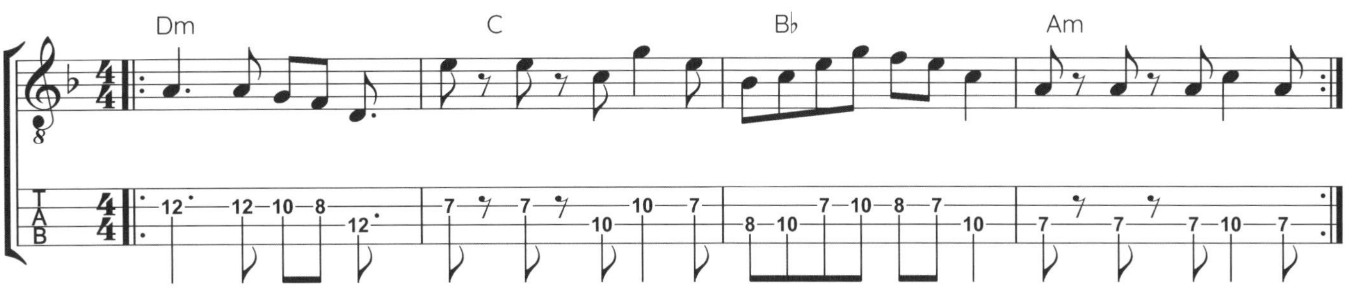

With a looper pedal, recording device, or friend who can play these chords, practice your own melody lines. Keep your melodies simple at first concentrating on the groove as the first priority. Try playing freely in the F major scale, being mindful of key arpeggio notes as starting or landing tones to empansize the chords changes.

Once familiar with playing in this region of the neck try to find other places related to other chord shapes to extend your melodies across the neck.

Chapter 4-3: E-Shape 7th Chords and Arpeggio Exercises

E-Shape
7th Chord

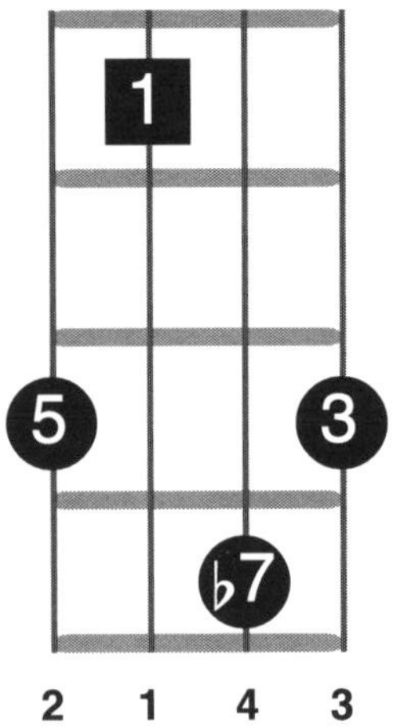

The easy way to remember the 7th chord and arpeggio is that it is exactly the same as the major chord arpeggio with the addition of one note, the ♭7. This is the note 1 step below the root note. This 7th chord shape has the root note on the D-string, which is how you locate your chord. For example, the note G is on the D-string at the 5th fret. If you use this shape with the one (1) note on the G at the fifth fret on the D-string, then you are making the G7 chord. Remember, to practice running this arpeggio up and down to get it memorized.

E-Shape
7th Arpeggio

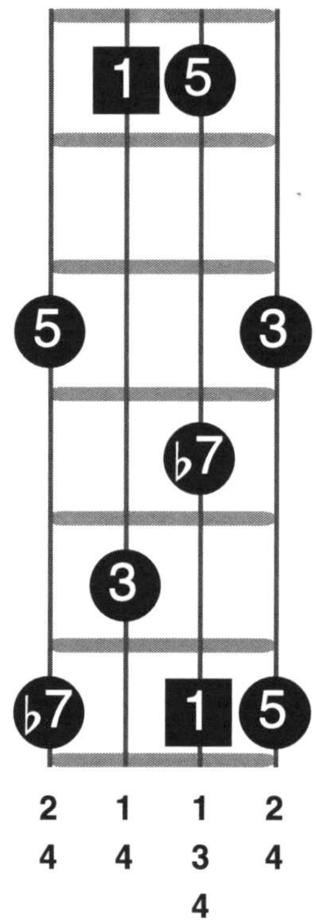

Alternative Chord Shapes

Here are some 7th chord variations made from this arpeggio. Try substituting these chord forms in songs that you know. Variation 1 emphasizes the high notes while Variation 2 emphasizes the low. With both Variations 3 and 4, I like to alternate using my pinky on and off of the 1 (root) note in gray. Try using one of these chords while strumming a rhythm lifting your pinky off and on with a catchy groove.

E-Shape
7th Chord
Variation 1

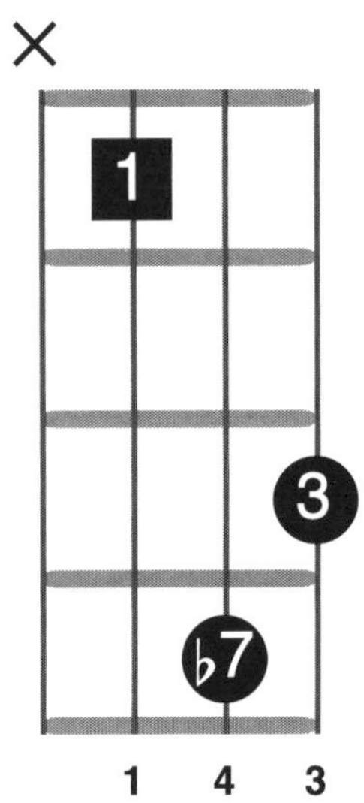

E-Shape
7th Chord
Variation 2

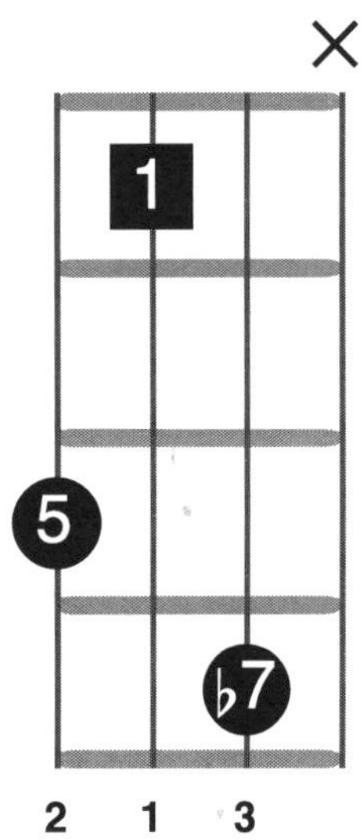

E-Shape
7th Chord
Variation 3

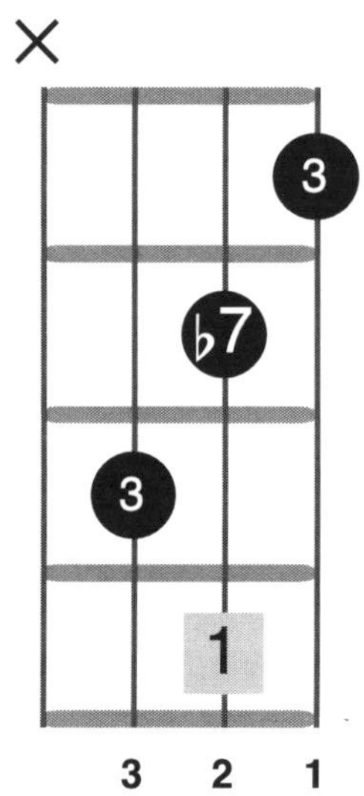

E-Shape
7th Chord
Variation 4

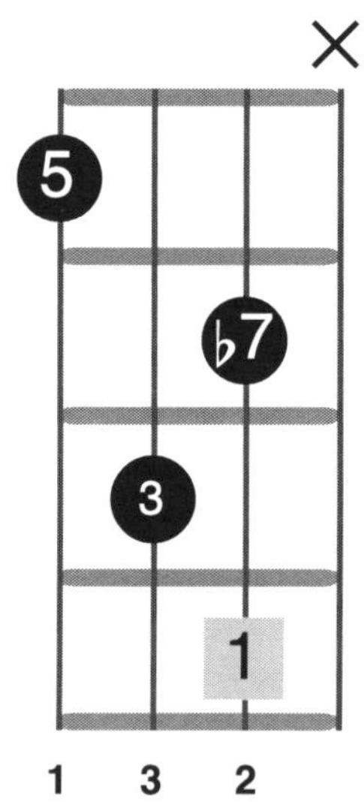

E-Shape 7th Exercise 1: The focus in this exercise is to learn the 7th arpeggio in small sections as an extension of the chord. We will shift from the chord to melody phrases within the arpeggio. Remember that each of these exercises can be moved anywhere up and down the neck. If you learn phrases like this as connected to the chord, you will be able to quickly find the “good notes” under any E-shape 7th chord.

46

E-Shape 7th Exercise 1

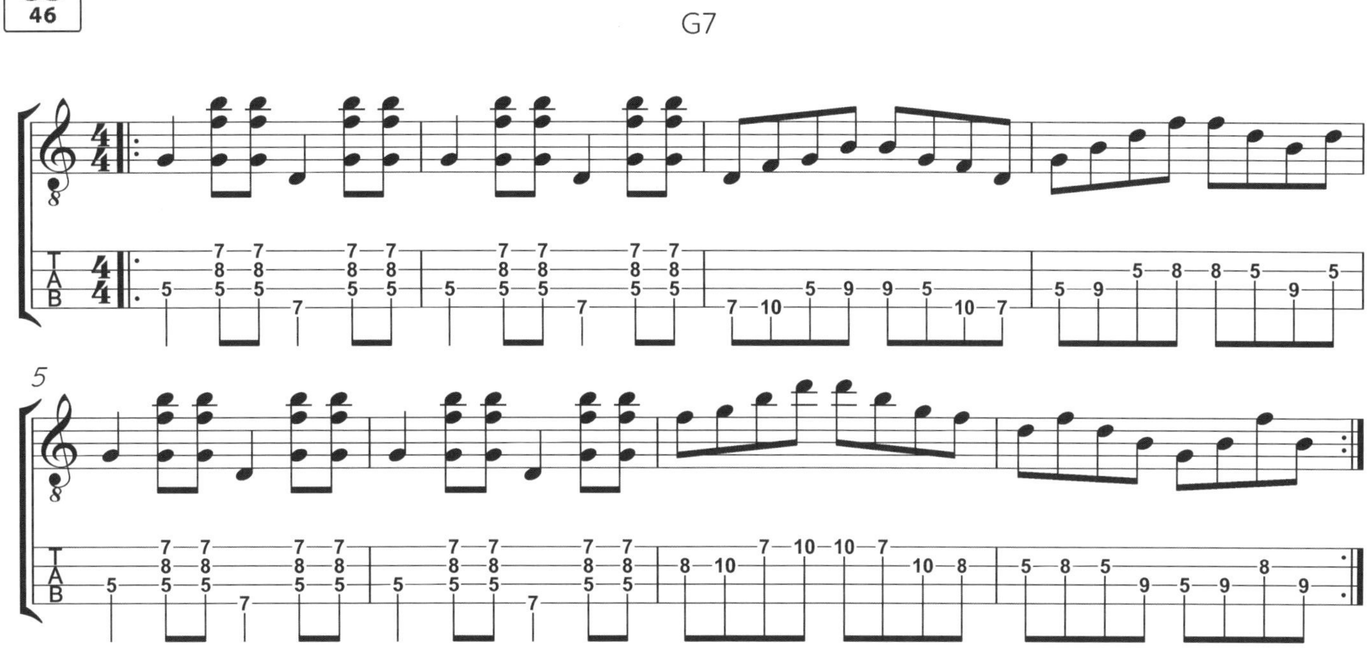

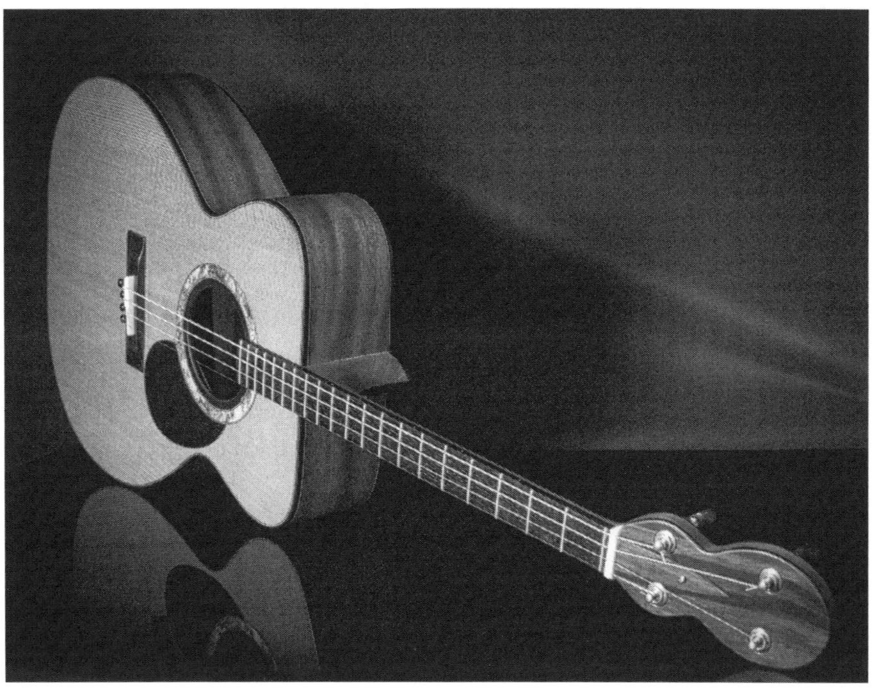

Nigel Forster-Tom Kimber signature tenor guitar

E-Shape 7th Exercise 2: Let's work on some licks in E7. The stretch is really too long to run the scale easily, but riff-like phrases that don't stretch too far are good to know. And, since E7 is a very common chord in folk and rock music, it'll come in handy.

47

E-Shape 7th Exercise 2

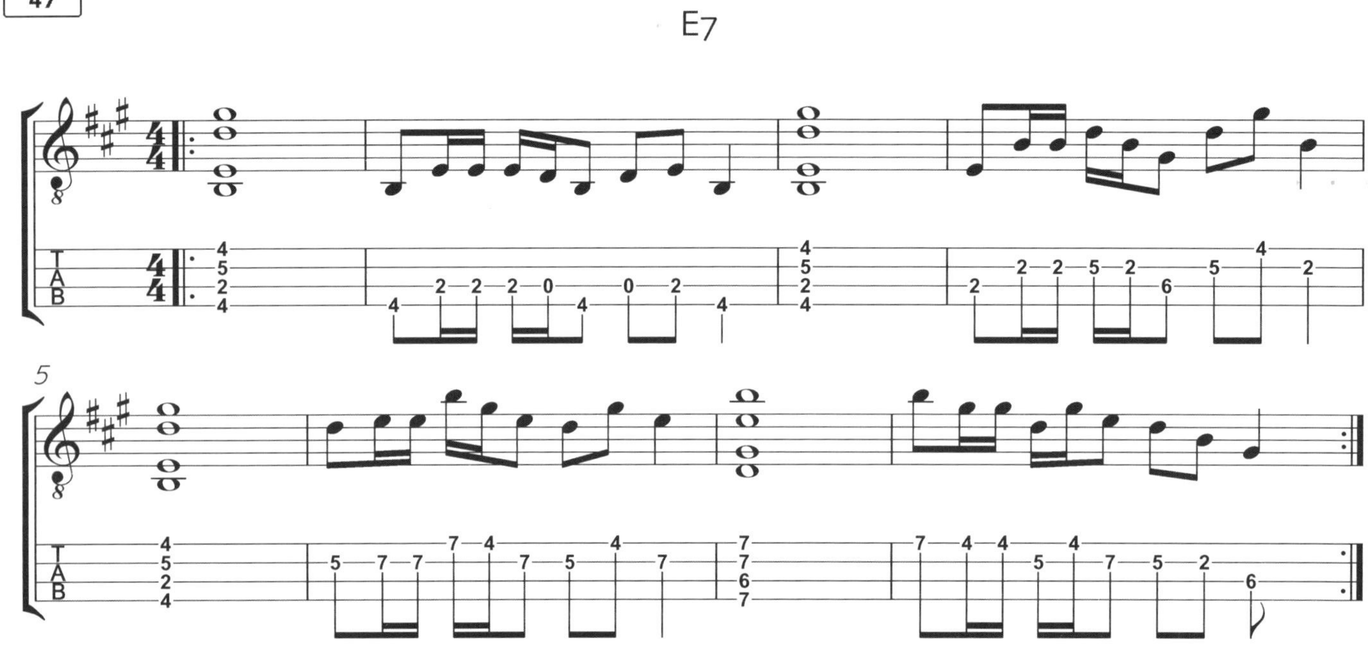

Practice moving between chords in the scale of E major. Let's use the C-shape E major chord at the 6th fret, the E-shape A major chord at the 7th fret and the E-shape B7 chord at the 9th fret. Here are the arpeggios for each with the chord indicated in gray-colored notes. We can also use notes of the E major scale.

C-Shape
E Major Arpeggio

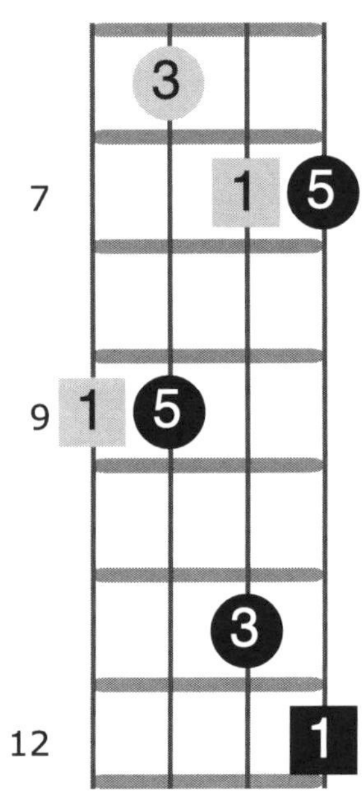

E-Shape
A Major Arpeggio

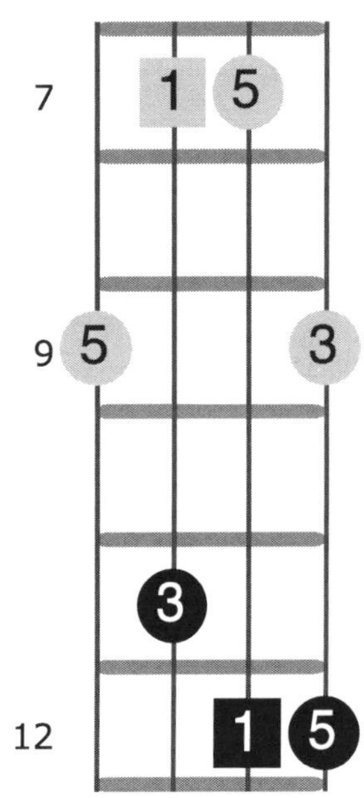

E-Shape
B7 Arpeggio

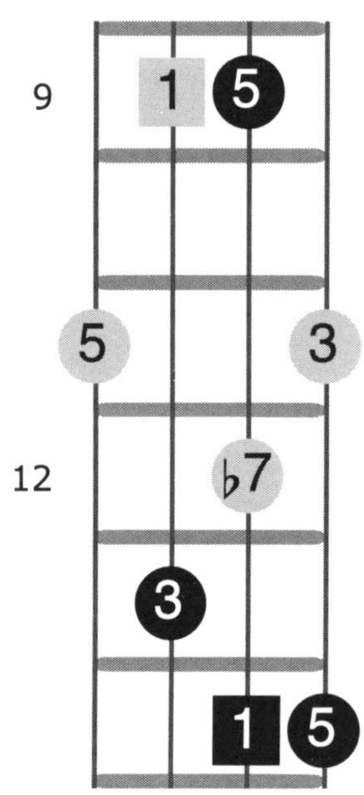

E Major Scale

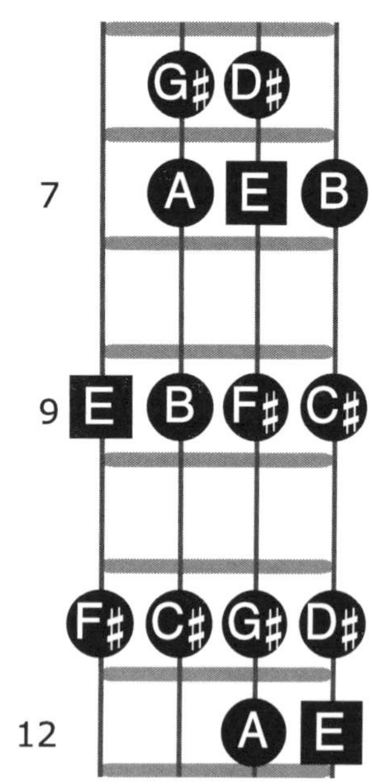

E-Shape 7th Exercise 3: For this exercise we will stick mostly to the arpeggio notes. In the first 4 bars the arpeggios are played straight up and down; in the next two times around the progression we learn different patterns to further memorize these arpeggios. But after you master these phrases, make up your own. Don't forget to throw in some chords from time to time. Or, base your melodic phrases on rhythm chord playing. Remember that you can add in some notes from the E major scale also.

48

E-Shape 7th Exercise 3

E Major - A Major - B7

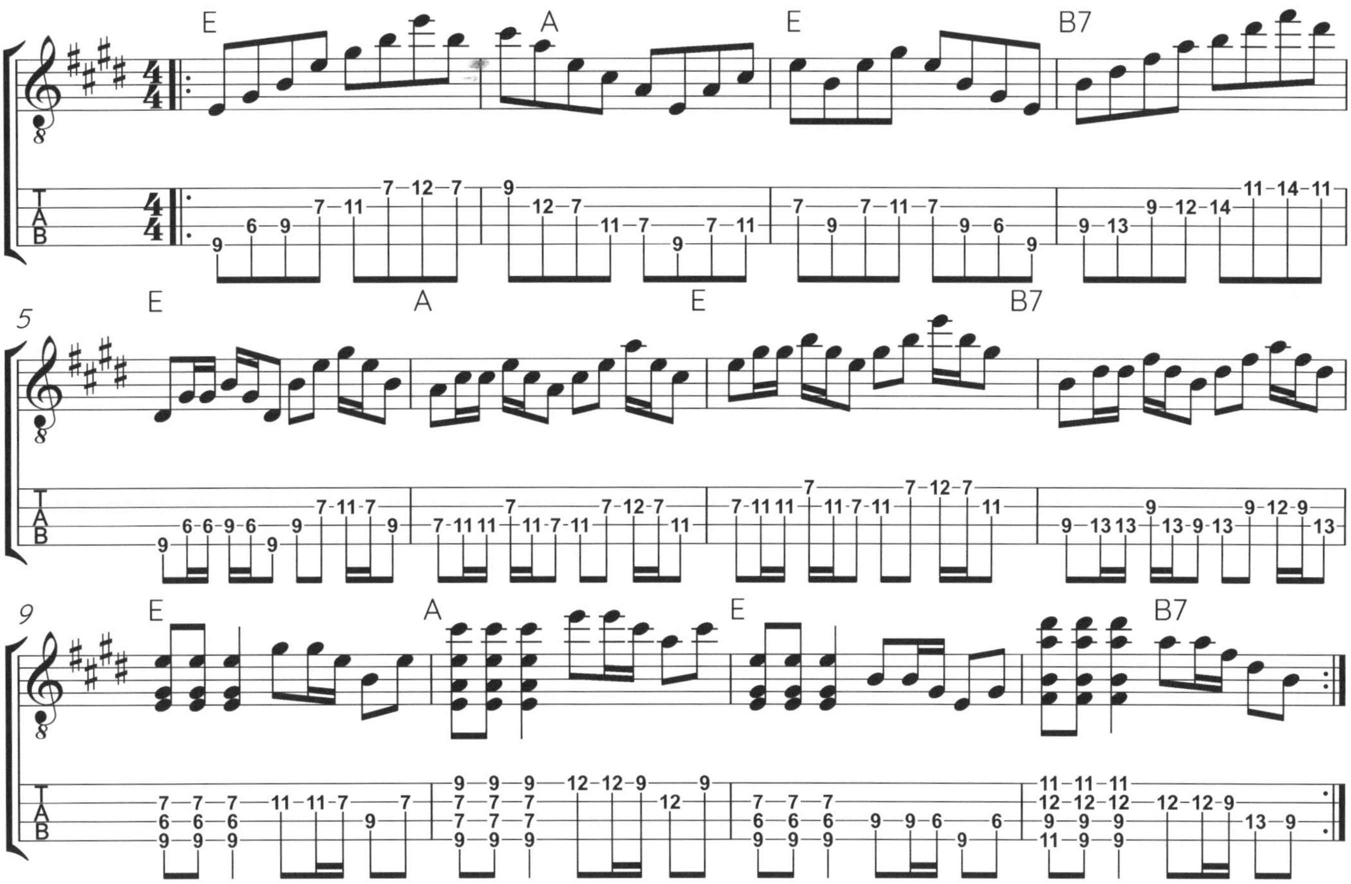

Chapter 4-4: E-Shape Melody Ideas

E-Shape Melody Exercise: Next, we will practice playing melodies over an A-G-D chord progression that uses the E-shape A major and G major chords at the 7th and 5th frets respectively, and the C-shape D major chord at the 4th fret. These chords are in the key of D, so we can use the D major scale and the arpeggios for each chord shape. As usual, we try to start or land on notes of the chord as we encounter them in the progression. Once you get more familiar with the location of the key notes of the chords, then experiment by starting and/or landing on notes outside of the chord notes. Experiment, experiment, and then do more experimenting.

E-Shape
A Major Chord

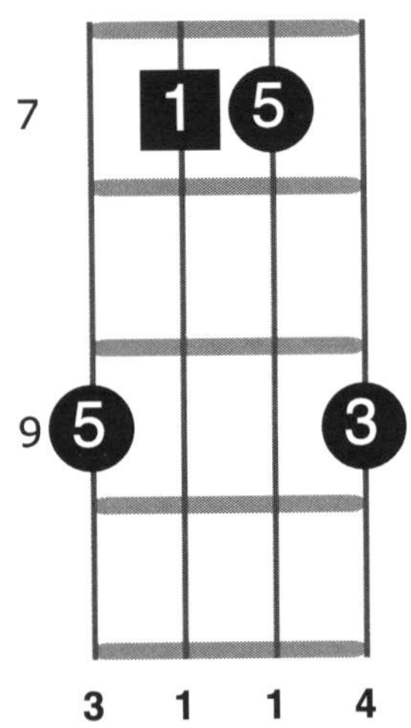

E-Shape
G Major Chord

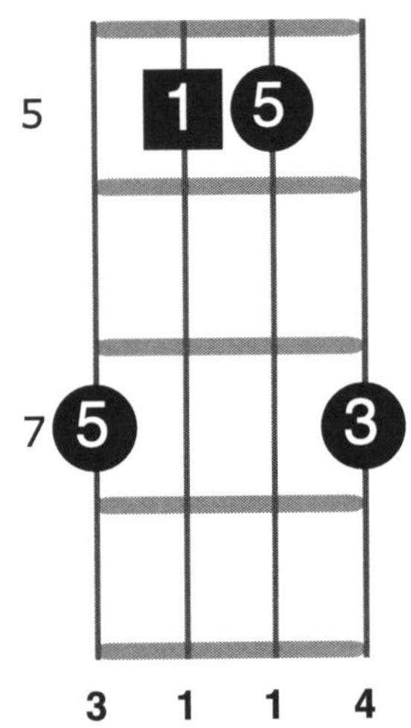

C-Shape
D Major Chord

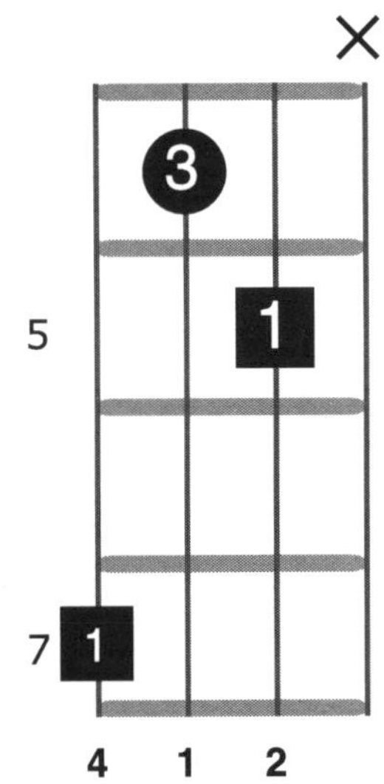

E-Shape
A Major Chord

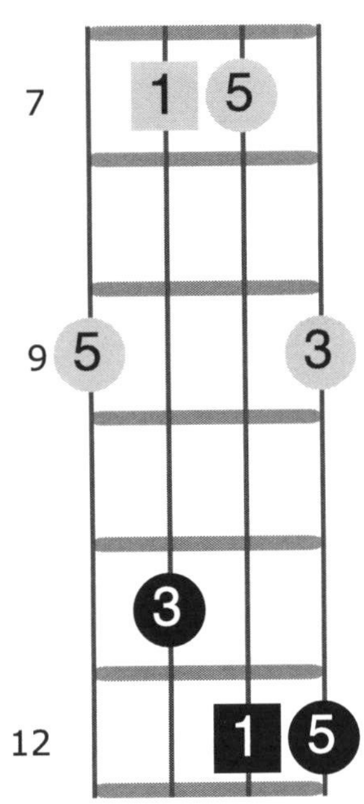

E-Shape
G Major Chord

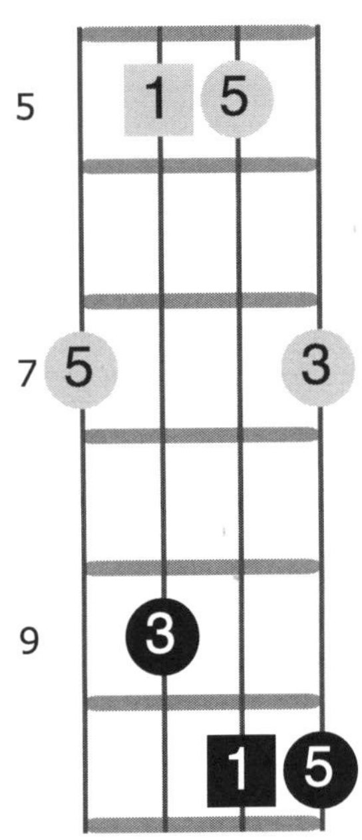

C-Shape
D Major Chord

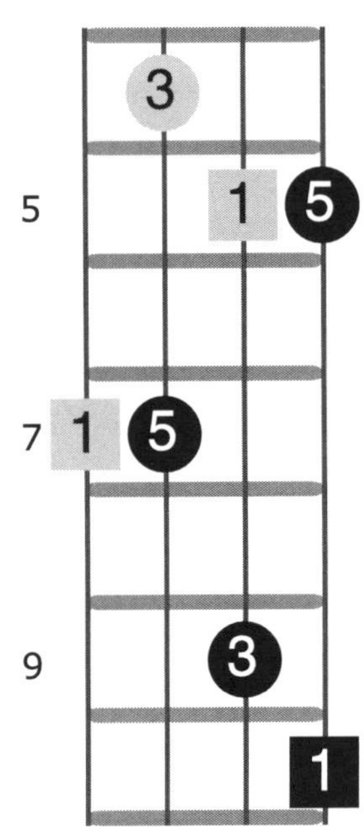

D Major Scale

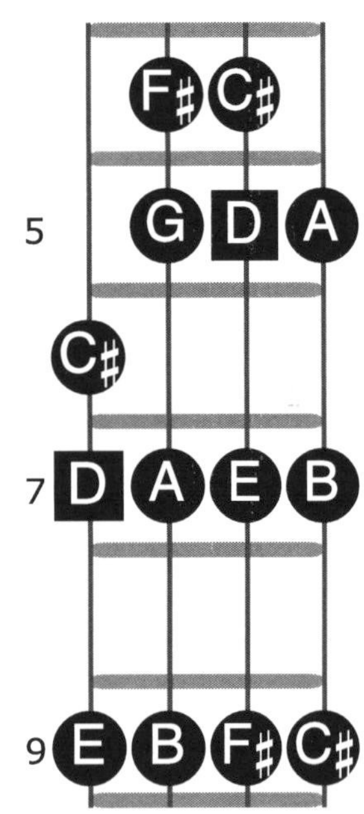

49

E-Shape Melody Application Ideas

A - G - D Major Progression: D Major scale

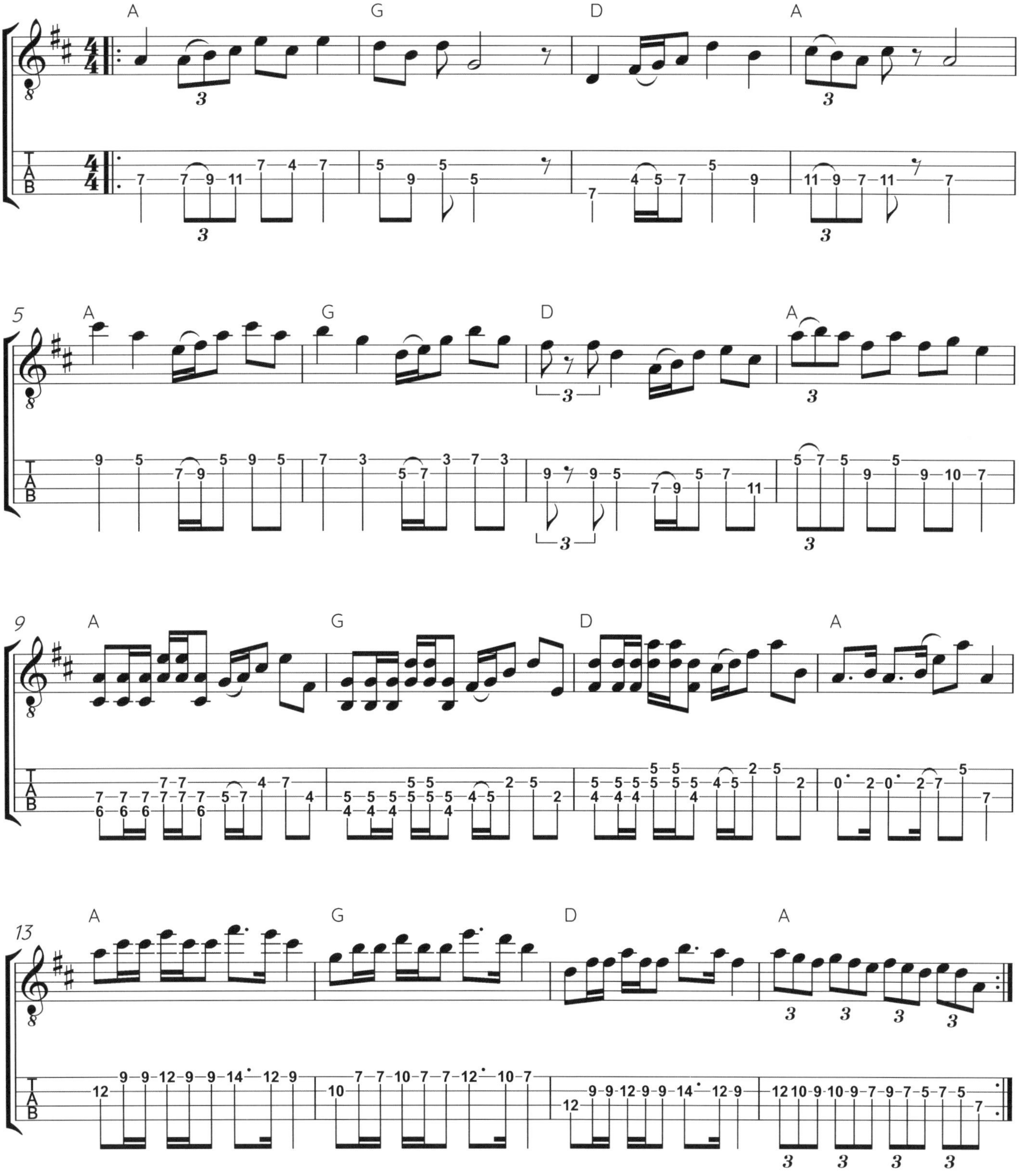

Chapter 5-1: D-Shape Major Chords and Arpeggio Exercises

D-Shape Major Chord

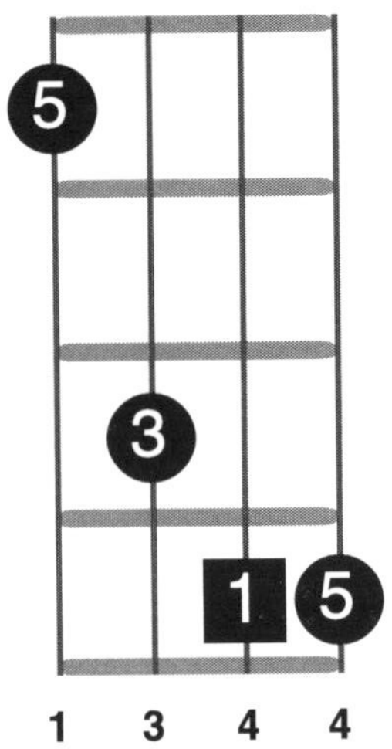

Here is the D-shape major chord. All the other chord shapes we have learned have their root notes on either the G or D strings. This shape has the root note on the A string, which gives it a unique voicing. It may sound less rooted due it's root note being on a higher string. But, it has the complete triad, the 1, 3, and 5 notes, and is very useful for giving a progression some variety. You position this chord by the note that you are fretting on the A string. When practicing this arpeggio, it's good to start from the 1 note on the A string to lock it in to the chord shape. Another tip for memorizing these arpeggios is to look for repeating patterns. Notice the 1, 3, 5 notes on the lower two strings and how the pattern repeats one step lower on the high two strings.

D-Shape Major Arpeggio

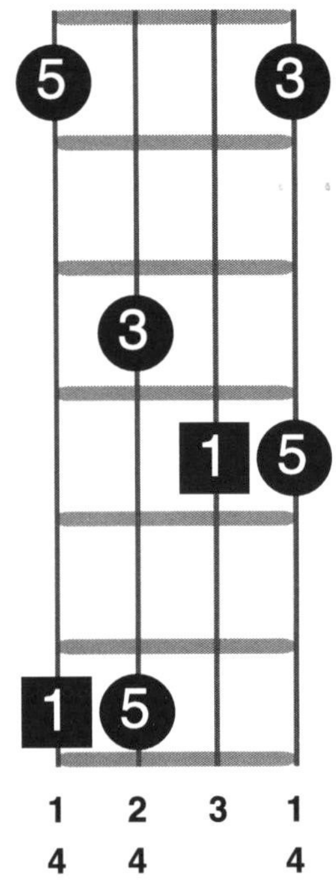

Alternative Chord Shapes

If you are playing with others, you may need to communicate which chord you are playing. They may hear the 5th or the 3rd as the root note. Variation 1 emphasizes the 3rd note, while variation 2 features the complete triad with the 5th note on bottom. Variation 3 can serve as a major or minor chord since the defining third note is missing. Variation 4 also has the complete triad, but emphasizes the high strings

D-Shape Major Chord Variation 1

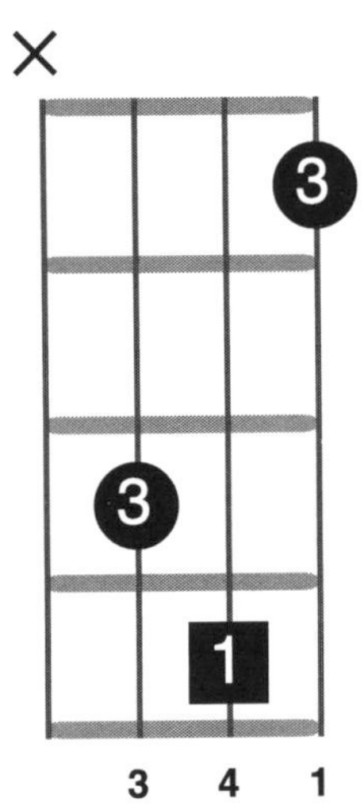

D-Shape Major Chord Variation 2

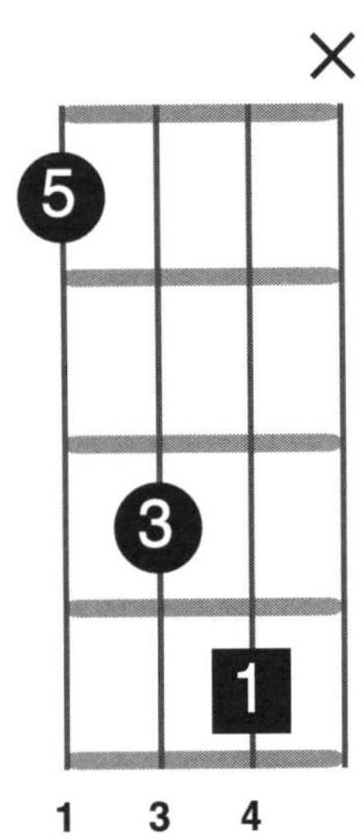

D-Shape Major Chord Variation 3

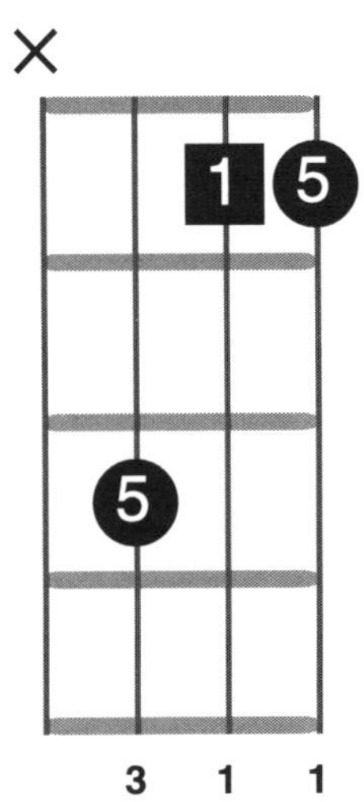

D-Shape Major Chord Variation 4

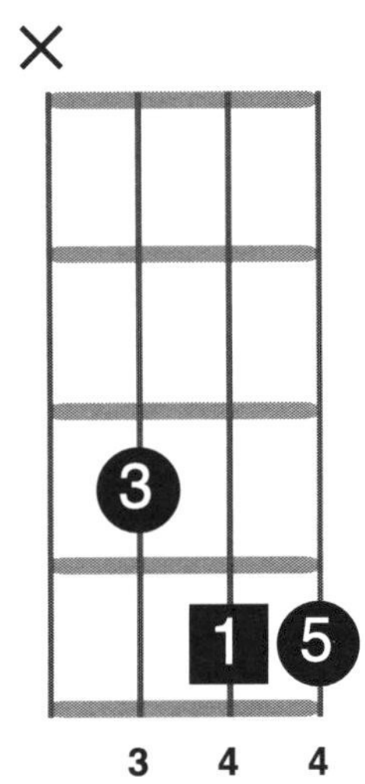

D-Shape Major Exercise 1: Become familiar with the arpeggio as it relates to the chord shape. Experiment with holding your fingers down and letting notes ring out longer than notated, especially in bars 1, 2, 7 and 8.

50

D-Shape Major Exercise 1

D Major

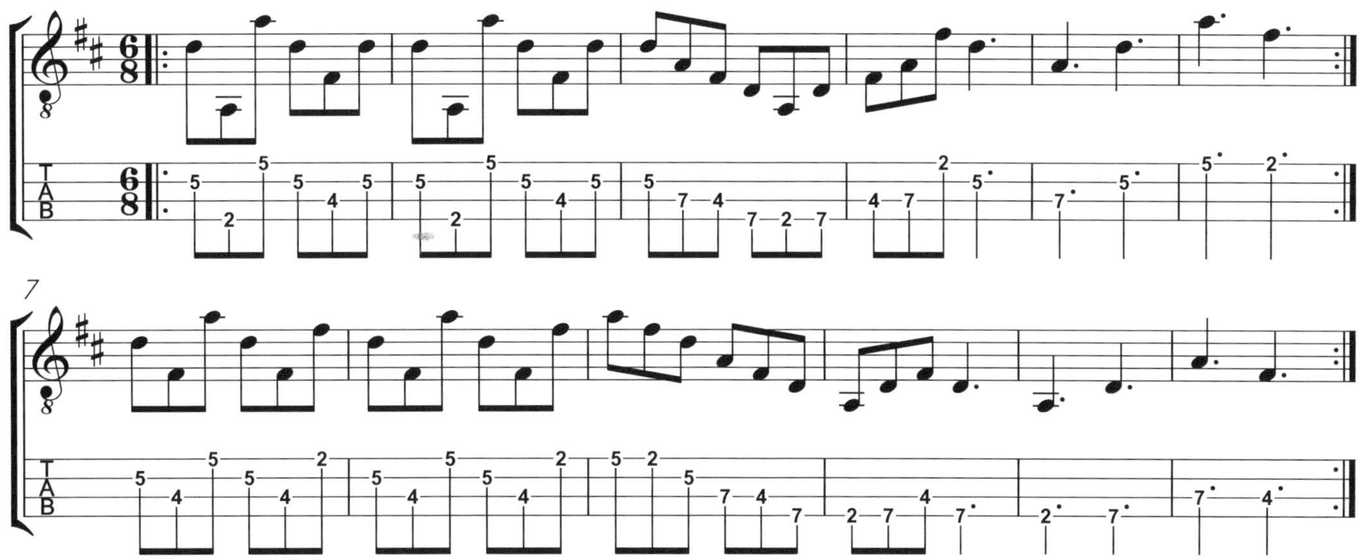

D-Shape Major Exercise 2: Practice moving between F and G major. This time we'll break the arpeggios into chunks of melodic phrases. This exercise is based on the F major chord at the 5th fret and the G major at the 7th fret in the D shape, of course. To repeat, as your fretting hand fingers are already in position from just having plucked these notes, it's often easier to leave them down-fretting the notes just plucked instead of trying to always lift your fingers off the neck after each note.

51

D-Shape Major Exercise 2

G Major - F Major

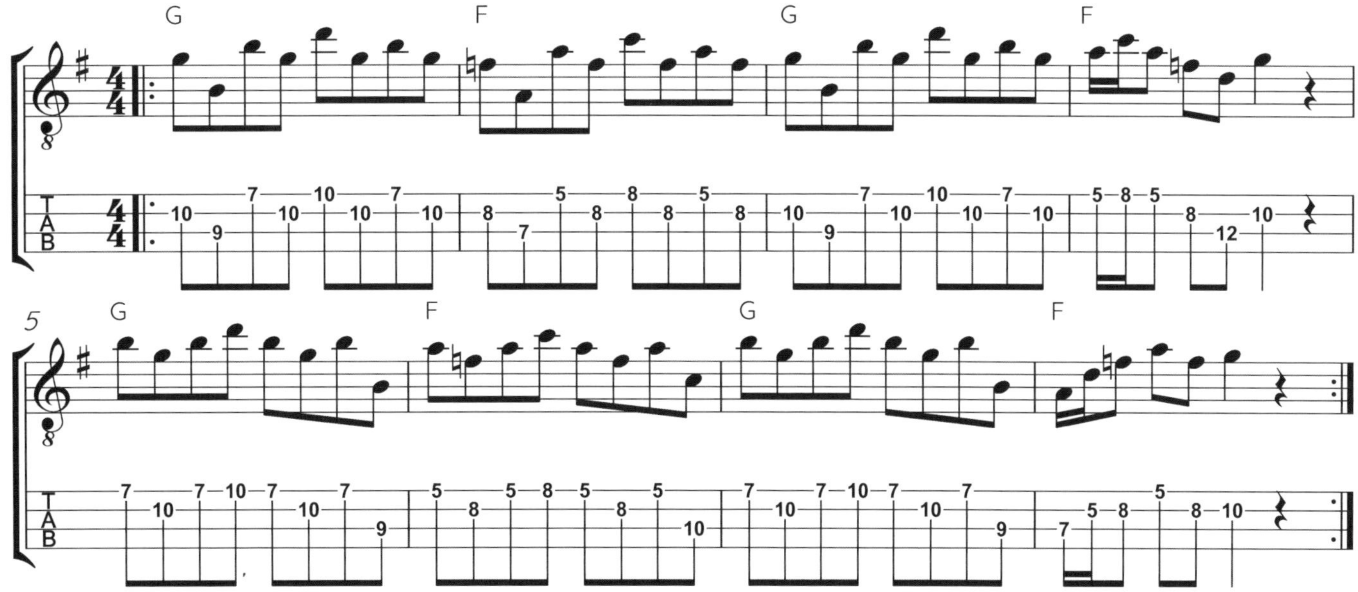

D-Shape Major Exercise 3: Play through a progression, G-Am-D7. Let's use our D-shape G major chord, an E-shape A minor chord and an A-shape D7-all at the 7th fret. Remember, these chords and arpeggios are movable. For example, if you slide this progression down one step, you'll have F-Gm-C7. This is why we want to memorize the key notes as related to each chord shape, so that they will be readily available under your fingers no matter where you play on the fretboard. Here are the chords, arpeggios (with chord shapes in gray) and the G major scale pattern for this exercise.

D-Shape
G Major Chord

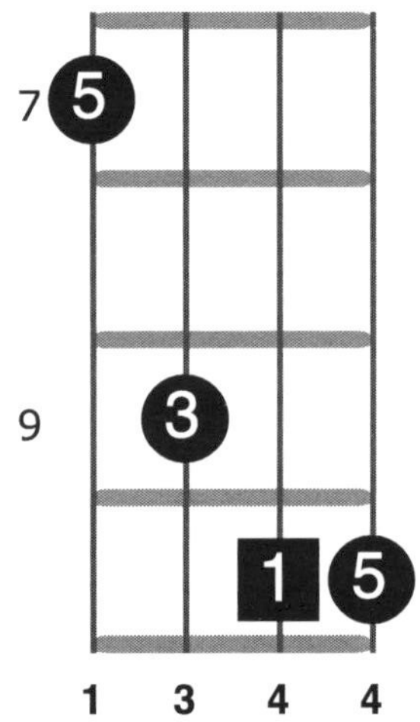

E-Shape
A Minor Chord

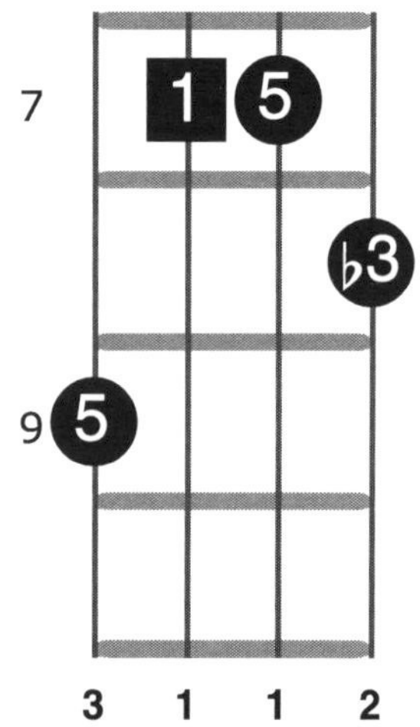

A-Shape
D7 Chord

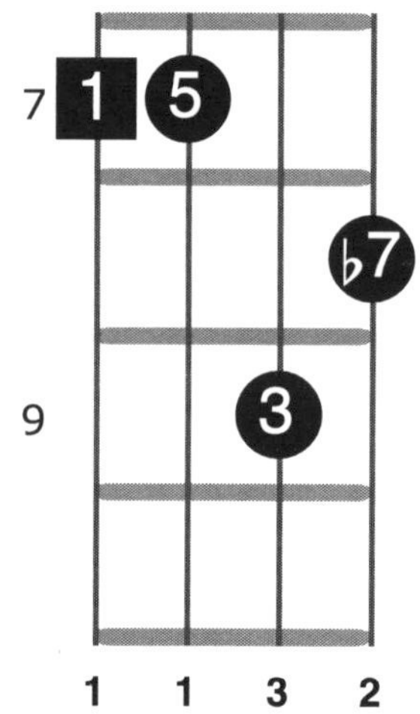

D-Shape
G Major
Arpeggio

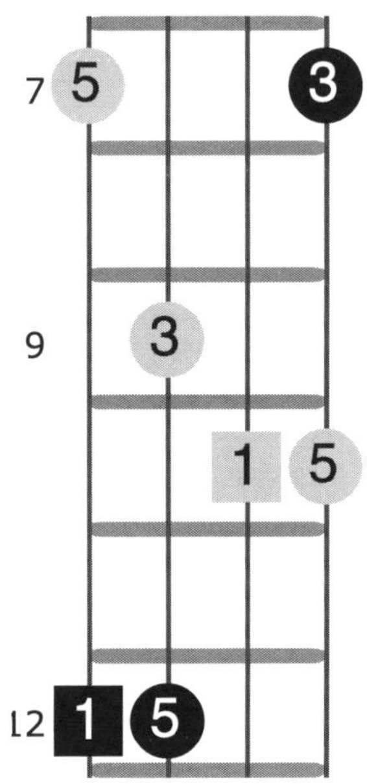

E-Shape
Am Arpeggio

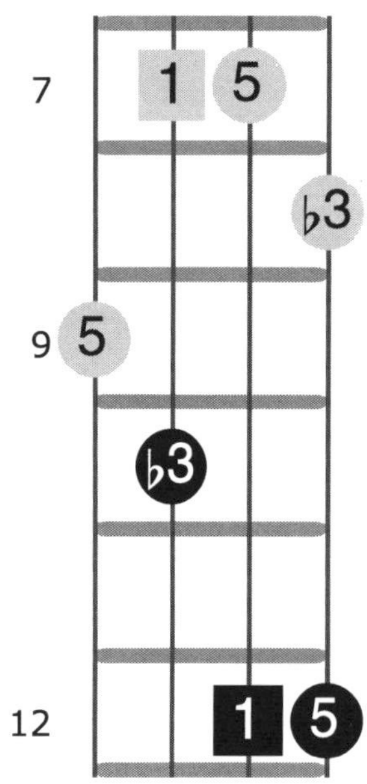

A-Shape
D7 Arpeggio

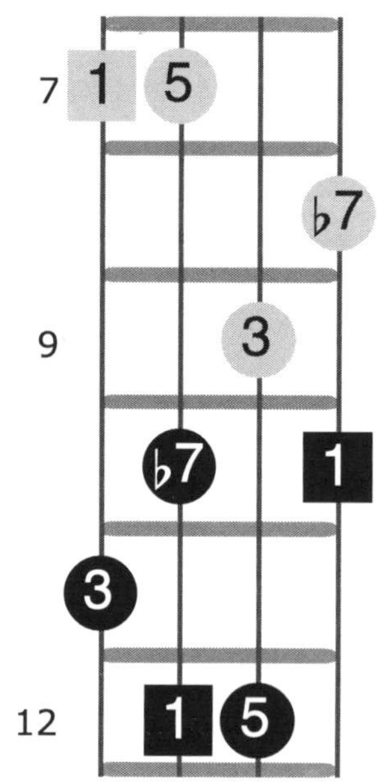

G Major Scale

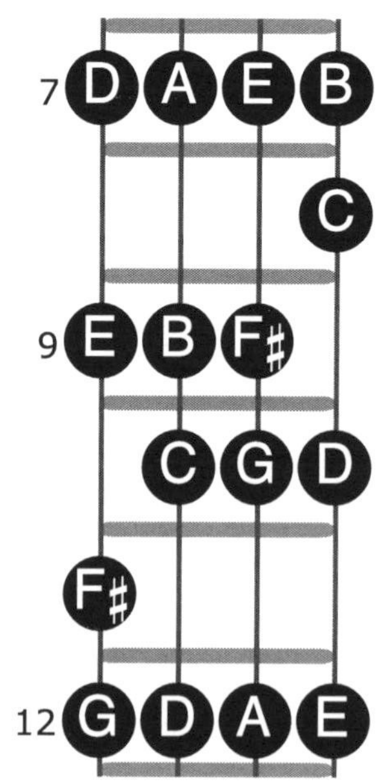

Repeat each bar as often as needed to play cleanly with the notes ringing until the next note is plucked.

52

D-Shape Major Exercise 3

G - Am - D7

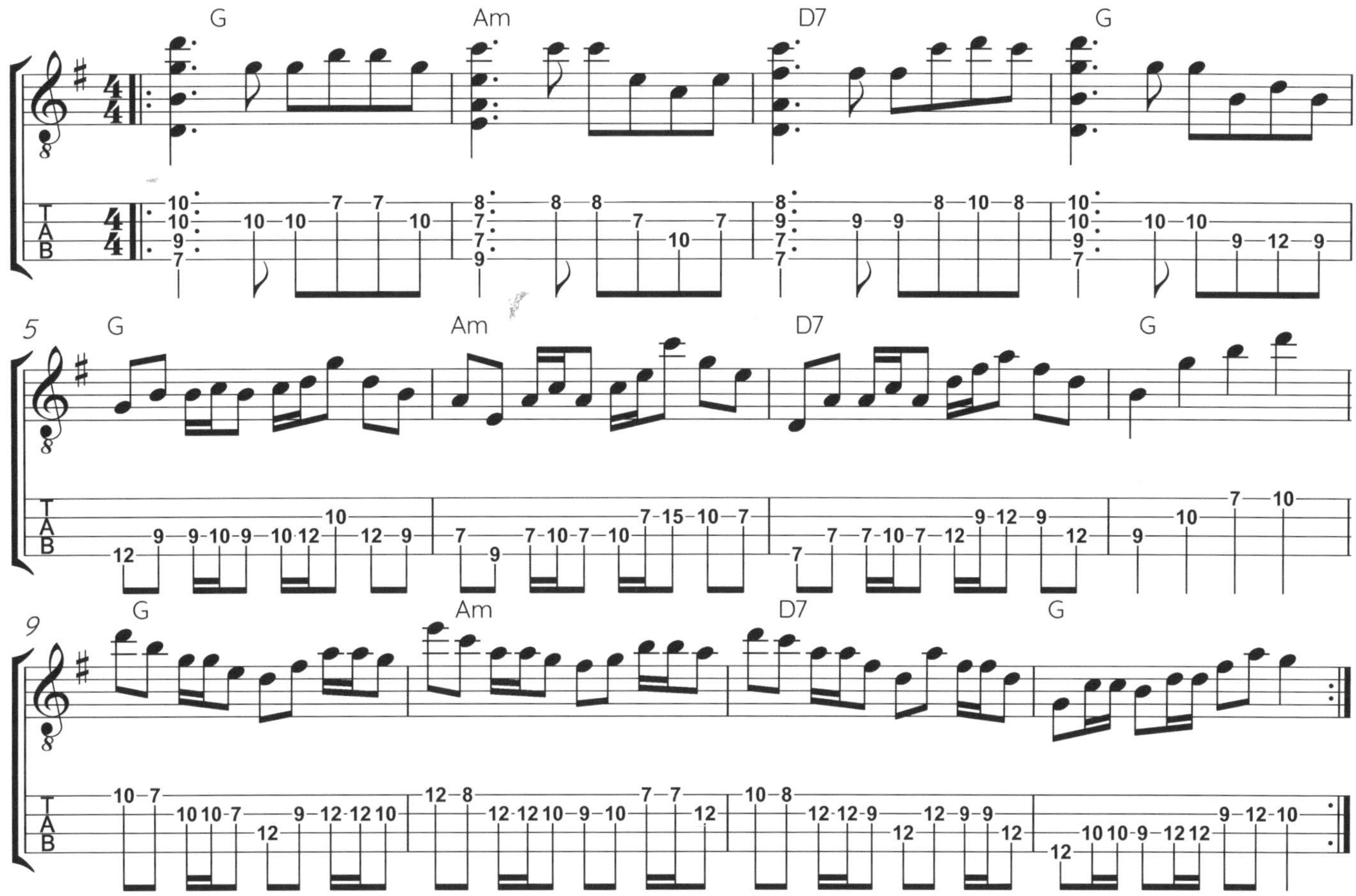

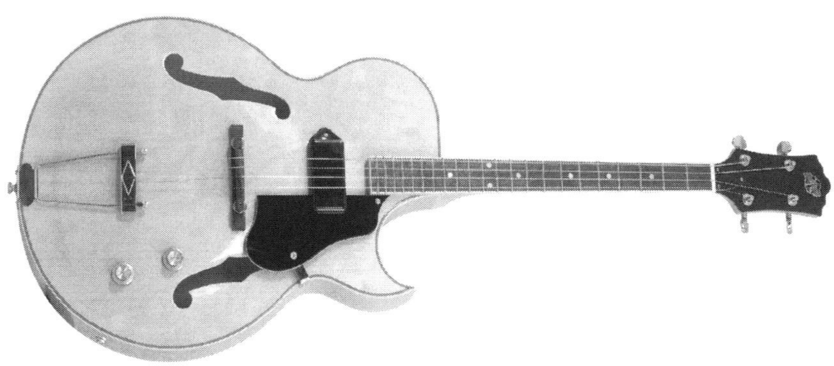

Eastwood TG-150 Tenor guitar

Chapter 5-2: D-Shape Minor Chords and Arpeggio Exercises

D-Shape Minor Chord

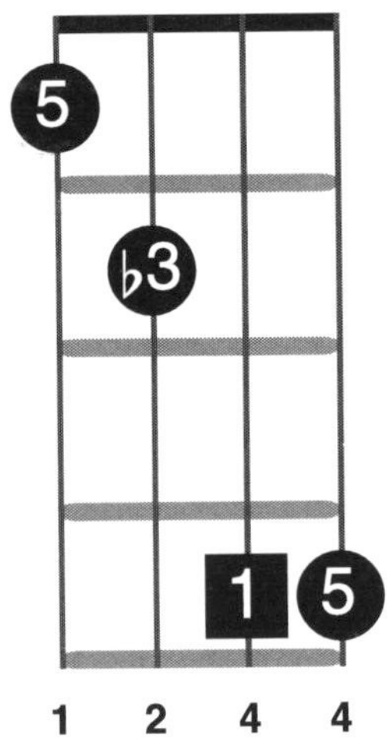

Here is the D-shape minor chord. Even though the root note is not on the low end, this chord shape is often the most convenient and unique sounding inversion in certain chord progressions.

The root note is on the A-string. If we fingered this chord at the 2nd fret, which would put the "1" note at D at the 5th fret on the A-string. We would be playing D minor.

Running this arpeggio is a finger-stretch challenge. If you fingers aren't long enough to reach, then practice quickly shifting your hand as needed. Use a metronome set at a very slow speed. Plan your fingering and stretches. Repeat until you can play cleanly and smoothly!

D-Shape Minor Arpeggio

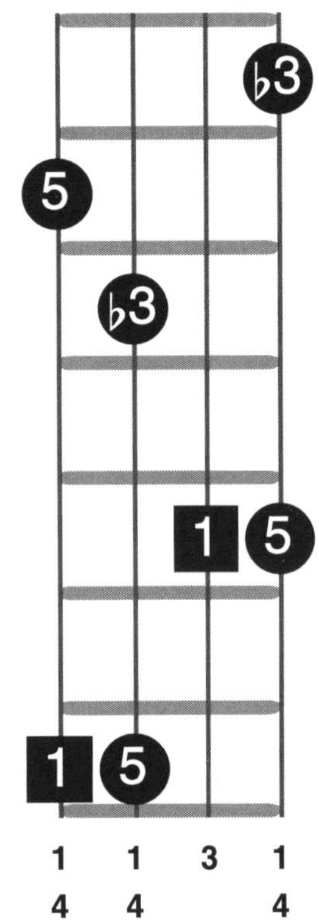

Alternative Chord Shapes

Here are some D-shape minor chord variations made from the arpeggio. Variation 1 is our handy double stop on the low end. Variation 2 has a unique voicing. Variation 3 is the power chord that can be used for a minor or major as its "3" tone is missing. And variation 4 is another double stop this time on the middle two strings.

D-Shape Minor Chord Variation 1

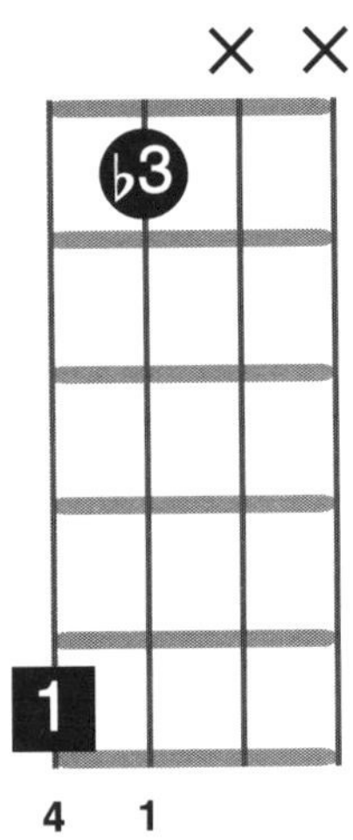

D-Shape Minor Chord Variation 2

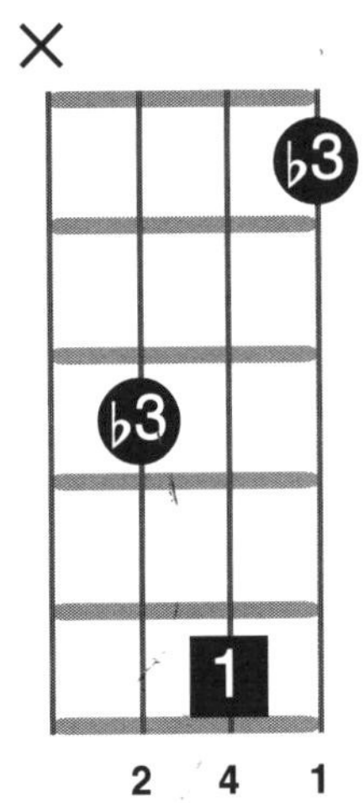

D-Shape Minor Chord Variation 3

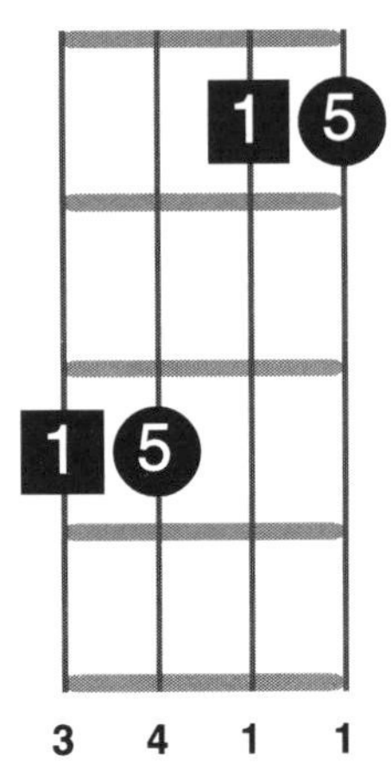

D-Shape Minor Chord Variation 4

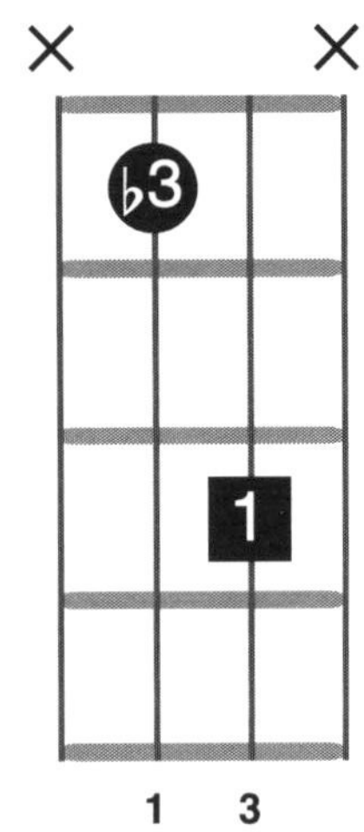

D-Shape Minor Exercise 1: Practice stretching those fingers while we learn this arpeggio. We will start higher up the neck, but later practice this arpeggio on lower frets where the stretch is greater. This exercise is built from the D-shape F♯ minor chord at the 6th fret. The most challenging bars are 8 and 11. For these, I like to use the pinky on the D-string 11th fret, the ring finger on the A-string 9th fret, and the first finger on the E-string 5th fret. Rehearse each bar over and over until you can play them confidently.

53

D-Shape Minor Exercise 1

F♯ Minor

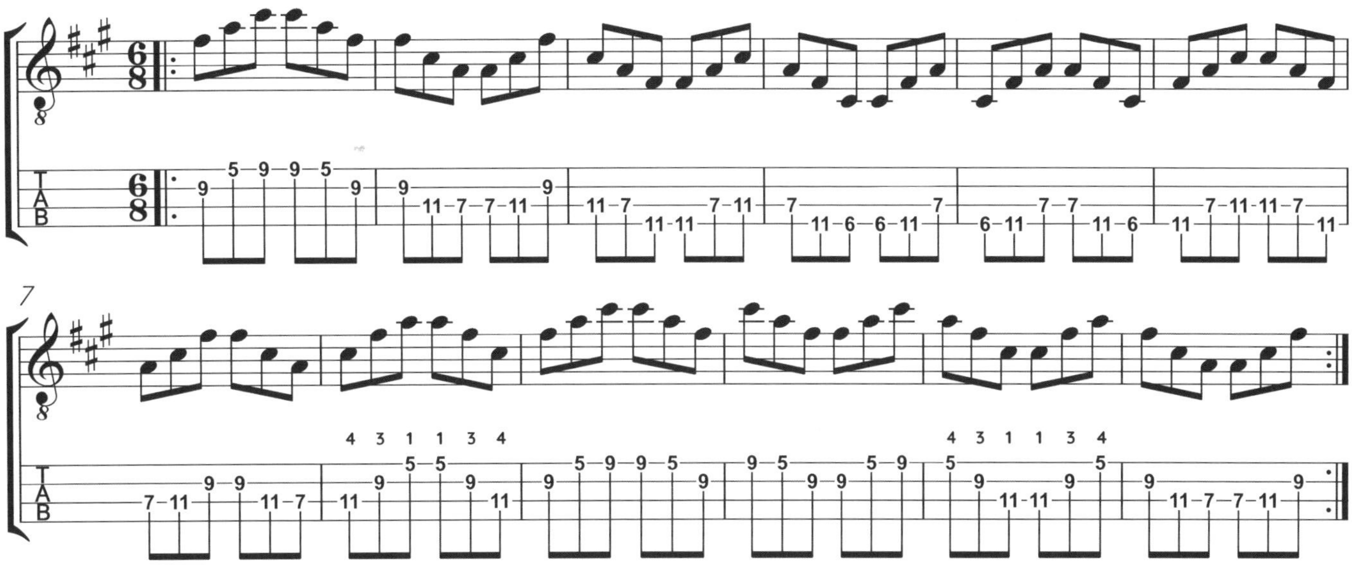

D-Shape Minor Exercise 2: We will cover a lot of territory as we practice the E minor arpeggio in the D-shape, C-shape, E-shape, and A-shape. The more you practice your arpeggios, the more you will find the connections between the chord shapes. This opens up the whole fretboard for expression! Try this strategy with all the chord shapes as you learn them.

D-Shape
E Minor Chord

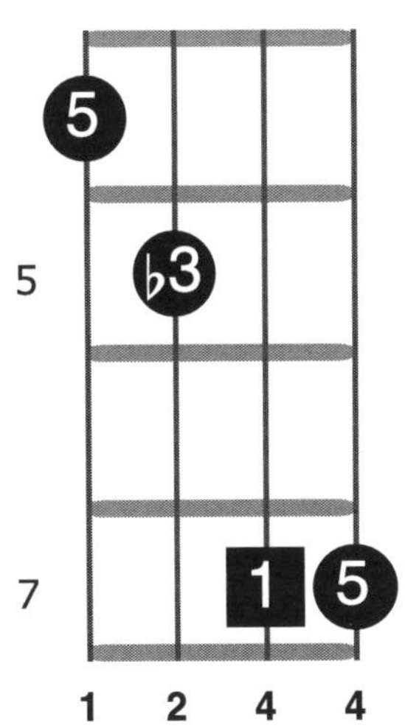

C-Shape
E Minor Chord

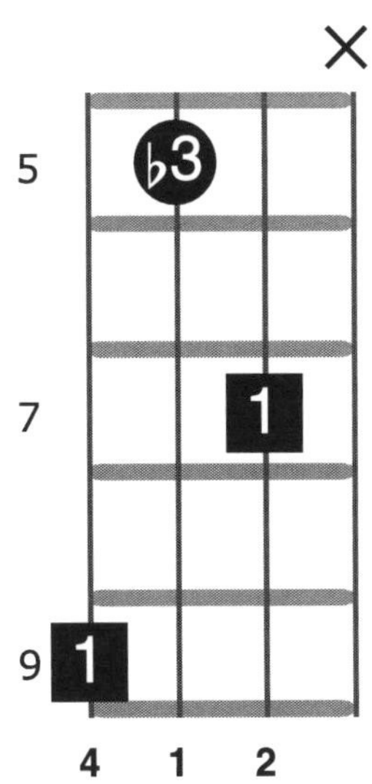

E-Shape
E Minor Chord

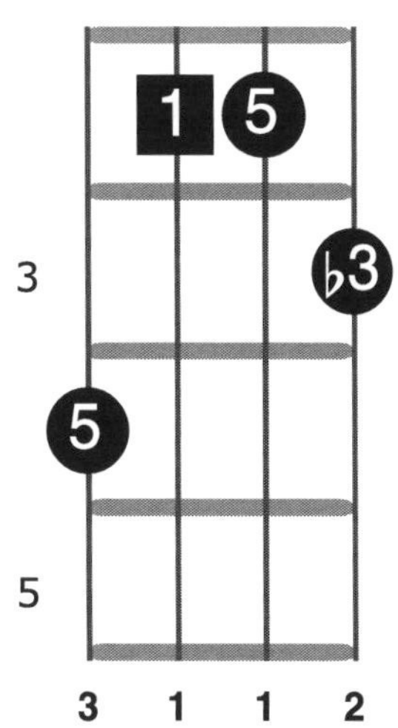

A-Shape
E Minor Chord

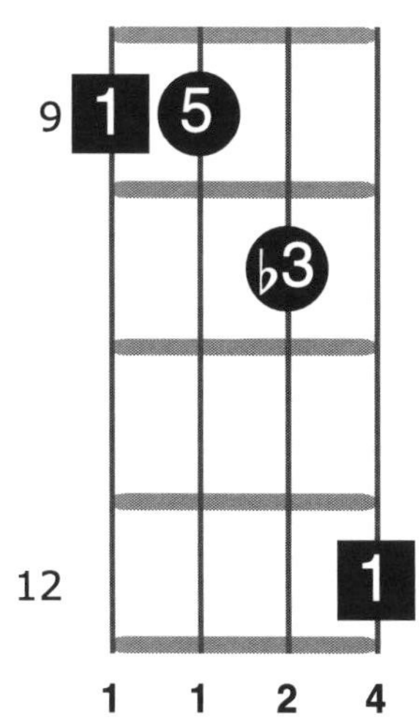

D-Shape Minor Exercise 2

Em Throughout the Fretboard

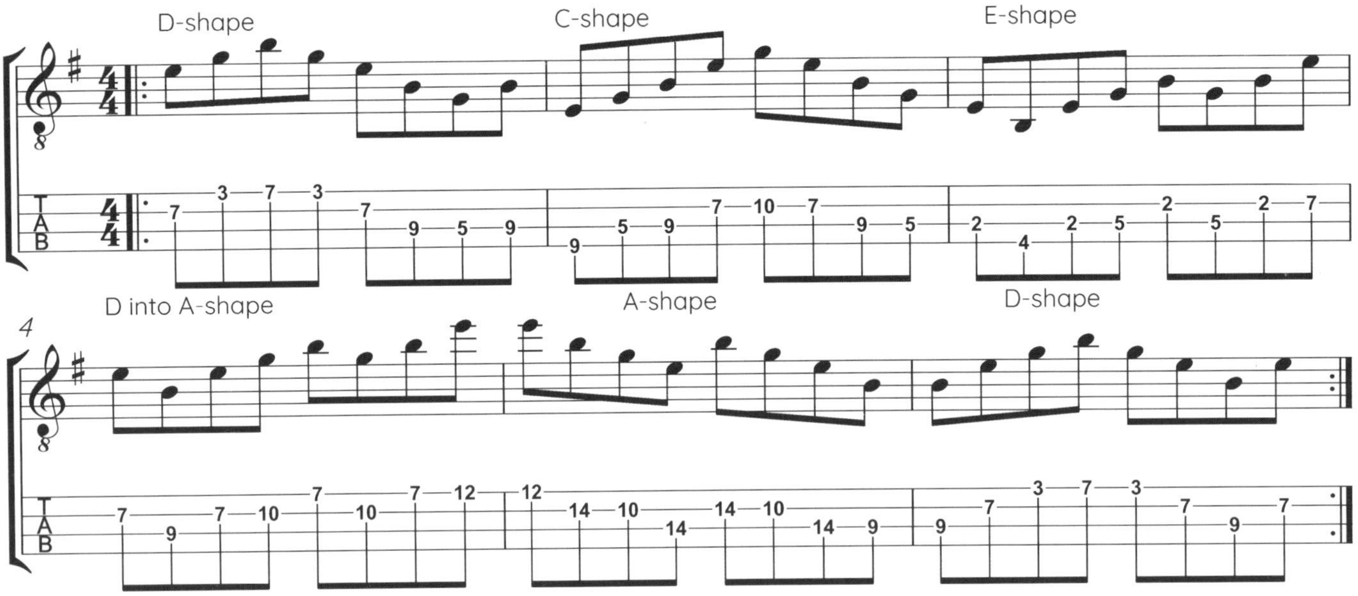

D-Shape Minor Exercise 3: Here is a progression with E minor in the D-shape and B major in the A-shape both at the 4th fret, and A minor in the D-shape with E major in the A-shape at the 9th fret. On the following page you'll find the arpeggio notes for each chord; we'll use these in our melody practice. Remember the gray notes are the chord shapes on the arpeggio charts.

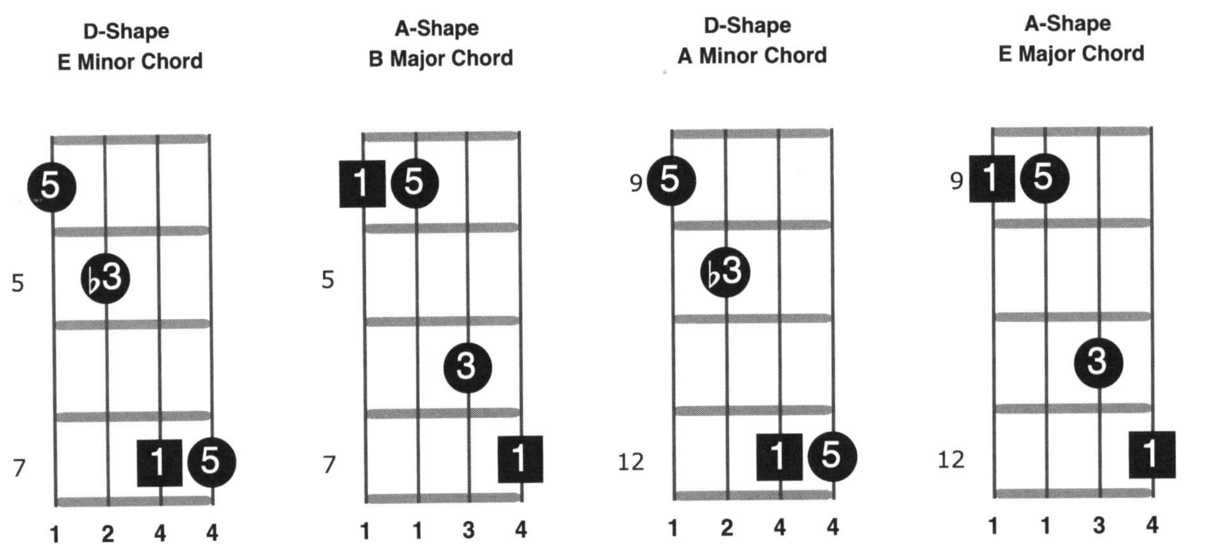

Practice fretting this E minor chord to the B major chord strumming any pattern you like. You can see how nice it is to have an interesting chord change right under your fingers in the same position! Remember, as we practice these progressions-they are just skeleton ideas of how to quickly find useful notes in your own progressions whatever they are. Here are the arpeggio notes for the Em-B-Am-E progression. As usual, it's super helpful to run the arpeggios up and down, over and over, and as cleanly as possible. If you do this enough times so that they are automatic, you will find yourself creating melodies over chord progressions without really thinking too much about it.

D-Shape
Em Arpeggio

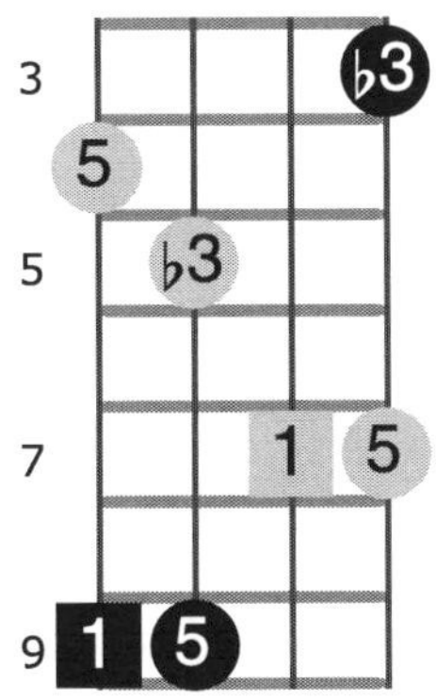

A-Shape
B Major Arpeggio

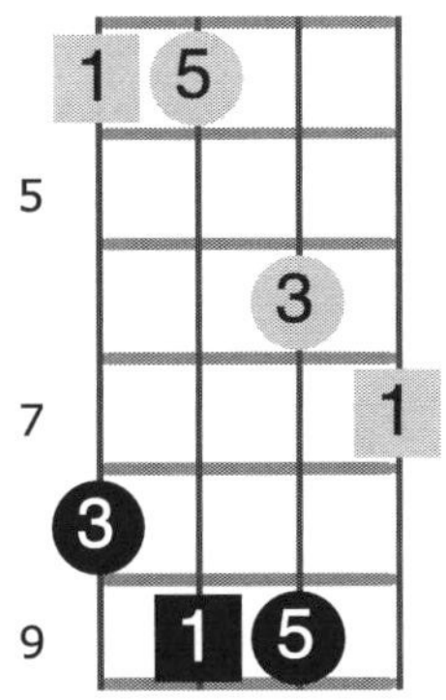

D-Shape
Am Arpeggio

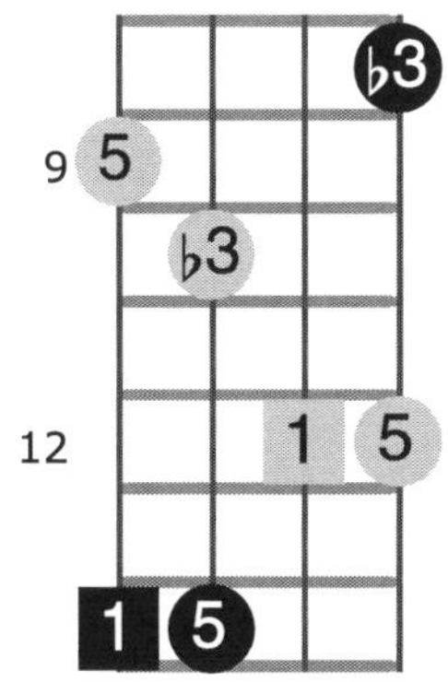

A-Shape
E Major Arpeggio

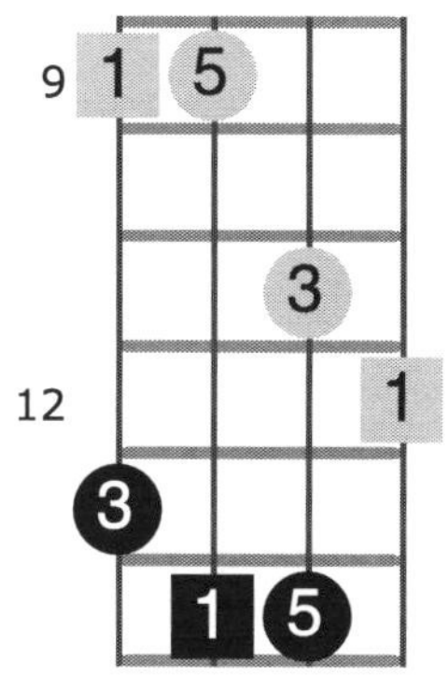

55

D-Shape Minor Exercise 3

Em - B - Am - E

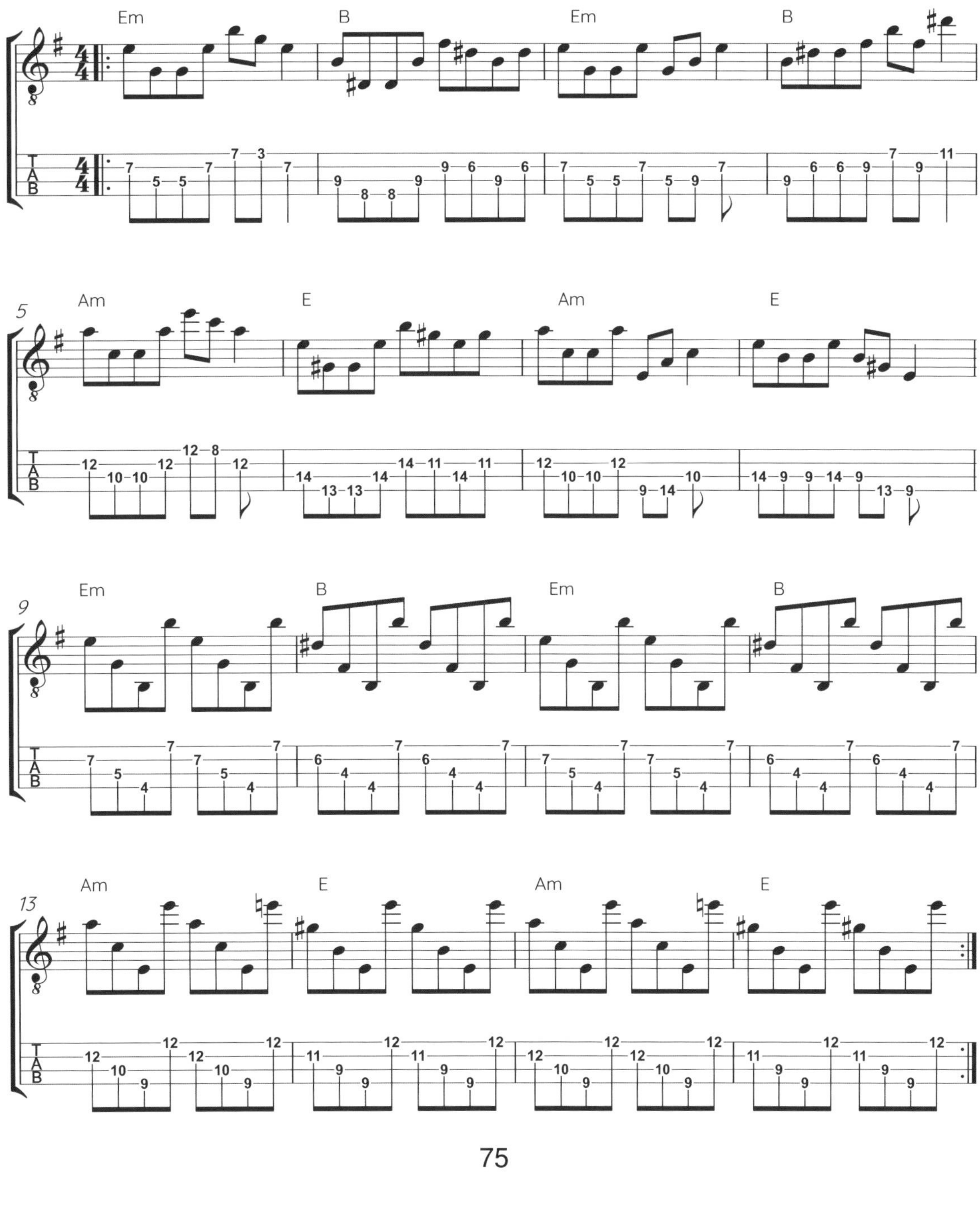

Chapter 5-3: D-Shape 7th Chords and Arpeggio Exercises

D-Shape
7th Chord

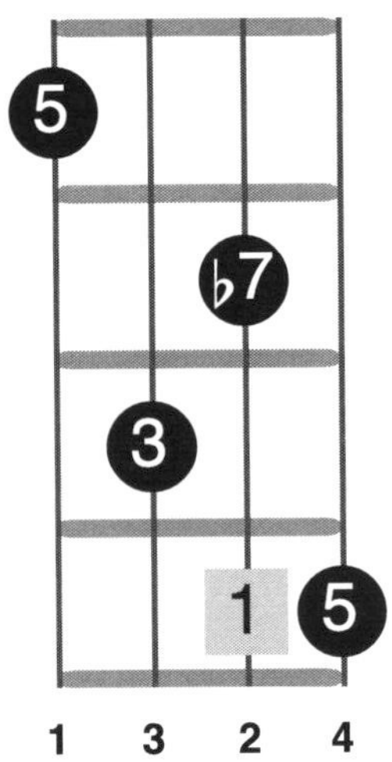

Here is the D-shape 7th chord on the left. Notice that the root is indicated in gray, but finger only the black notes. You can see that this shape doesn't have the root note in it at all! Sometimes, however, it's helpful to play the root note periodically to emphasize the key. Locate the 7th chord from the location of the root note on the A-string.

This 7th shape is very handy when playing a I - IV7 progression, like B major to E7 for example. Play the B major chord in the A-shape, then the E7 chord in this particular D-shape at the 4th fret. We will practice this in one of the exercises below.

Remember, the 7th arpeggio is the same as the major but with the flat-7th added.

D-Shape
7th Arpeggio

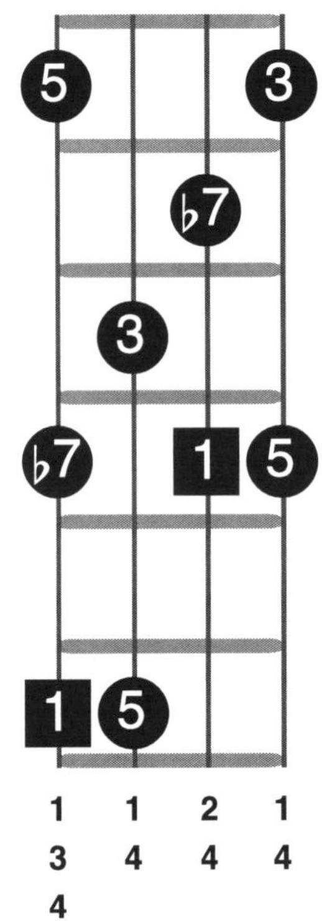

Alternative Chord Shapes

"Variation 1" features the classic "staircase" 7th shape that we have seen many times already, and of course you can add the next "step" on the low string too. "Variation 2" does have the root note, but not the 5th. "Variation 3" might be easier to locate by root note on the low string, but requires a larger stretch. "Variation 4" is great for rhythm comping with strings semi muted with the palm of the strumming hand in short percussive beats. Try it!

D-Shape
7th Chord
Variation 1

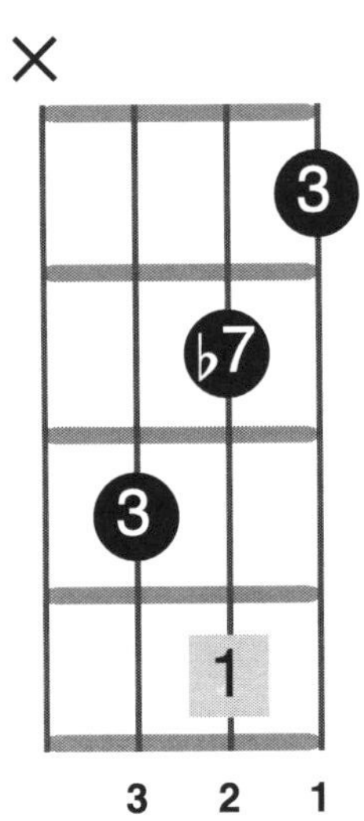

D-Shape
7th Chord
Variation 2

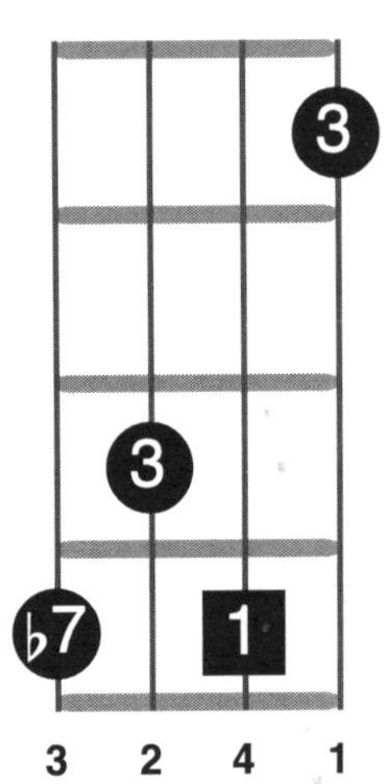

D-Shape
7th Chord
Variation 3

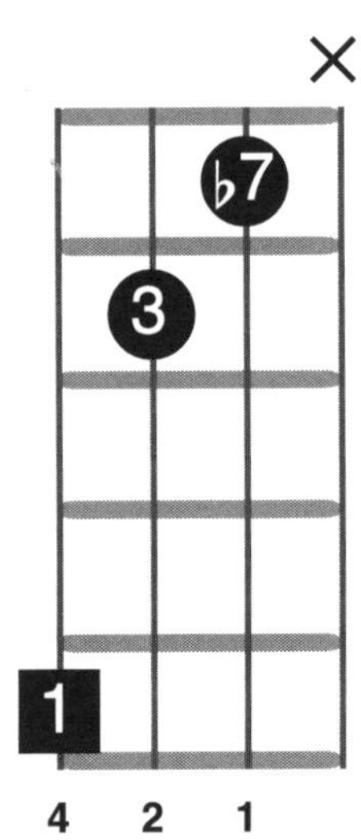

D-Shape
7th Chord
Variation 4

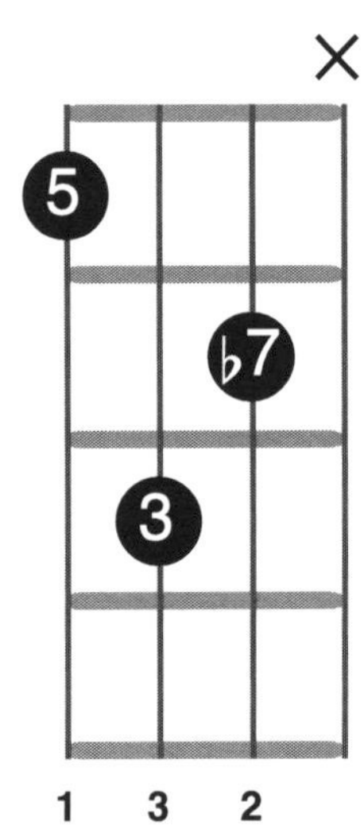

D-Shape 7th Exercise 1: Start by fingering the D-shape G7 chord at the 7th fret as we simultaneously become more familiar with the 7th arpeggio.

56

D-Shape 7th Exercise 1

G7

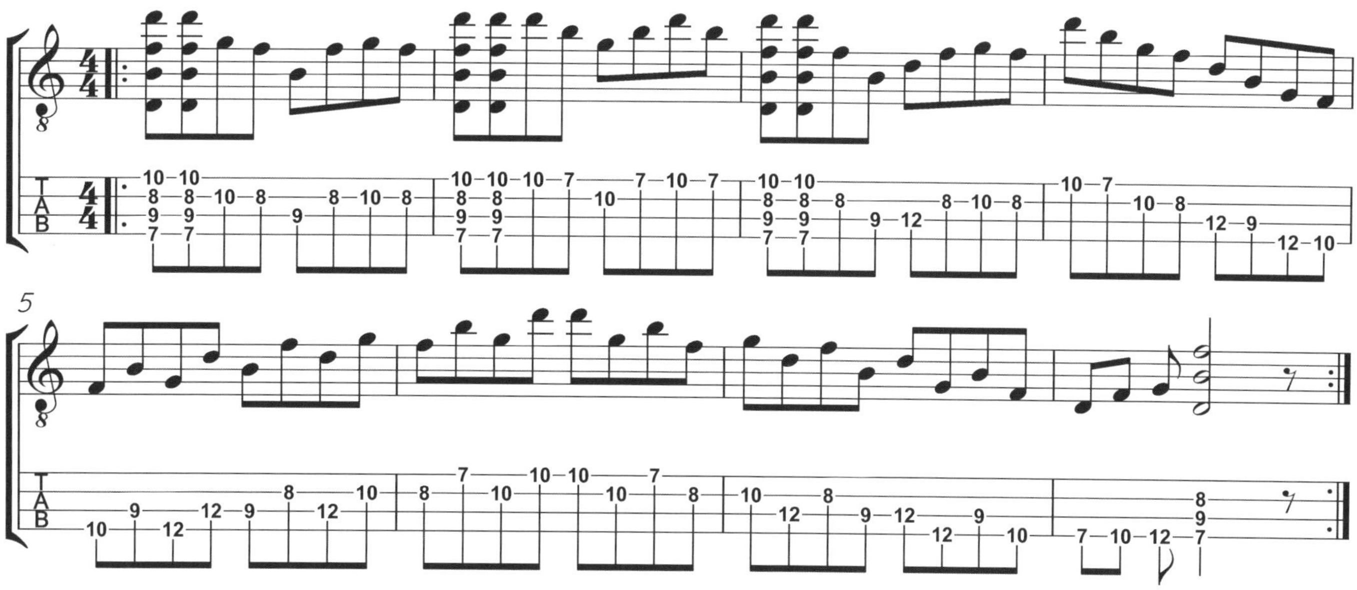

D-Shape 7th Exercise 2: Now let's work on moving 7th arpeggios between two chord shapes: the D-shape E7 at the 4th fret and the A-shape A7 at the 2nd fret.

57

D-Shape 7th Exercise 2

E7 - A7

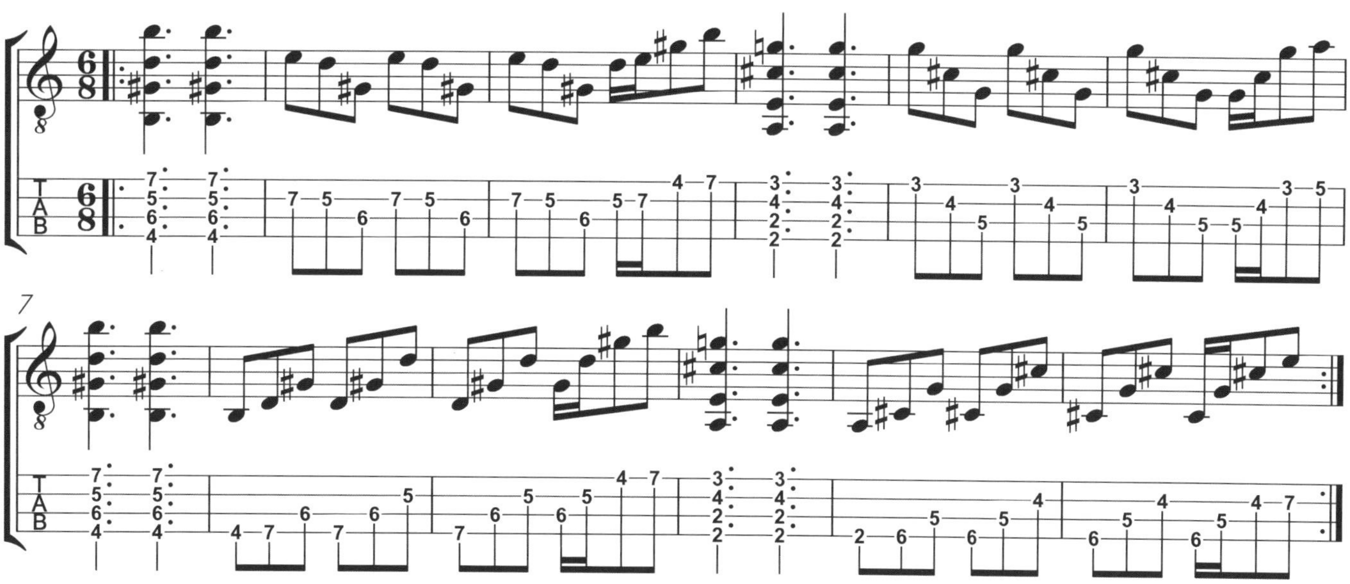

The 7th chords and arpeggios are special because they have that extra note. They are just like the major arpeggios, but a little more tangy with that flatted 7th. The 7th position is also special because it has that extra "pull" that wants to resolve. Therefore, it is a great harmonic tool to have handy for creating tension, release and movement. So far in this section, we've worked on A7 in the A-shape, and E7 and G7 in the D-shape.

D-Shape 7th Exercise 3: Let's continue focusing on the D-shaped 7th chord in exercise 3 with an all-7th progression using an A-shape D7, and D-shape G7 and A7 chords. Remember, you can see the corresponding chord shape in gray in the arpeggio charts. Don't forget to first practice running these arpeggios.

A-Shape
D7 Chord

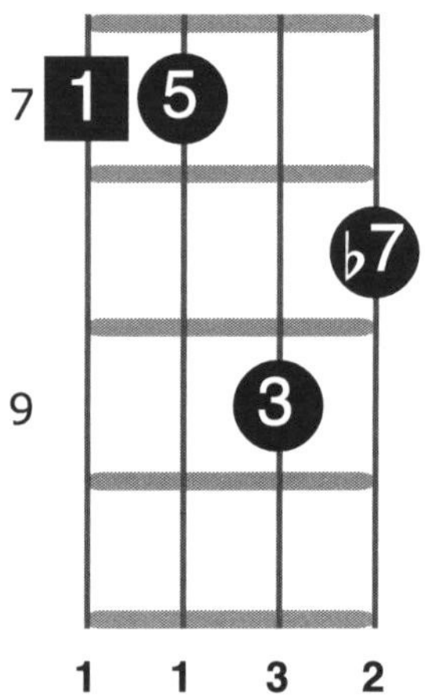

D-Shape
G7 Chord

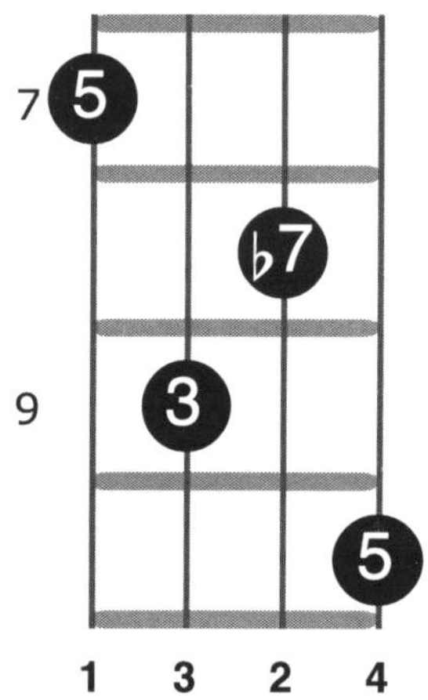

D-Shape
A7 Chord

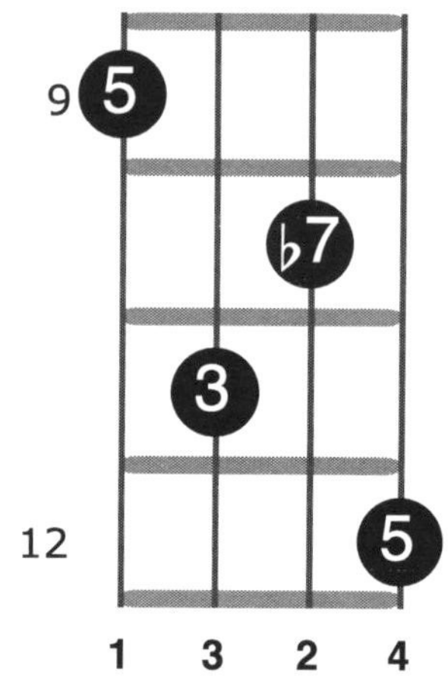

A-Shape
D7 Arpeggio

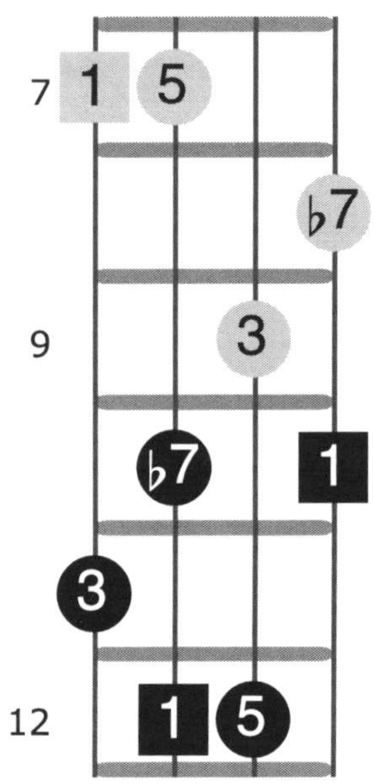

D-Shape
G7 Arpeggio

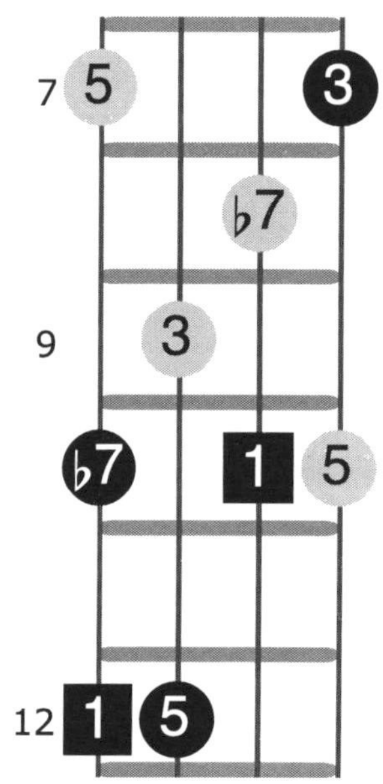

D-Shape
A7 Arpeggio

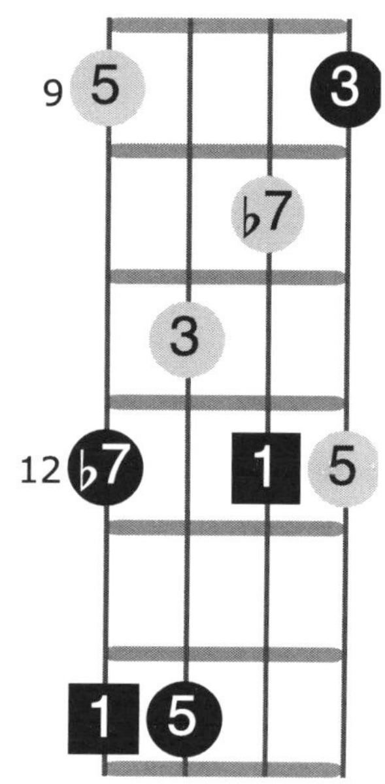

In this exercise the focus will be with more riff-like phrases over each chord rather than focusing on playing the arpeggios in order up and down. Practice making your own riffs and melodic phrases using these 7th arpeggio notes.

58

D-Shape 7th Exercise 3

D7 - G7 - A7

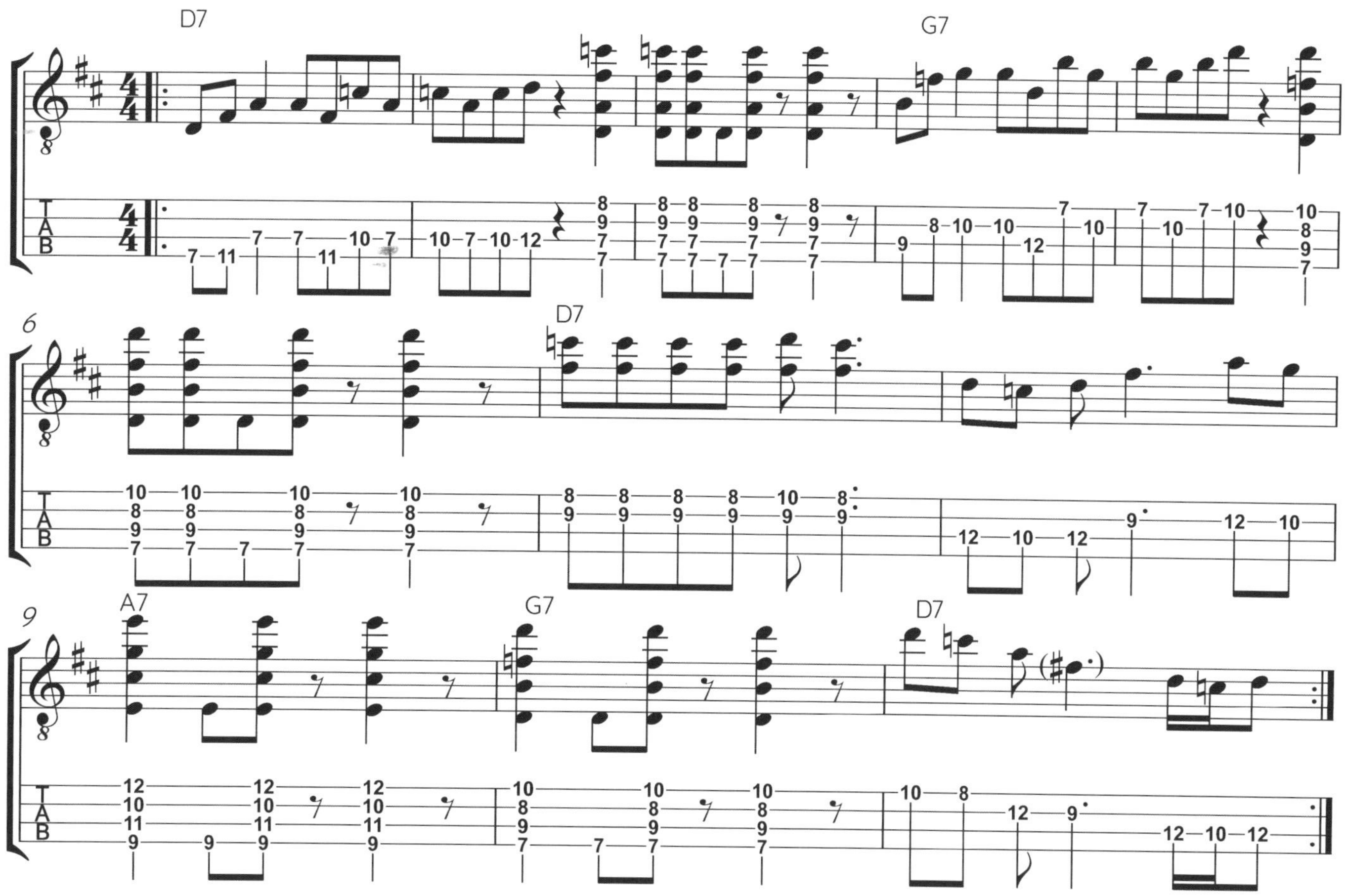

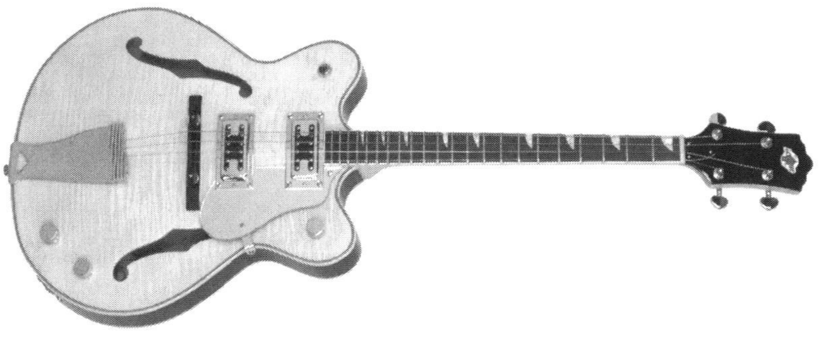

Classic tenor guitar by Eastwood

Chapter 5-4: D-Shape Melody Ideas

The next exercise will use 2 of 3 chord shapes that differ some from the shapes we have used so far: the 5-chord D5, the A-shape D6, and D-shape G minor. The 5 chord is one of the chord variations mentioned a few times in this book that uses only the 1 and 5 notes. This chord is neither major nor minor in character, so can be substituted for either one. We will practice mixing strong rhythmic chords with melodic phrases that use arpeggio notes and bits of related scales. This is a good exercise to practice keeping the chords/rhythm going while adding single-note phrases. Sometimes, it's helpful to view the chords together with the single-note lines as elements of the melodic totality. On audio track 59, the first 8 bars are chords for you to practice soloing over, and then I mix in single notes. Below are the chord shapes and related arpeggios and scales you might use. On the D5 chord, I like to keep the melody notes more related to the chord than playing notes that are firmly major or minor. Experiment with those more defined notes to hear how they work over a "5" chord. The D6 chord arpeggio uses major arpeggio notes with the 6th added.

A-Shape
D5 Chord

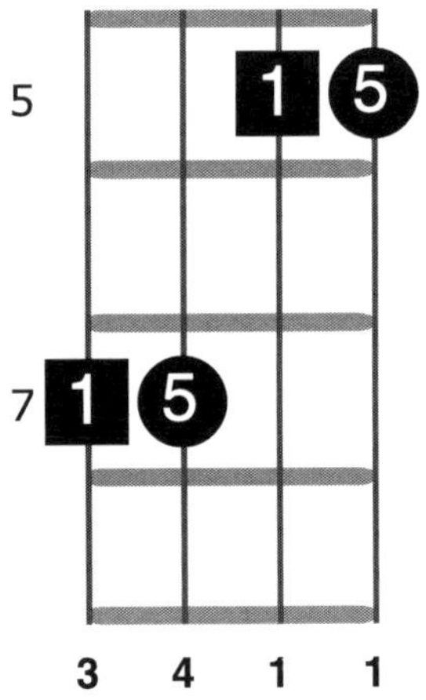

D6 Chord

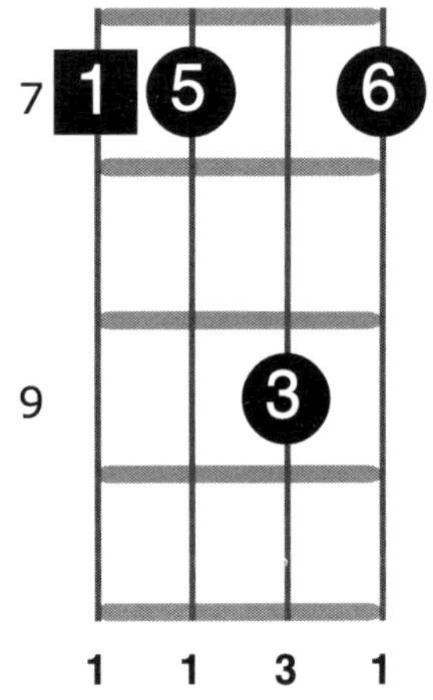

D-Shape
G Minor Chord

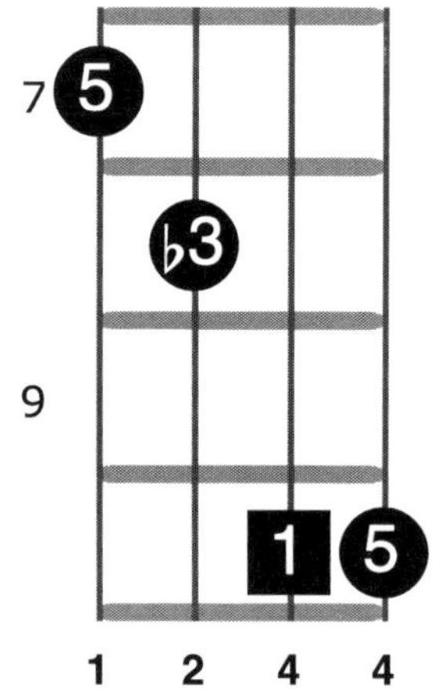

D5 Melody
Notes

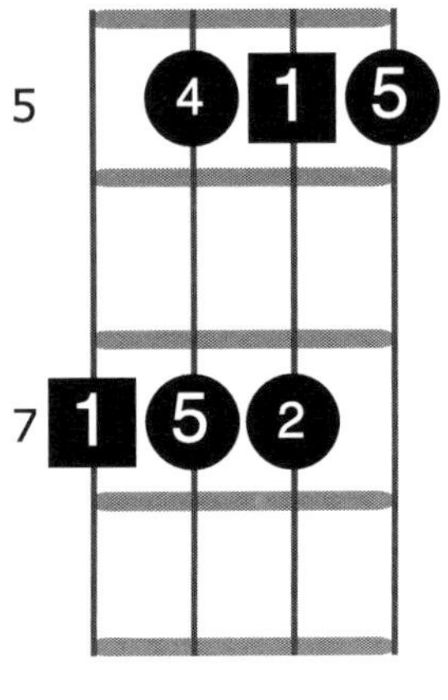

A-Shape
D6 Arpeggio

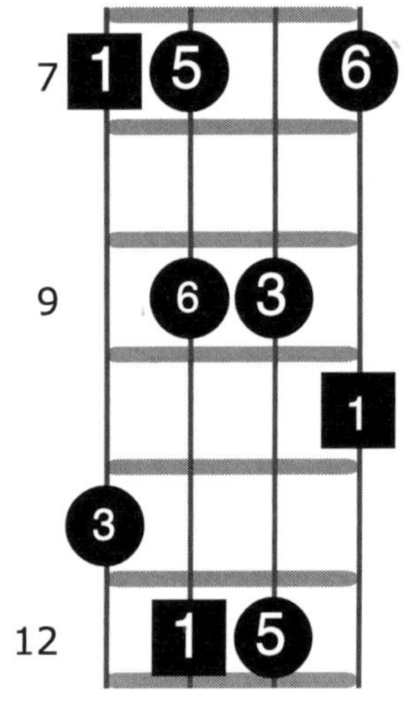

D-Shape
G Minor Arpeggio
and Scale Notes

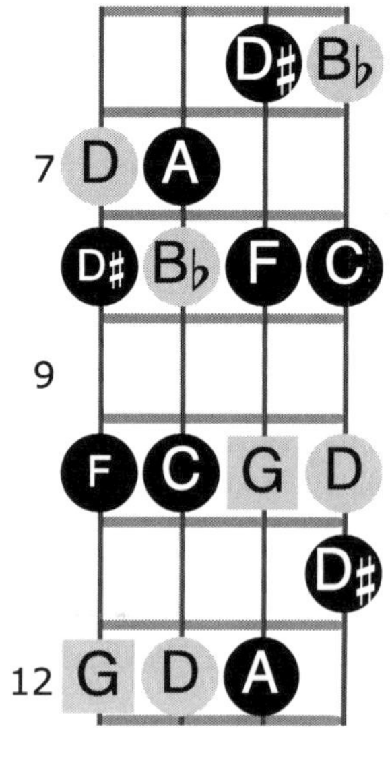

59

String of Jade

Melody Ideas

by Todd Montgomery

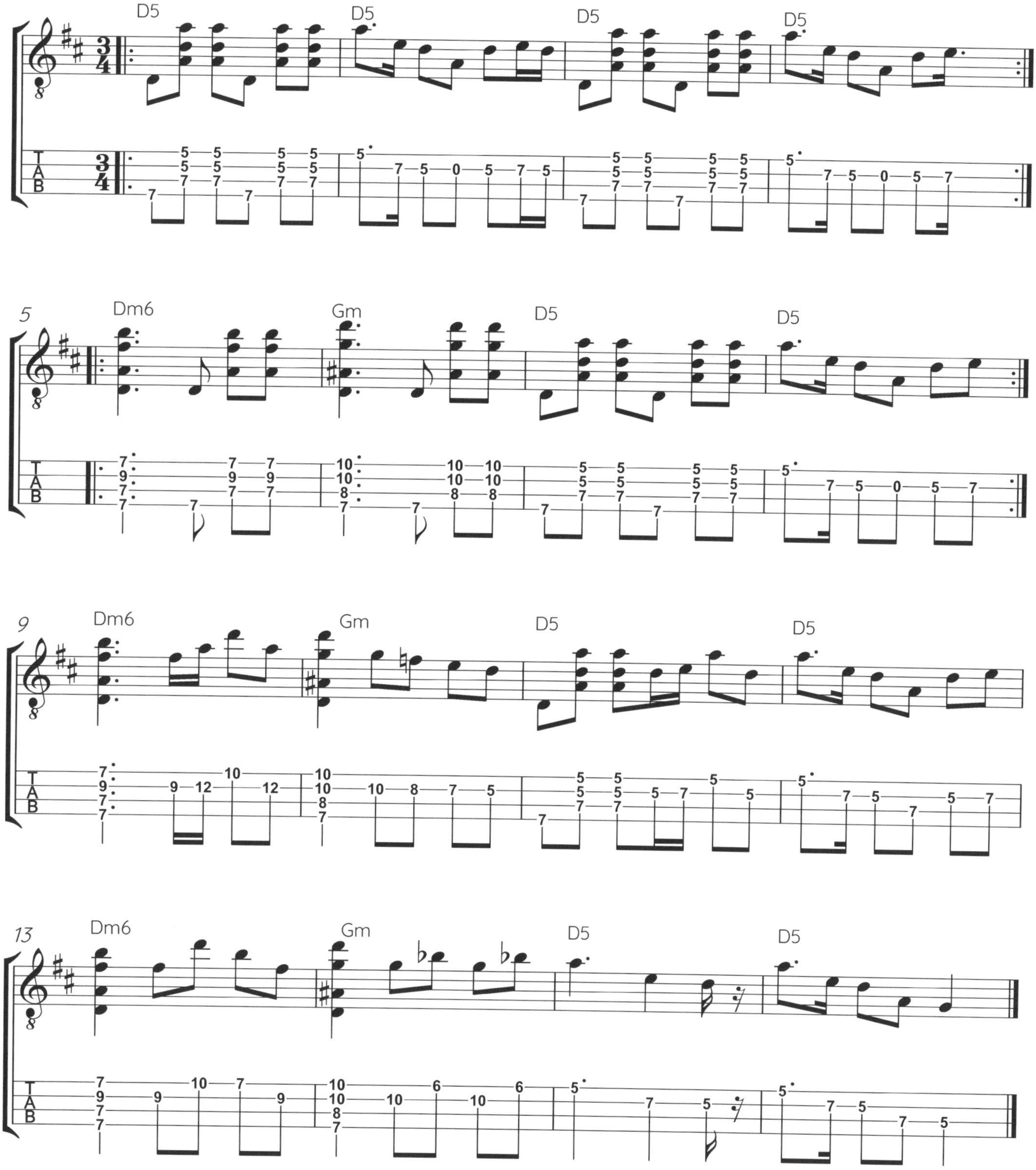

Chapter 6: Major Scale Exercises for Each Chord Shape

Now that you have learned all the chord shapes and their related arpeggios, it's time to expand beyond the arpeggios and add major scales to your practice. When creating melodies, the arpeggios are the most reliable notes to start or finish melodic phrases, but we will certainly want to add other notes as well. The following exercises will help you get familiar with the major scale notes connected to each chord shape. Let's learn a different note pattern to practice each major scale, but remember you can apply each exercise strategy to each chord shape major scale. Notice the chord shapes and the root notes in gray in each chart. It's always good to strum the chord and run the scale up and down in order to get warmed up.

C-Shape Major Scale Exercise: Try to position your hand with your third finger on the '1' note on the low string to start. This first exercise is in thirds, where you pluck one note, then the third note. Then go back to the second note and then to the third note from the 2nd and so on. Try to use your pinky on the notes at the eleventh fret. Once this pattern is part of your muscle memory, move the exercise to different positions up and down the neck. Don't forget to strum the root chord periodically.

C-Shape Major Scale

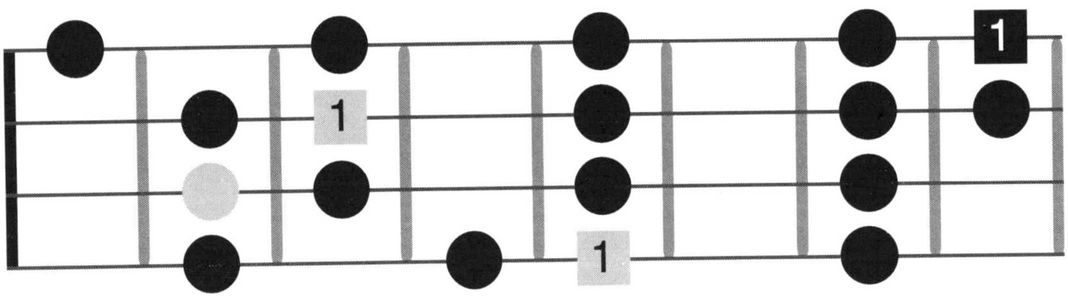

60

C-Shape Major Scale Exercise

E Major

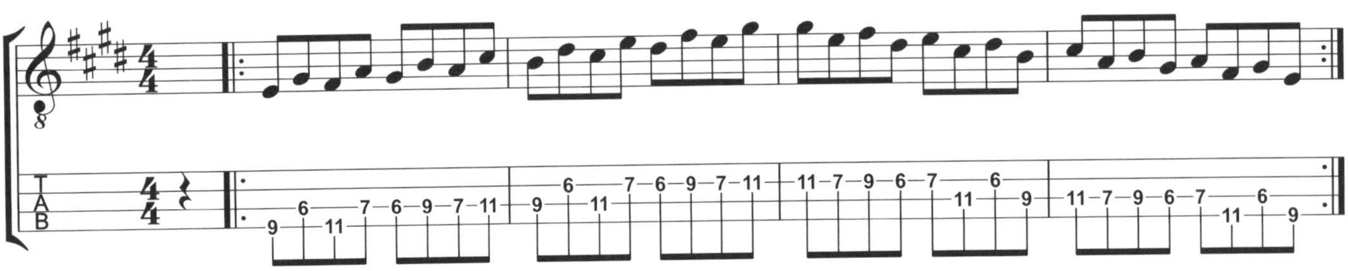

A-Shape Major Scale Exercise: Fret the A-shape D major at the 7th fret to start. Memorize this one from the perspective of the first finger at the root note on the low string.

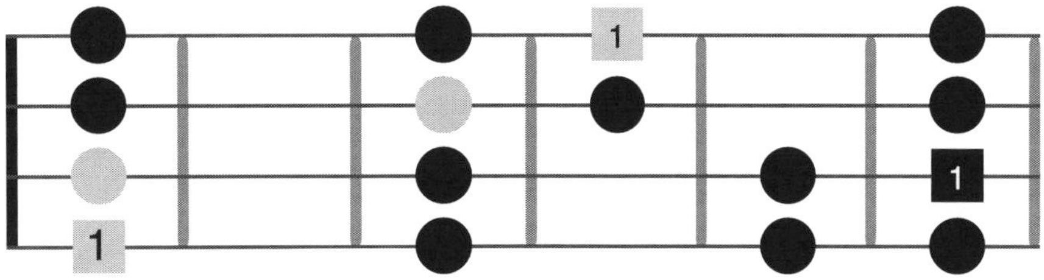

61

A-Shape Major Scale Exercise

D Major

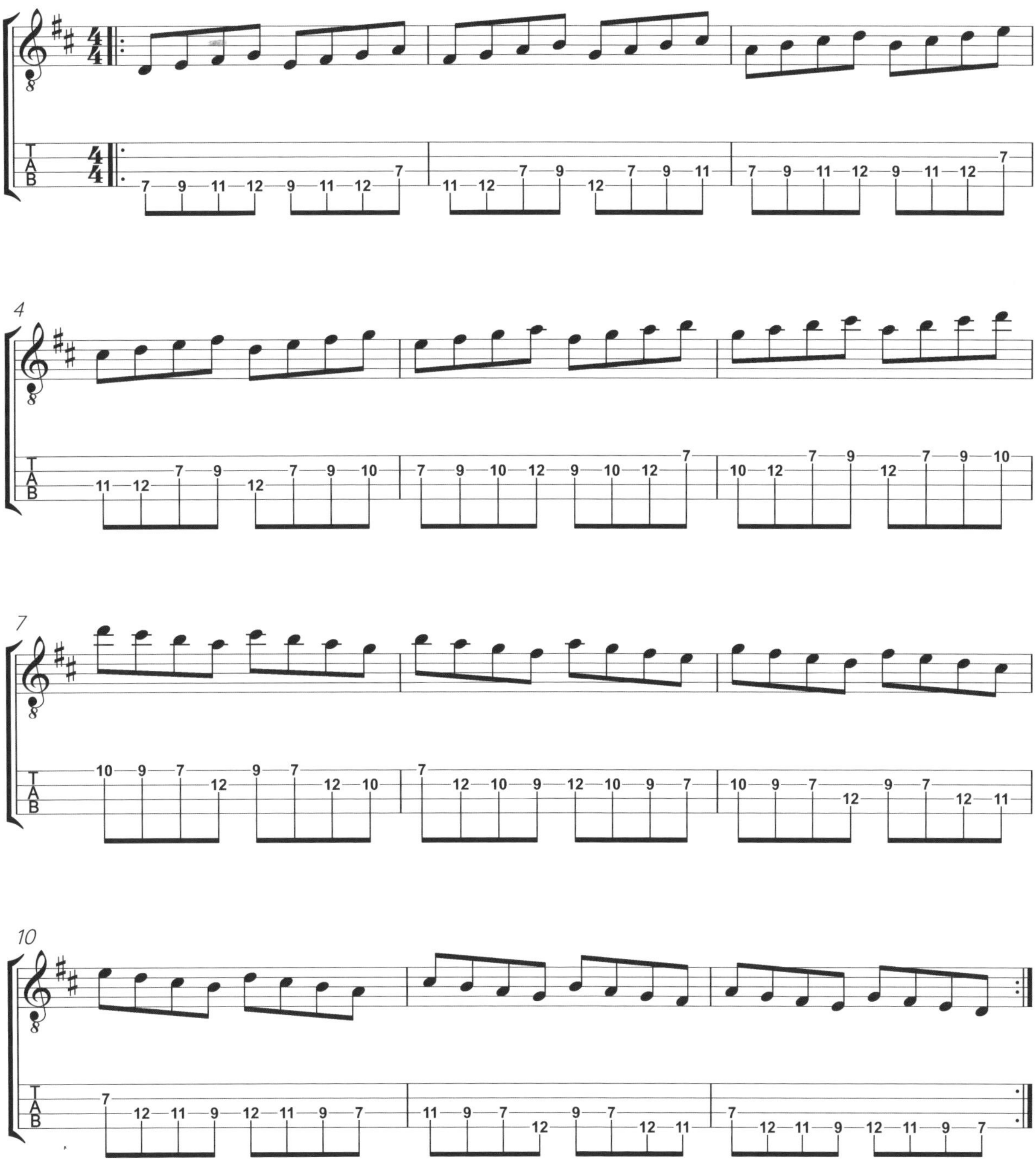

G-Shape Major Scale Exercise: Here's a different pattern for the this major scale exercise. It starts out ascending in order, but has a few direction changes. Start by fretting the G-shape chord. Let's try this one as C major at the 7th fret. Your third finger can start at the tenth fret on the D string.

G-Shape Major Scale

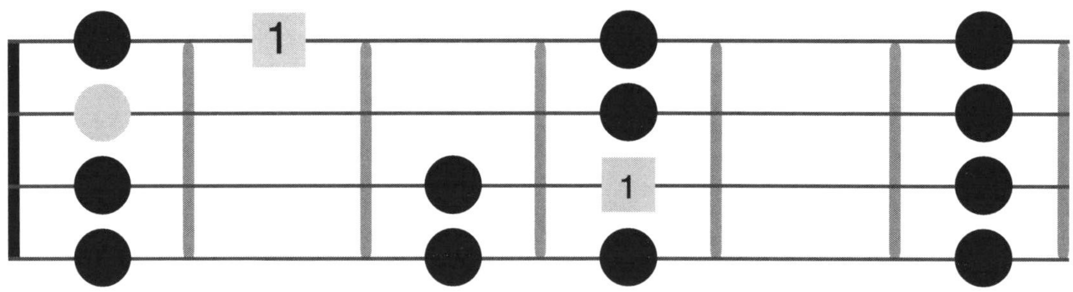

62

G-Shape Major Scale Exercise

C Major

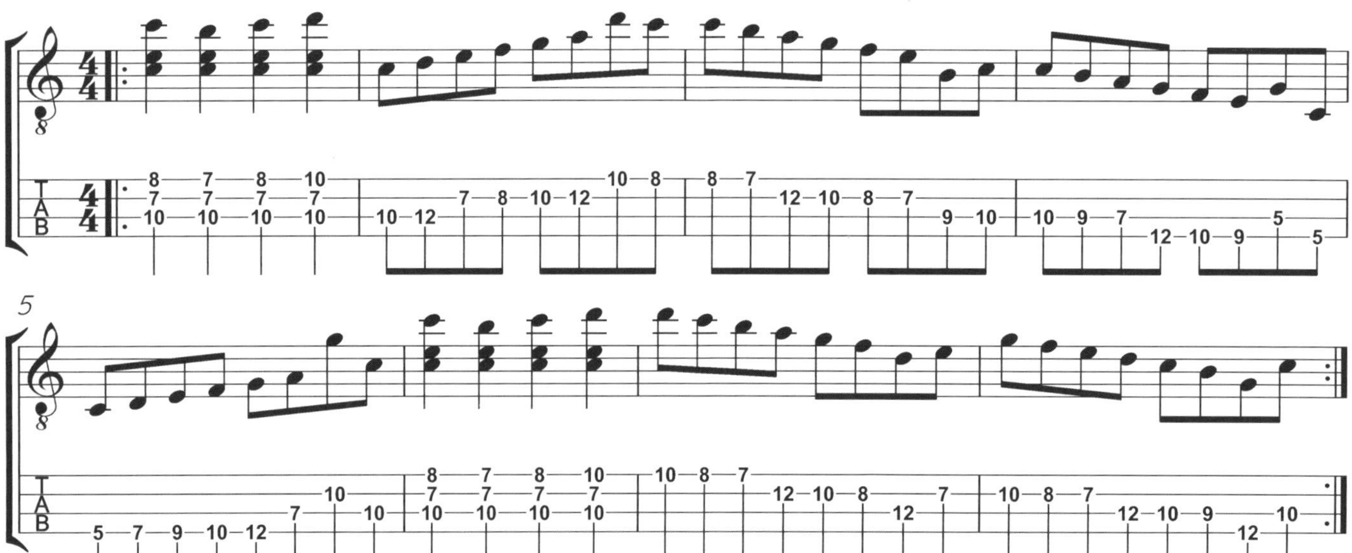

E-Shape Major Scale Exercise: Try to keep your first finger barred at the fifth fret on the D and A strings with a G Major scale as we bounce around the scale in 6/8 time.

E-Shape Major Scale

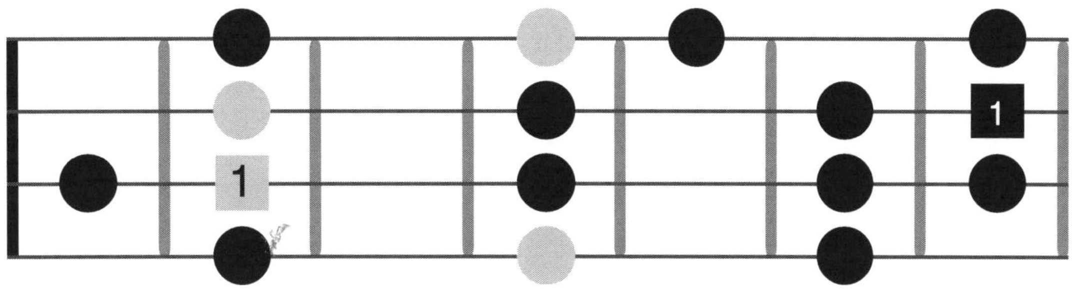

E-Shape Major Scale Exercise

G Major

63

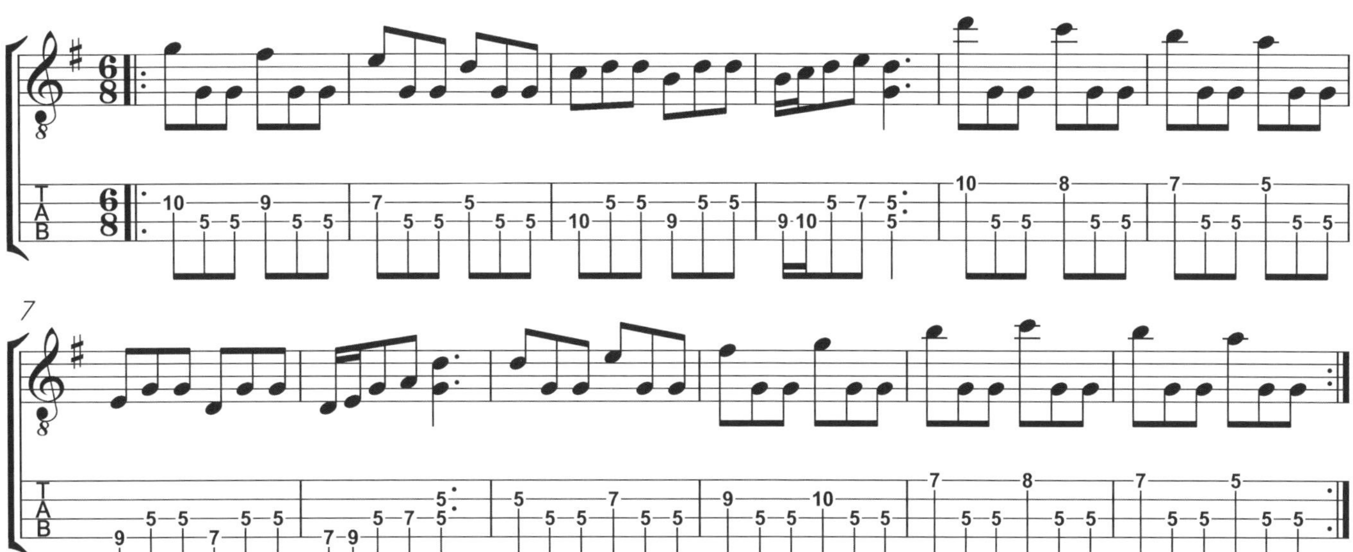

D-Shape Major Scale Exercise: We will use the G major at the 7th fret. This time we alternate the root note of the chord shape with all the other notes in this major scale.

D-Shape Major Scale

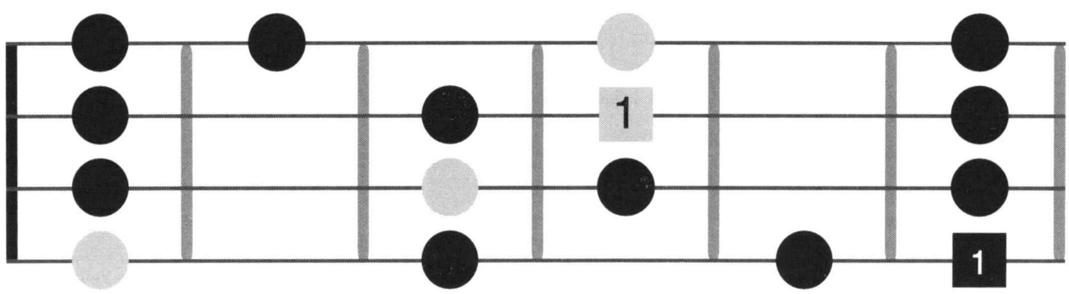

64

D-Shape Major Scale Exercise

G Major

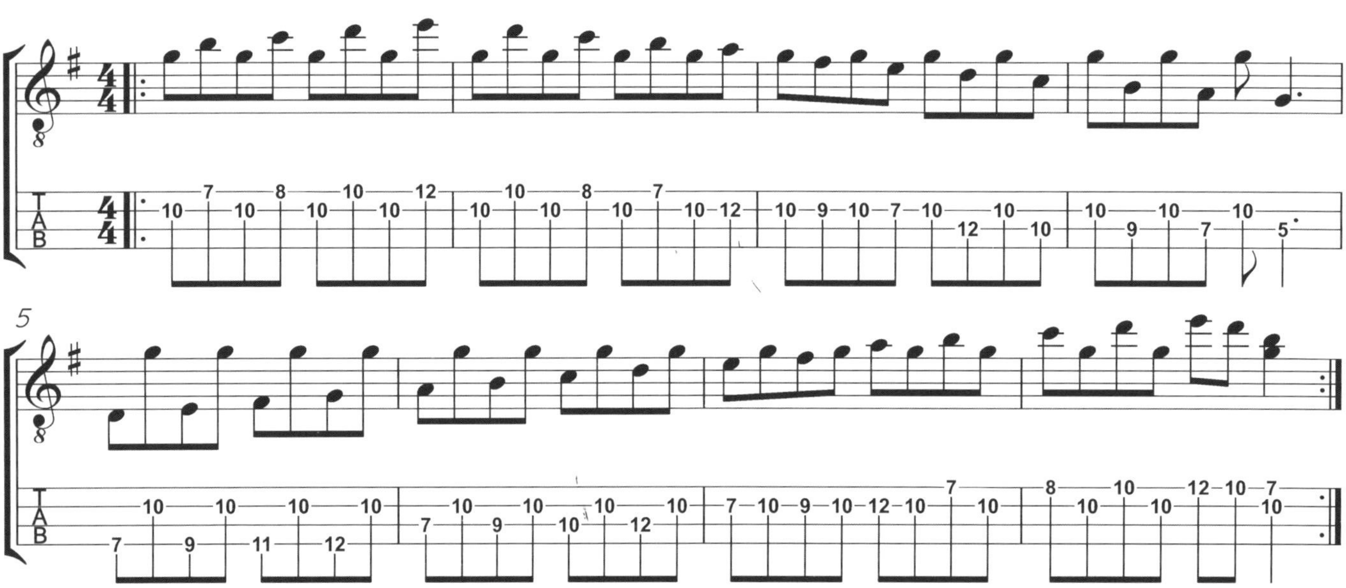

Chapter 7: Putting It All Together to Make Melodies

I hope you wil continue to practice the arpeggio exercises. They are guidelines for improving finger dexterity while helping you to ingrain those identifying chord notes into your muscle memory so that whenever you play a major, minor, or 7th chord anywhere on the fretboard, your fingers know where the key notes are located without you having to think about it. If you practice those exercises, move them around the fretboard and spend time with them in various chord progressions, you will see the harmonic skeleton of the tenor guitar neck connect with new clarity.

I discovered an interesting thing when I really began learning arpeggios. When learning a new song, I would start by playing the chord progression using arpeggio patterns. Upon repetition, I began to see how the notes of each arpeggio overlap and connect to each other. Through this process, I noticed is that parts of the melody of the tune begin emerging under my fingers. I could hear by doing this type of practice, that composers often focus mostly on the arpeggio notes (notes of the chord) in their melody lines.

Most of my guitar heroes say that when they create and play solos, riffs and melodies the first concern is from the perspective of the chord, not from the perspective of scales. The great soloists mix in parts of any scale that suits them, but they know what chord they are playing over.

Now let's use our hard-won knowledge of the arpeggio notes of the chord shapes as the starting point for learning a more complex song that has more chords. The following exercises form a method that can be used to go about learning a song and creating a melody for it.

First, I like to take time trying out different chord shapes around the neck looking for "clumps" of chords that are located near each other. Then I try to build the architecture of the piece, choosing parts that I might play higher up the neck to give the piece movement and drama. Once I'm happy with my chord shape choices I then practice each arpeggio until I can play them smoothly, in time with the chord progression of the song. Once the arpeggios are mastered, I practice "dancing" around with these key tones and making small phrases using parts of arpeggios while trying out other notes in related scales that artistically transition from one arpeggio to the next. Of course, the melody might flow high to low, and have interesting rhythmic and dynamic elements as well.

Let's apply this method to one of my tunes, "Waiting for Penny", which uses some jazzier chord shapes, and arrange chords and a solo to this more complex song. Let's try applying the method I just described starting with choosing chord shapes that have appealing movement throughout the progression. The chord grids on the following page are in order that they appear in the song.

Play along with the practice track while looking at the chord charts on the following two pages. Once you can strum the chord progression while listening to the song, practice running through the arpeggios for the verse, chorus, and bridge chord progressions in the next two exercises.

65

Waiting for Penny-Verse Chords

1	2	3	4	1	2	3	4

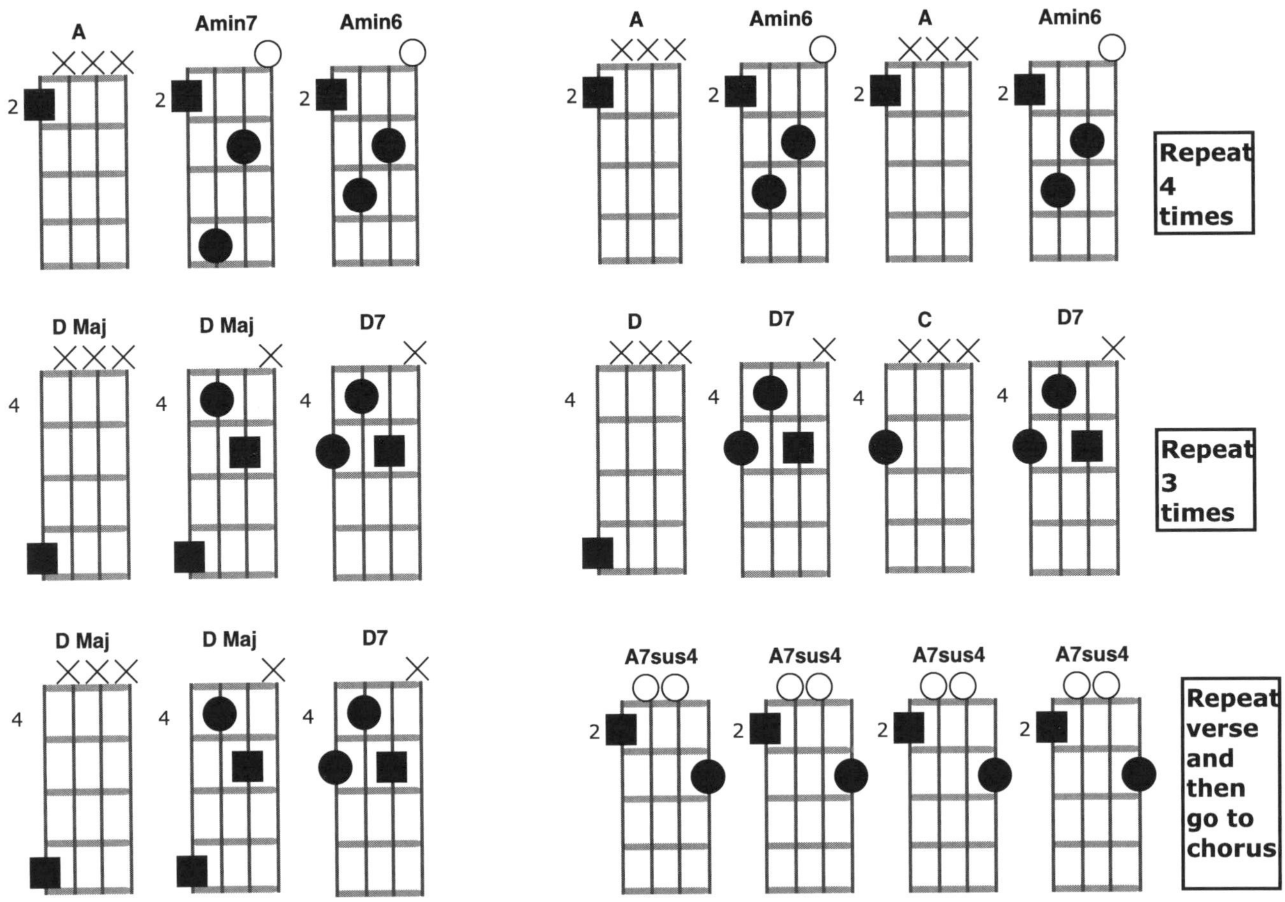

Waiting for Penny-Chorus Chords

1	2	3	4	1	2	3	4

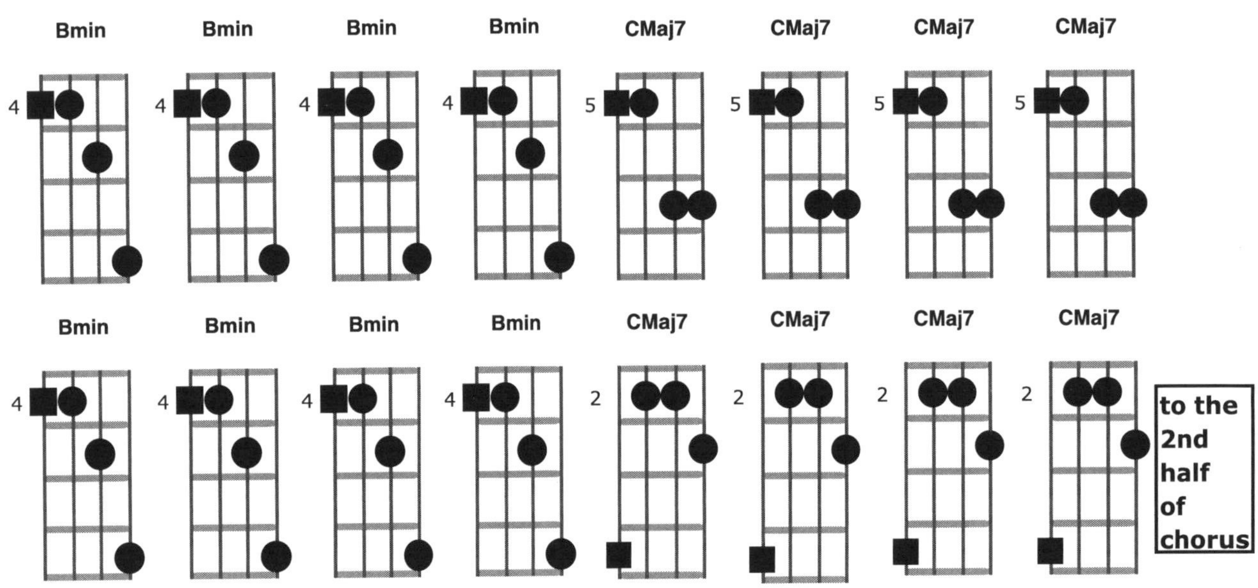

Waiting for Penny-Chorus Chords

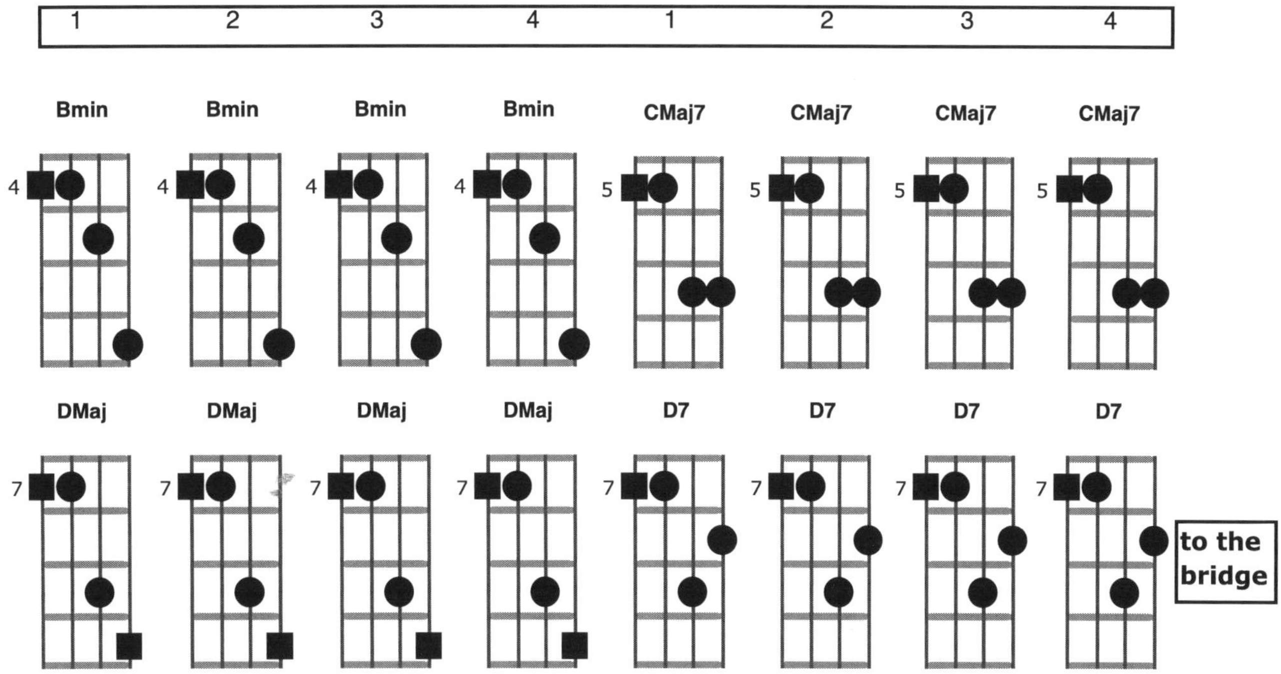

Waiting for Penny-Bridge Chords

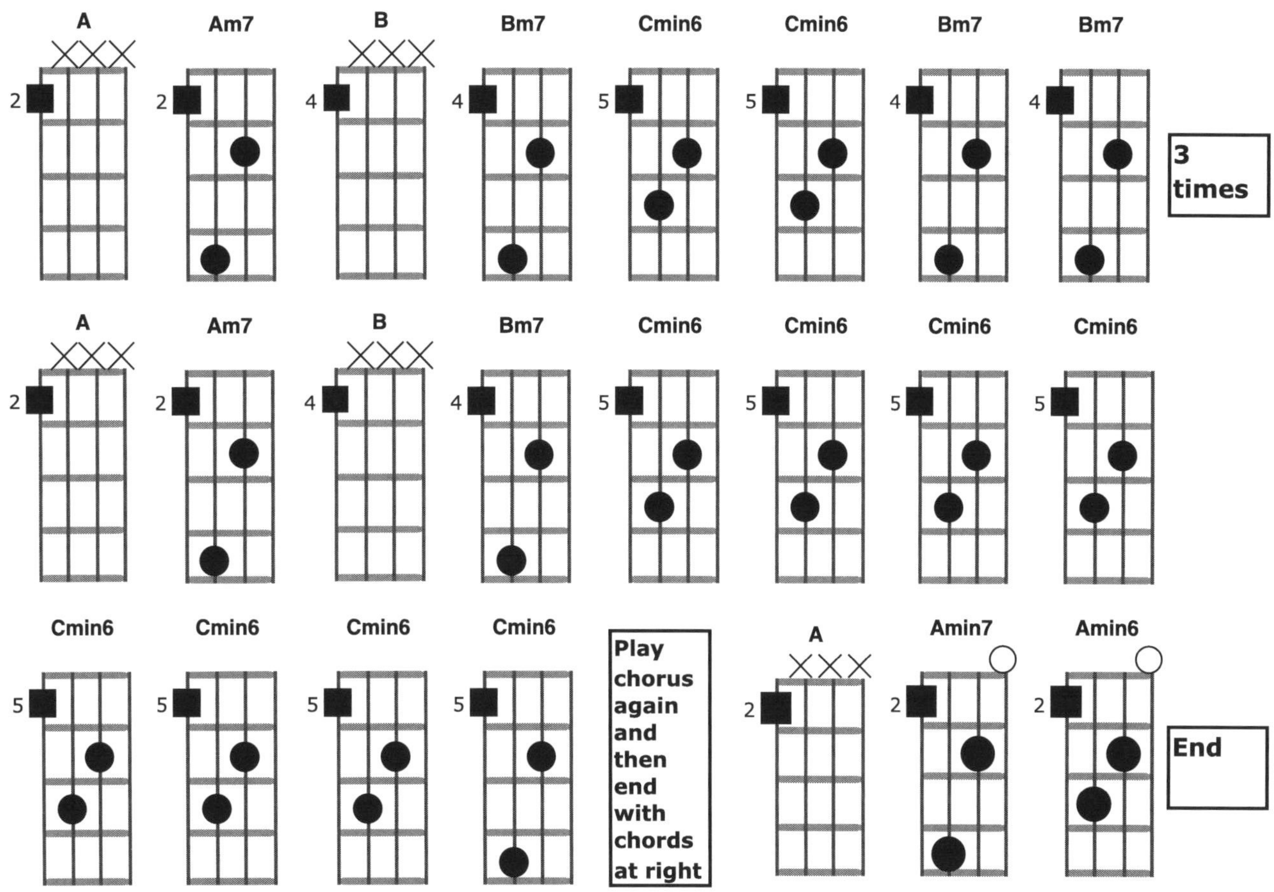

66

Waiting for Penny

Arpeggio Exercise

Music by Todd Montgomery

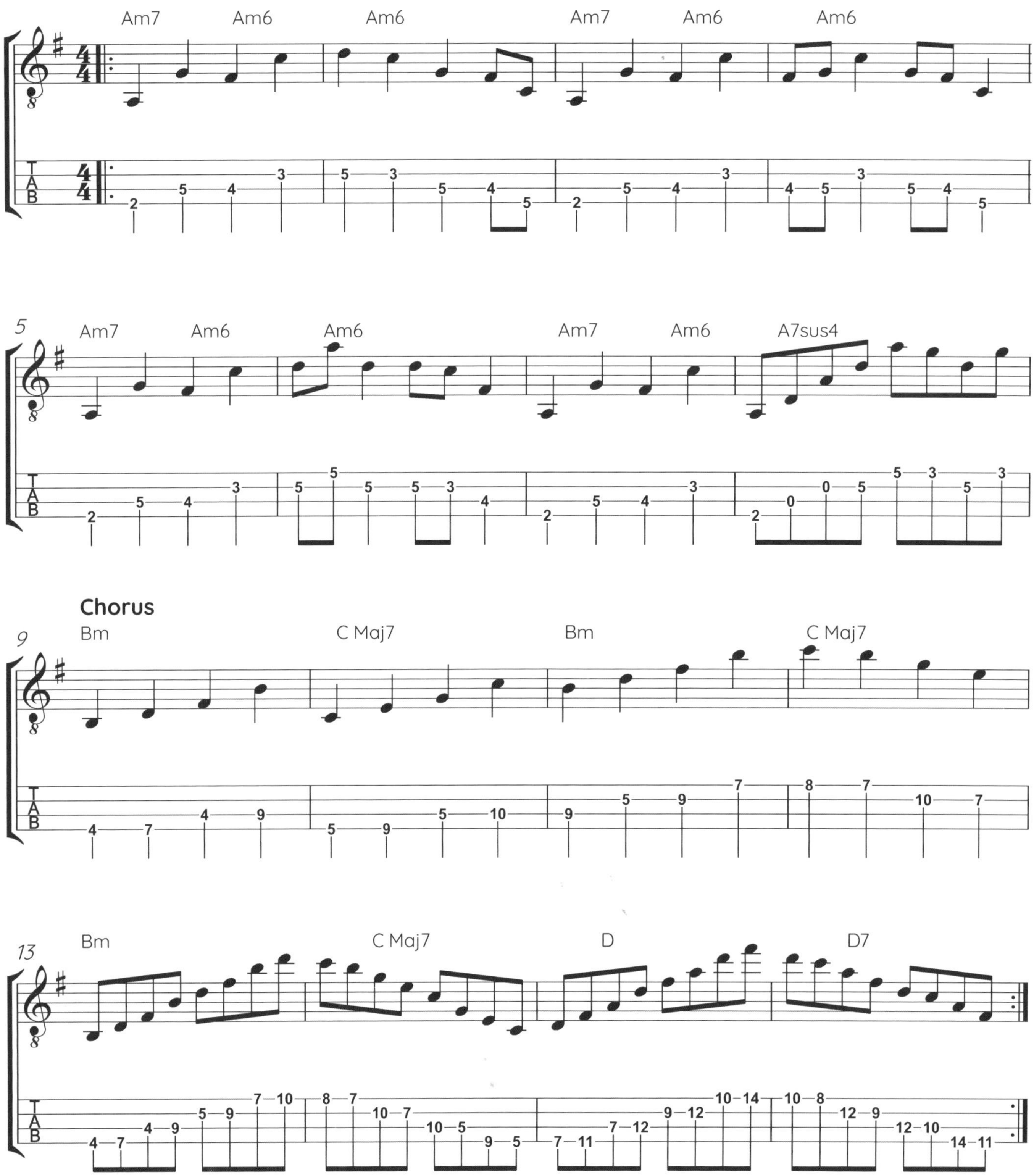

67

Waiting for Penny

Bridge Exercise

Music by Todd Montgomery

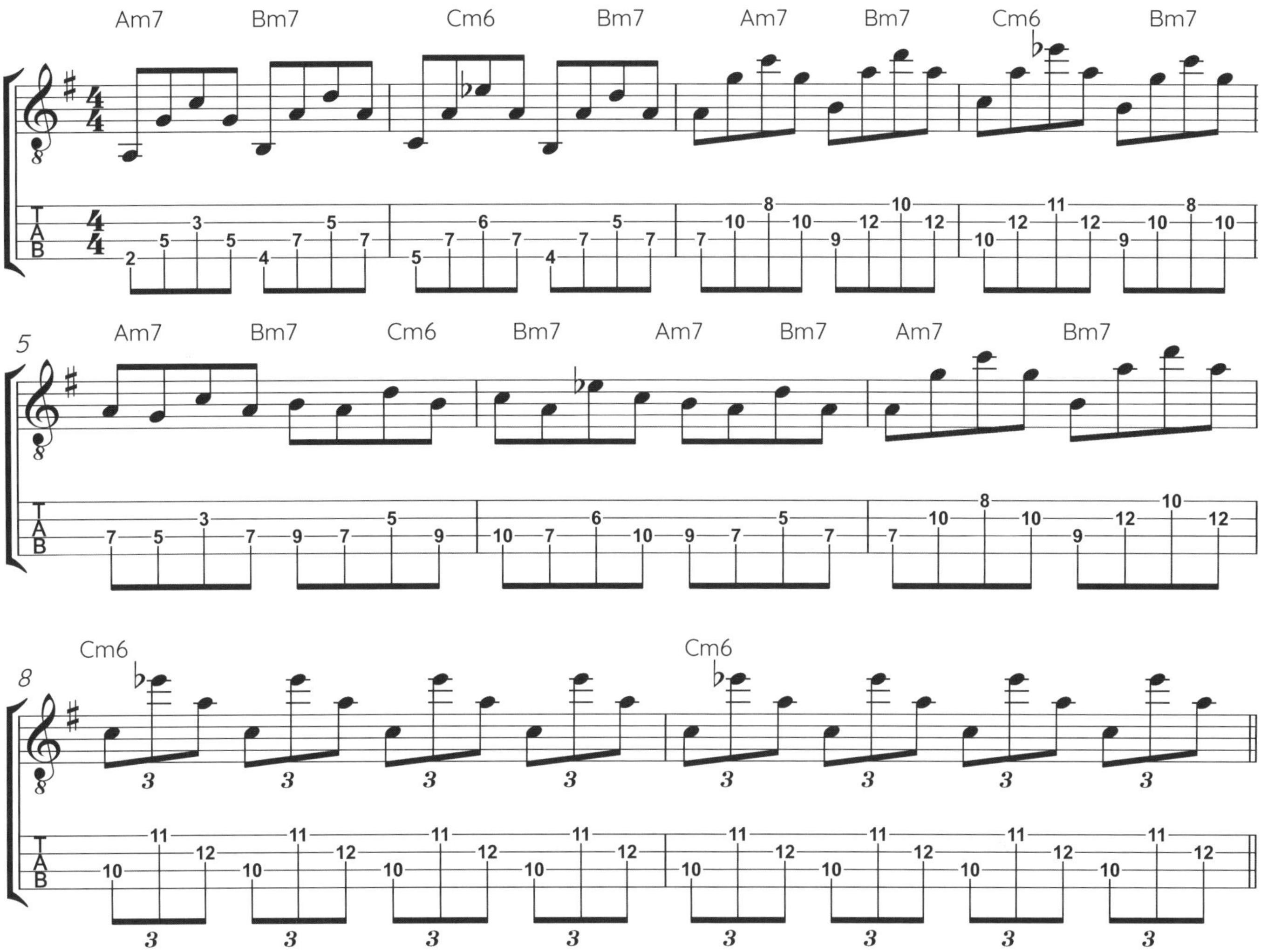

Now let's try to "dance" around the arpeggios adding other notes of the G major scale along with some passing notes, and then play our melody with the chord changes. I almost always play with a swing rhythm rather than playing strictly by the music. Similar to the way you might approach playing Irish tunes to sheet music, the "dots" (notes) are really a guideline. It's up to the player to really make it musical. Once you can play "Waiting for Penny" as written, try making up your own melodies; keep in mind that chord notes are good to start with and to land on in your musical phrasing. Audio Track 68 includes the whole tune, "Waiting for Penny" Solo Exercise Parts 1, 2, and 3.

68

Waiting for Penny

Solo Pt. 1 Exercise

with Scale and Passing Tones

Music by Todd Montgomery

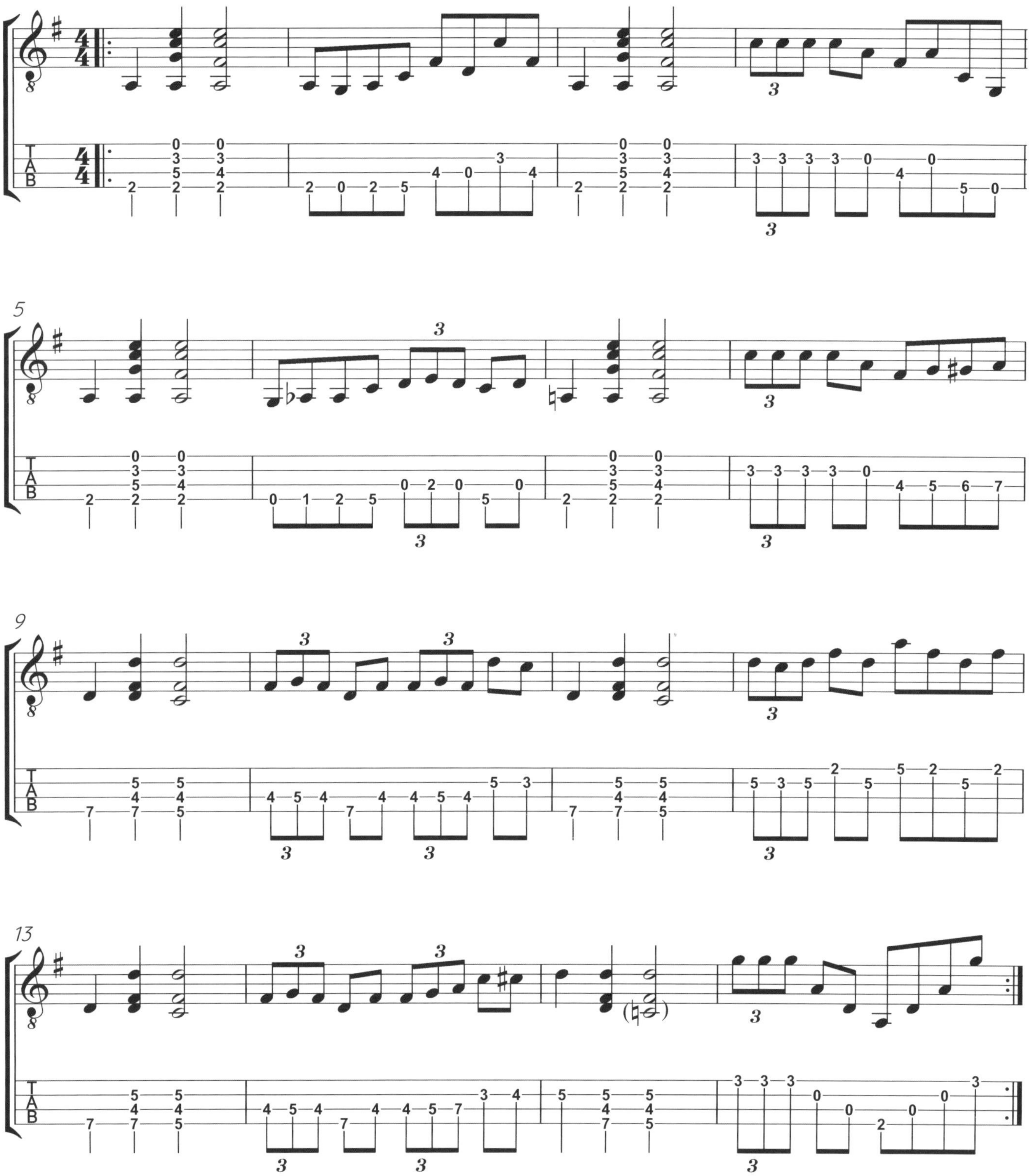

Waiting for Penny

Solo Pt. 2 Exercise

Music by Todd Montgomery

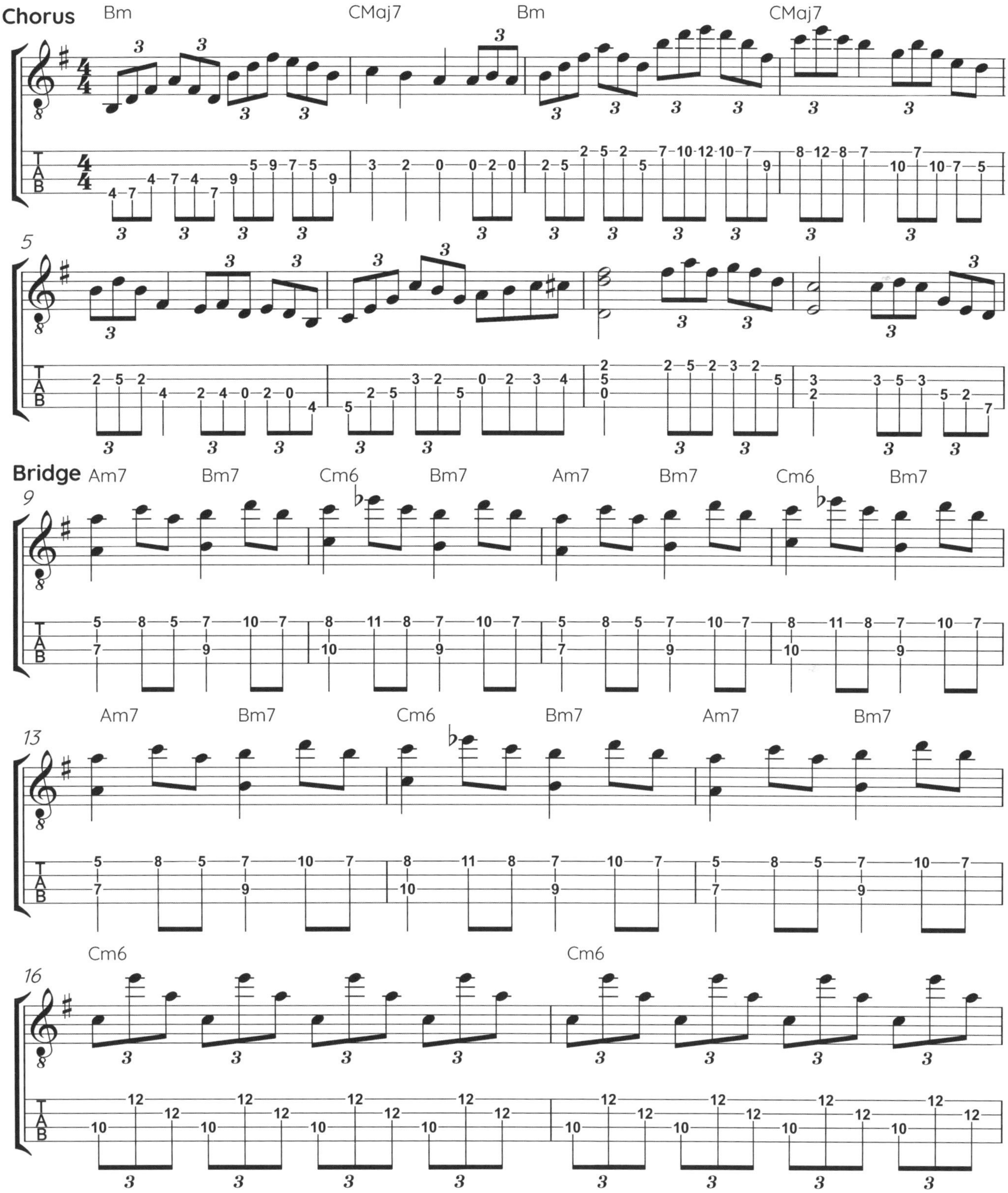

Waiting for Penny

Solo Pt. 3 Exercise

Music by Todd Montgomery

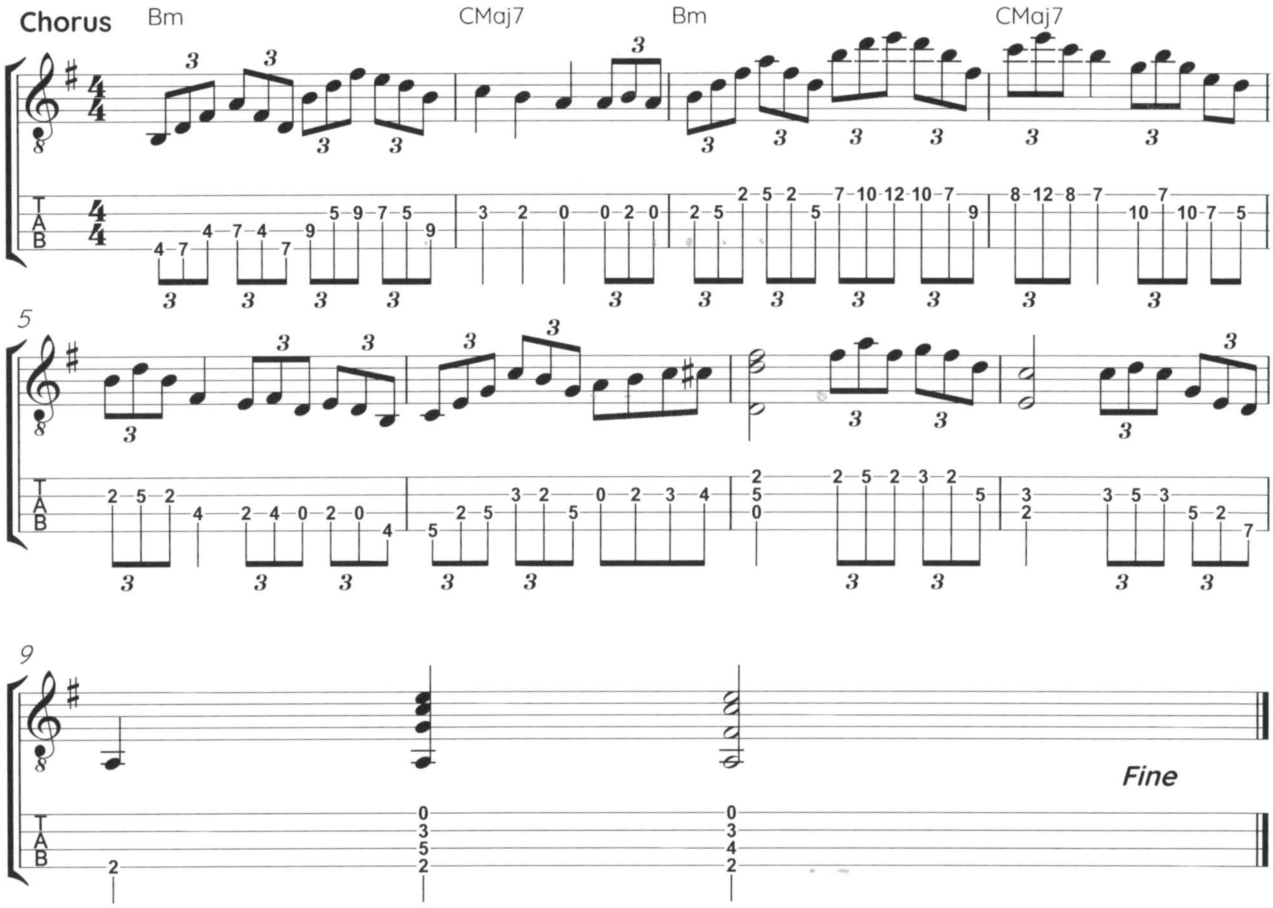

Moving Forward

Here are a few ideas about moving forward with your music that may be of use. First of all, and of course, most obviously is the idea that no matter what role music plays in your life, the more you practice, the better! It doesn't matter what level you consider yourself to be, absolute beginner to professional, you'll be happier and healthier if you play everyday. When we practice, the inner-dialogue slows down and the mind relaxes and becomes less distracted. Then you can listen more deeply and simply enjoy being in the present moment.

Remember to relax your hands as much as possible when practicing. If you are clenching your hands, you'll get tired faster and the notes won't ring out as sweetly. It's not a bad idea to learn some basic yoga-like stretches for the back, neck, shoulders, and hands. Be aware of your posture and if you are gripping or clenching shoulder, back or neck muscles. Now that I'm a bit older, I have a routine of stretches I do before and after playing so that I can play longer.

Whether you are using an acoustic or electric tenor guitar, make sure that it's set up by a professional. Big guitar stores usually have a repair department that can do this. I prefer to find well-respected independent guitar specialists because, in my experience, they'll spend more time and usually do a better job. When a guitar is set up correctly, it will be easier to play and in tune everywhere on the fretboard. Therefore, you'll enjoy playing it more often, it will sound better and you'll likely make progress faster.

Even though many of the exercises in this book may be relatively easy to play, there's still much to enjoy and learn by practicing them. Take the very first C-shape arpeggio exercise for example. It stays on one chord and there are no tricky fingerings to work out. Nevertheless, there are many ways to appreciate and grow by practicing a simple sequence of notes. For example, try to play them as slowly as possible while making sure that each note rings out, uncluttered by finger squeaks, until the next note is cleanly plucked; then gradually speed up while still keeping it clean and musical.

You might also practice to different rhythms and tempos. Try using a metronome that can be set without an emphasis beat, where all clicks are of equal volume. Then try to play to different beat cycles, such as odd numbered patterns. I like practicing to 5 and 7 beat cycles. It's challenging and it opens up new ideas. Players with more experience can mix ornaments, notes from related scales, exotic chords, key changes and fast tempos, etc. The possibilities are endless when a player knows the defining notes within each chord shape, and can use them from the bottom to the top of the fretboard.

More Chords

Adim | Asus2 | Asus4 | Am7 | AMaj7 | Adim7 | A6

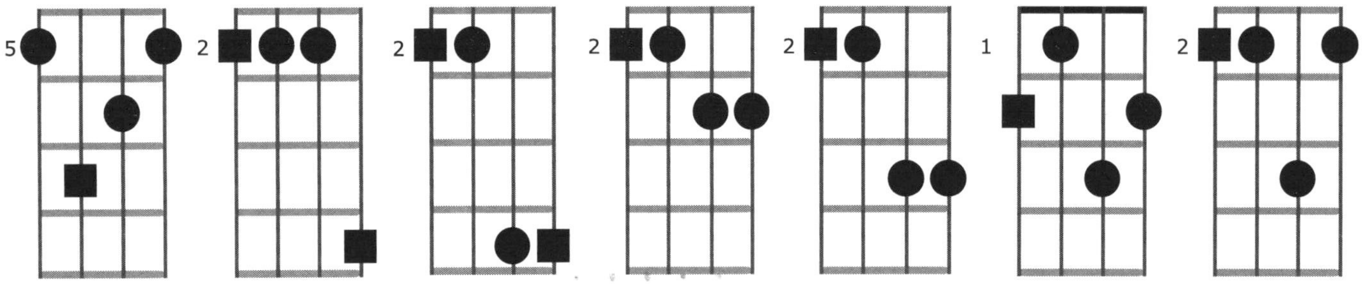

Am6 | A6add9 | Bdim | Bsus2 | Bsus4 | Bm7 | BMaj7

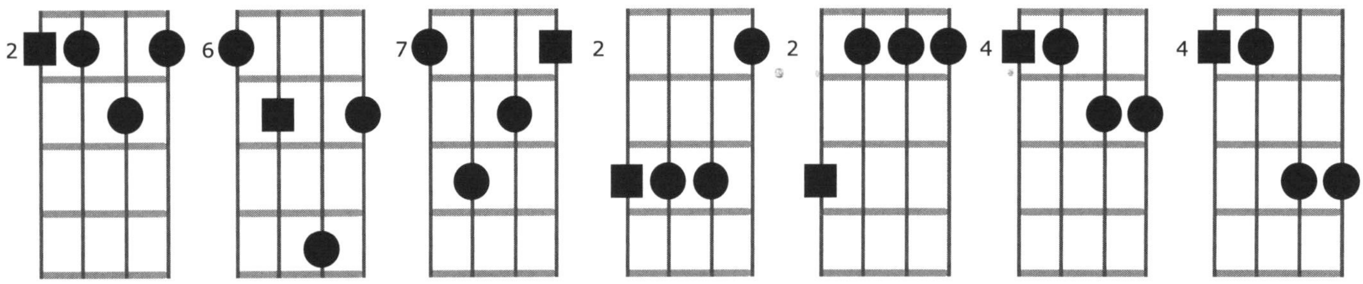

Bdim7 | B6 | Bm6 | B6add9 | Cdim | Csus2 | Csus4

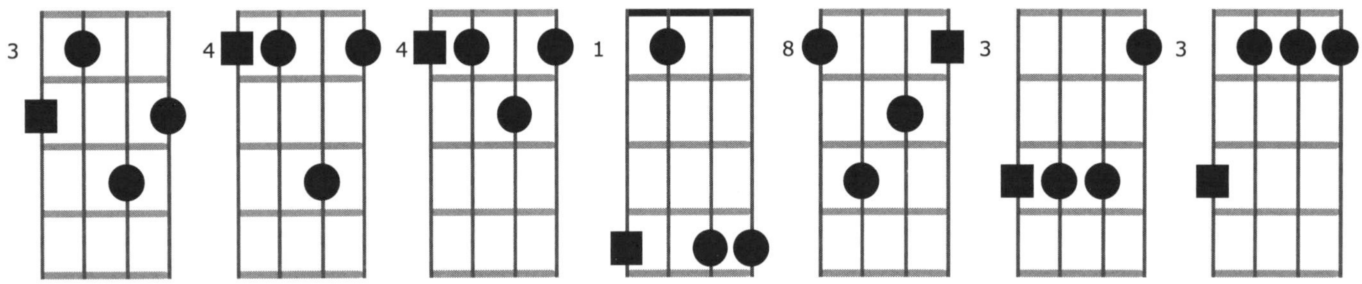

Cm7 | CMaj7 | Cdim7 | C6 | Cm6 | C6add9 | Ddim

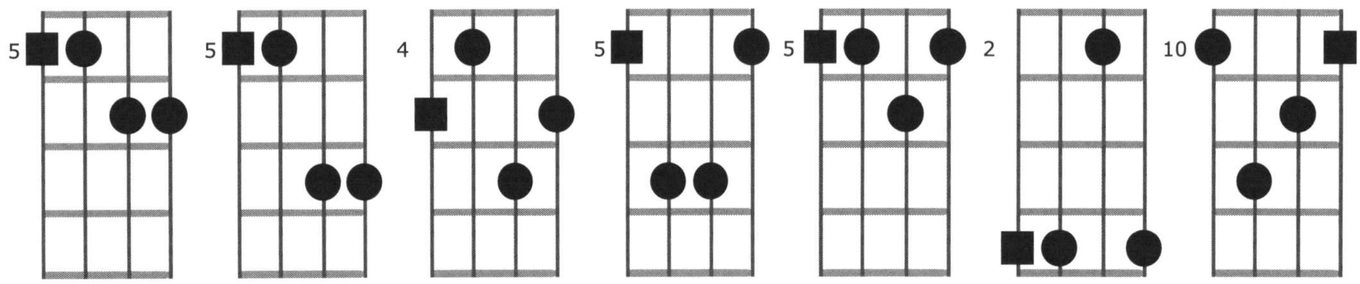

Dsus2 | Dsus4 | Dm7

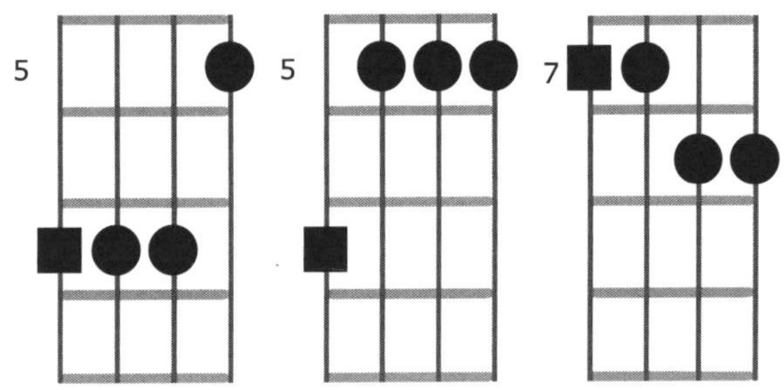

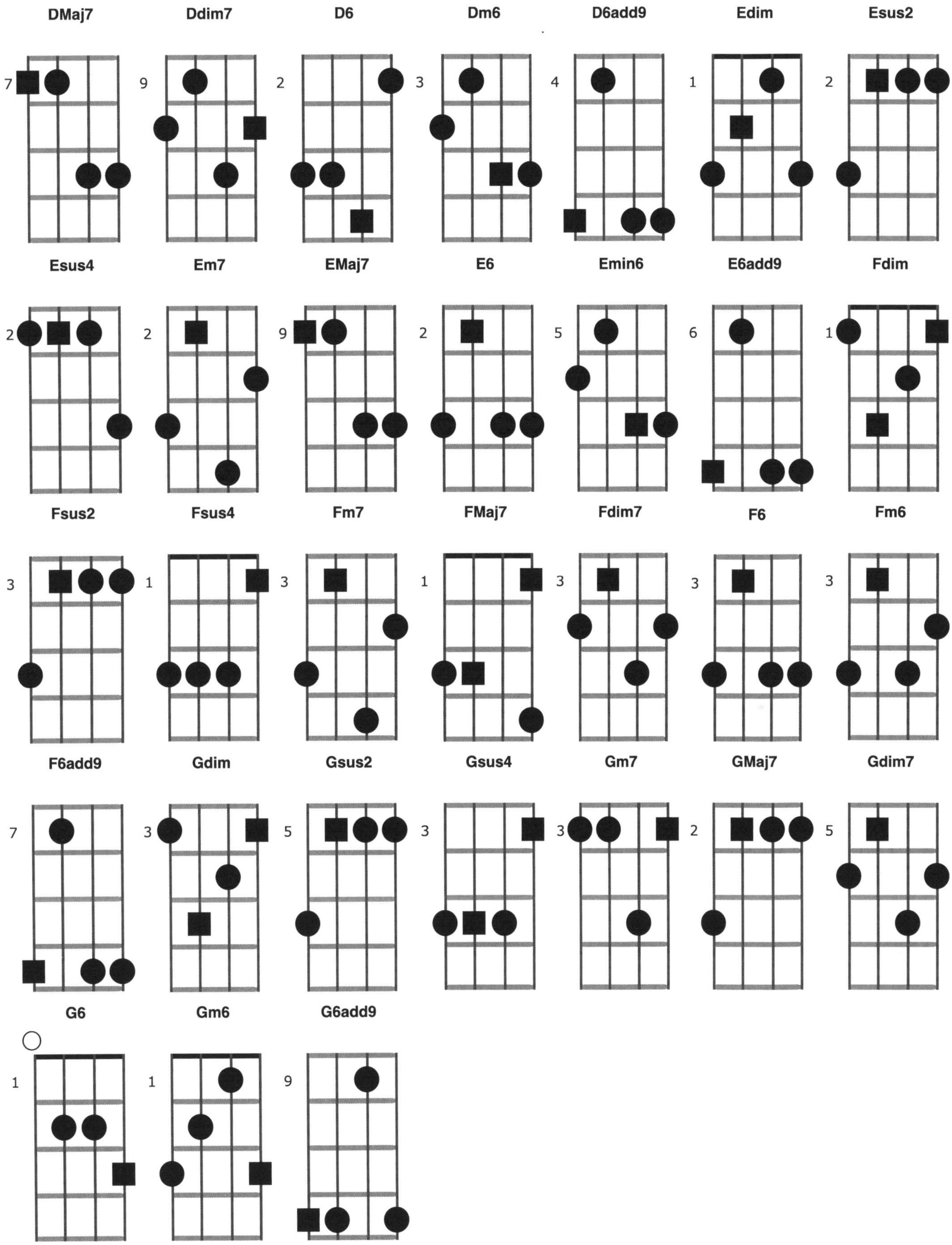

DMaj7
7
Ddim7
9
D6
2
Dm6
3
D6add9
4
Edim
1
Esus2
2
Esus4
2
Em7
2
EMaj7
9
E6
2
Emin6
5
E6add9
6
Fdim
1
Fsus2
3
Fsus4
1
Fm7
3
FMaj7
1
Fdim7
3
F6
3
Fm6
3
F6add9
7
Gdim
3
Gsus2
5
Gsus4
3
Gm7
3
GMaj7
2
Gdim7
5
G6
1
Gm6
1
G6add9
9

About the Author

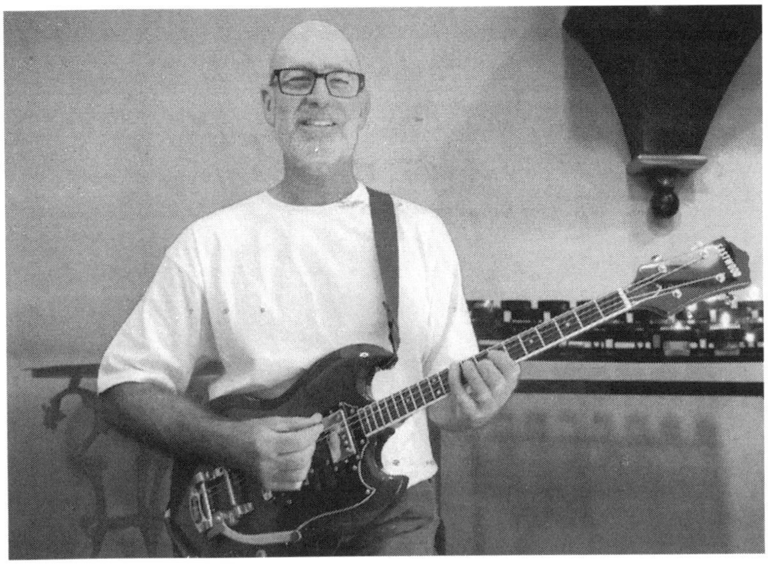

Todd Montgomery began learning guitar chord changes at age 9 using a strip of wood shingle with frets and strings drawn on it. In the fifty years since then he hasn't stopped exploring different stringed instruments. Most of that time was spent with the GDAE fingerboard, but he has also studied guitar, mandolin, Irish bouzouki, and sitar. He has played in bands in the genres of rock, folk, Irish dance music, classical Indian sitar and world music. He composed and produced original world, folk and rock music for 4 critcally acclaimed albums (Fernwood: *Almeria* 2008, *Sangita* 2009, *Arcadia* 2015 with Gayle Ellett, and with the Kelp Dwellers, *Surfacing* 2020, he composed all tunes on the electric tenor guitar).

He had the good fortune to study classical Indian sitar with Harihar Rao, who was Ravi Shankar's oldest student and collaborator, and he learned how to play Irish tunes from Cait Reed in Los Angeles. He earned a master's degree in teaching, and recently retired from 30 years as a high school special education teacher in public schools and is now focused primarily on teaching, composing and recording music. You can find him teaching lessons online at Tenor Guitar Time.

WWW.MELBAY.COM